D1577182

From Anarchy to Power

From Anarchy to Power

The Net Comes of Age

Wendy M. Grossman

NEW YORK UNIVERSITY PRESS
New York and London

NEW YORK UNIVERSITY PRESS
New York and London

Library of Congress Cataloging-in-Publication Data
Grossman, Wendy, 1954–
From anarchy to power : the net comes of age / Wendy M. Grossman.
p.   cm.
Includes bibliographical references and index.
ISBN 0-8147-3141-4 (cloth : alk. paper)
1. Informational technology. 2. Internet—Economic aspects.
3. Internet—Social aspects. 4. Electronic commerce.   I. Title.
HC79.I55 G765 2001
303.48'33—dc21   00-012775

New York University Press books are printed on acid-free paper,
and their binding materials are chosen for strength and durability.

Manufactured in the United States of America

10 9 8 7 6 5 4 3 2 1

For my mother, Lee Merian Grossman

Contents

Introduction   ix

1   The Internet Gets the Bomb   1
2   Selling Community   14
3   Who Owns the Net?   32
4   The Heart of the Net   42
5   A Thousand Points of Failure   59
6   The Empire Strikes Back   67
7   Free Speech, Not Free Beer   80
8   The Innocent Pleasure of Reading   95
9   The Future of Public Information   117
10 Falling into the Gap   128
11 Divide by Zero   140
12 The Haunted Goldfish Bowl   154
13 Twenty-first Century Snow   177

Acknowledgments   187
Notes   189
Selected Bibliography   217
Index   219
About the Author   223

Introduction

He used often to say there was only one Road; that it was like a
great river: its springs were at every doorstep, and every path was
its tributary. "It's a dangerous business, Frodo, going out of your
door," he used to say. "You step into the Road, and if you don't
keep your feet, there is no knowing where you might be swept off
to. Do you realize that this is the very path that goes through
Mirkwood, and that if you let it, it might take you all the way to
the Lonely Mountain or even further and to worse places?
—J.R.R. Tolkien, *The Lord of the Rings*

At the beginning of 1997, when I was finishing *net.wars*,
Netscape was the hot tech stock. Amazon.com only sold books and
had yet to become a public company. Yahoo! was proud of losing less
money than *Wired*. Freedom of speech activists were waiting for the
Supreme Court to overturn the Communications Decency Act. A battle
was raging over the deregulation of strong cryptography. And the
dancing baby had not yet found stardom on *Ally McBeal*.

Three years later, as I finished this book, Netscape had lost out and
been acquired by America Online; Amazon.com had moved into CDs,
toys, consumer electronics, auctions, patio furniture, and hosting small
shops; Yahoo!'s stock was selling at more than a thousand times its
earnings; *Wired*, split off from its digital arm, had been sold to Conde
Nast; and "Hampster Dance" had hit number one on the Christmas
singles list in Britain. The battles over freedom of speech, privacy, and
the deregulation of strong cryptography remained the same. And the
Internet's user base worldwide had tripled.

Many of the big Internet issues from 1994 to 1997 concerned the
cultural shift as the Net culture defined by a decade of academic and
research use tried to assimilate a massive wave of immigration. In those

years, most battles *about* the Net grew directly out of battles *on* the Net. There wasn't so much money flying around then, and the businesses that were growing—Netscape, the Internet Movies Database, Yahoo!—were founded by early Net users who at least understood the Net and began by creating something that would make a difference to the Net community. These days, you find a lot of large companies trying to look Nettish by sticking "community" buttons on their Web sites while failing to grasp that linking is what makes the Web. Meanwhile, the old-time grassroots activists are busy testifying in Congress or running start-ups rather than bashing things out on Usenet.

Around 1990, a couple of friends of mine got sick of "the Edinburgh rat race," so they packed up and moved to Crete to build an ornithological database, do specialist tours, and read in the sun. This would be unremarkable, except that one of them, John Henshall, was part of a leading team researching and developing networking protocols. His work on Open Systems Interconnection (OSI) was, of course, largely superseded by the widespread adoption of the TCP/IP Internet protocols. In 1997, when he emerged from his email-less existence on Crete, I pointed him at the Amazon.com site long enough to find a book he'd long been told was out of print; he was fascinated to find out that all the issues he and other Net users had debated theoretically in the 1980s—censorship, cooperation, standards, intellectual property rights, community—were being fought out for real, not just by a handful of theorizing academic researchers, but by thousands of people all over the world, including government officials, policy makers, and economists. In that sense, the Internet has scaled remarkably well—that is, it has maintained its structure while growing dramatically.

Many early predictions about the Internet and its impact were dismissed, often rightly, as hype. These included wild predictions about the volume of electronic commerce soon to come; the claim in the early days that copyright was dead; the hype that the Internet would level society, remove class barriers, and facilitate democracy; and the fear that the Net would destroy privacy. Many of these of these predictions clearly have not played out the way the early Netheads thought they would. But the underlying issues remain consistent. Equality, access, the future of democracy, public information, copyright, and especially privacy are now the stuff of congressional debates and international treaties.

Not that the Net has stopped paying attention to these issues. As governments push, Netizens still push back. So censorship attempts are followed by the development of anti-censorship servers, encryption regulations beget continued development and deployment of free software products, and judgments demanding that Web sites be pulled down inspire mirror sites located outside the jurisdiction of those particular courts. Similarly, major corporations find themselves battling the Net. Microsoft must live with an "Evil Empire" tag and a burgeoning community of antagonistic free software developers. AOL is still loathed by many, and even a Net-savvy company like Yahoo! finds itself besieged when it forgets whom it's talking to and imposes a widely disliked copyright grab on the "homesteaders" of its Geocities subsidiary.

The big difference now is that everyone's involved. Few people in the United States talked about privacy five years ago, other than in book reports on Orwell's *Nineteen Eighty-four*. Now, the question of how to protect our lives from government and commercial scrutiny is the stuff of presidential candidates' speeches and stories in, of all newspapers, *USA Today*. The same goes for the future of intellectual property, cryptography regulations, and even the issue of how the technology industry should be regulated (in the example of the Department of Justice's suit against Microsoft). Five years ago, these were all arcane subjects, but today they get play-by-play coverage in the mainstream media.

For anyone who's traveled much, the national blinders the United States currently seems to be wearing are embarrassing. These are not domestic issues. The U.S. Congress can't simply legislate away online indecency or decide that it's OK for U.S. companies to ignore European data protection laws. We are living in a world where privacy advocates warn that there may be a trade war between the United States and Europe over privacy. The European Community's privacy directive, which came into effect in October 1998, places strong restrictions on how companies may use the data they collect on consumers, and it bans European companies (even if they're U.S. subsidiaries) from transferring personal data to countries where there is no similar legislation in effect. The United States insists that its long-standing regime of self-regulation by the market is sufficient, but European privacy commissioners disagree.

It's easy to imagine that another threat to international trade will come from the United States' insistence on regulating the use and export of strong cryptography. In December 1998, the U.S. government claimed that all thirty-three countries that signed the export restrictions in the Wassenaar Arrangement agreed with the American view that cryptography exports should be restricted. It's become even clearer than it was at the time that the other thirty-two countries interpreted the agreement quite differently. Even U.S. businesses aren't cooperating: RSA Data Security announced in early 1999 that it was opening an Australian subsidiary just to get around the American export laws.

Many of the issues that haven't changed—how online communities bond, how copyrighted material can be protected in the digital era, and how the pioneer spirit of those who created software and gave it away for free can survive the commercialization of the Net—have professionalized. Copyright in particular is likely to be the most bitterly embattled area in the first decade of the twenty-first century, as the music and film industries seek to profit from the Net and digital distribution while finding technological ways to lock up their products to prevent piracy.

Then there's the software business. Five years ago, the challengers to Microsoft were other software companies: Lotus, Novell, WordPerfect, Borland. Now, the biggest challenge is coming from free software such as the operating system Linux and the Web server Apache, along with the many governments' antitrust actions (besides the United States, Japan and the European Union are also investigating Microsoft).

But the media haven't changed. Hype and new moral panics still abound, from push media and Amazon.com, the hot new technology of 1997 and hot new stock of 1998, respectively, to 1998's headlines about Internet addiction and depression among online users (both greatly overestimated), to 1999's headlines about the "outing" of more than a hundred names and addresses personnel from MI6, Britain's most secret service. And yet, what's often overlooked amid the sensationalist stories about cyberwar is the Net's own vulnerability: designed as an information-sharing system, the Net's infrastructure still lacks security that could protect it from sabotage. Meanwhile, important stories, like the revamping of the domain name system, fall through the cracks because they're deemed too esoteric for the general press, too techie for the business pages and political magazines, and too policy-oriented for the computer magazines.

Nonetheless, the Net is beginning to change the world, though not (of course) quite in the way people expected. One of the biggest impacts has been in finance. The ready 24/7 availability of information such as the buy/ask spread on individual stock prices or research reports that a decade ago would have been available only through a full-service broker has made it possible for ordinary people to lose money like professional stockbrokers. The upshot is that Wall Street's finest are having a hard time predicting what's going on with the market.

Many businesses have been slow to figure out how to use the Net effectively. While everyone's got their ecommerce site up, many companies haven't figured out that they have to cooperate. To take simple example: in the summer of 1999, I went athletic-shoe-shopping online and stopped in at the Ryka Web site. Helpfully, the site lists four major retail chains that stock its shoes. It did not link to any of them, even though three of the four had set up shopping sites and were selling the company's shoes through them. Companies outside the technical fields typically do not link to their partners, their suppliers, or their customers, even though they could gain greatly by doing so. "Community" to them means a way to get consumers to spend more time on their site and maybe buy more of their stuff; these businesses aren't used to thinking of themselves as being part of their own community of suppliers, customers, and even competitors.

In the early days of the Net, it was possible to imagine that at some point the infrastructure would be "finished"—that there would be enough bandwidth to do anything you wanted, from free long-distance voice telephone calls to movies on demand. By late 1999, that idea seemed to be receding. By then, it seemed as though the Net would always need another bandwidth upgrade to accommodate another new technology to supply yet another new service no one had thought of before.

Perhaps this atmosphere of constant change is just the experimentation that happens when any technology is young. In that case, we may be on the verge of seeing the Net harden into something like its final shape. Or perhaps the Net and its computer bedrock will remain, as they have been so far, the most versatile of tools and open to tinkering. It's certainly more interesting this way. I would hate to have missed these years.

—Wendy M. Grossman
Millennium Eve

1

The Internet Gets the Bomb

We'll try to stay serene and calm, when Alabama gets the bomb.
—Tom Lehrer, "Who's Next?"

Can you catch a virus from your computer?

That used to be one of those questions a technical support person would tell you about to make you understand how little the people they dealt with knew about the computers they were trying to use. But in August 1999, this was the headline on a Reuters story that got picked up by everyone from ABC News to *Nando Net*: "Syphilis Outbreak Traced to Chat Room."[1] In fact, the story was that a number of men diagnosed with syphilis had met their last sexual contacts in a gay America Online chat room (confusing AOL with the Internet yet *again*). This story fails the "phone test" some of my editors like to use: if you substitute a telephone for the Internet, would it still be a story? The one aspect of the story that didn't fail the test was the privacy question: Should AOL protect the identities of the men using the chat room as public health officials tried to trace and alert contacts? In the end, staff from the online gay and lesbian community service PlanetOut spent a couple of weeks visiting the chat room and posting warnings. Another interesting follow-up that didn't get much play offline was the story that the publicity made the chat room's users targets of hate email.

There is barely a human disaster story of the last five years that hasn't been blamed on the Internet for at least the first day or two. The Heaven's Gate UFO cult's group suicide: one of their number first researched the group via its Web site. The school shootings in Littleton, Colorado: those kids played Doom and used the Internet. Naturally, it's the experience of shooting things on-screen in Doom that flipped them over the edge, rather than the ready availability of guns.

This is, of course, not peculiar to the Internet. Every new technology is society's prime demon for a while. What's maddening is that it's so inconsistent. One day, kids are logging on to learn how to blow up their teachers; the next, wiring every classroom to the Internet is going to solve all our educational problems. One year, Oprah is claiming that 90 percent of the time people aren't who they say they are online (nonsense); the next, she's sympathetic to the cause of free speech when a couple of women get fired for posting nude pictures of themselves on the Web. One day, NBC News is warning of the prevalence of dangerous medical misinformation on the Net; the next, it's telling people to research online to protect themselves against doctors' mistakes. Like the media-friendly serial killer Mickey Knox said in *Natural Born Killers*, "Media is like the weather—only it's man-made weather."

All subcultures, as large parts of the Net still are, tend to feel misunderstood by the rest of the world. When I was on the folk scene, a lot of people thought "the media" failed to appreciate any music that wasn't slick, commercial, and heavily hyped. Among skeptics, it's accepted wisdom that "the media" prefer the sensational story of a paranormal claim to the more sober, rational truth that usually emerges if you investigate carefully enough. Many newspapers, for example, ran the story in early July 1999 about Nostradamus's prediction that the world would end on July 4. So for geeks and Netheads to feel misunderstood and sensationalized is not surprising. What's funny is realizing that even after ten years as a journalist, for me the media are still always "them."

On the other hand, there is a reason why the 1998 Computers, Freedom, and Privacy conference had a panel entitled "What Have the Media Been Smoking?" Trivial, stupid, and just plain wrong stories make the rounds, as if all the media were in lock-step. Why *did* every outlet have to cover Nostradamus, anyway? The man's been dead for five hundred years. Didn't anybody think it was ridiculous to write a story about the world ending on July 4 while planning the July 5 edition? What follows is a small sample of the more popular Internet stories of 1998 and 1999.

Spies under threat. In July 1999 the news broke that the names and addresses of 115 members of the MI6, Britain's secret service, had been posted on the Net. The media were alerted to the story by the Department of Defence, which sent out a notice asking newspaper editors not to publish the Web address where the information was posted. This provided good fodder for conspiracy theorists. One would think that in the event life-threatening information was leaked, the logical first move would be to move the endangered people, then alert the media. Since MI6 didn't do this, the natural conclusion was that they must have had an ulterior motive. Until the spooks had alerted everyone to the list's existence, few people knew it was out there. Found on the Lyndon LaRouche Web site, it was then posted to Usenet, where it could have gone extensively ignored for years.[2] Since we're supposed to think MI6 is made up of smart people, the logical conclusion was that they had acted deliberately to ensure maximum coverage. This way, the next time someone official wanted the Internet regulated, the evidence that it was necessary would be ready to hand. Said one newspaper editor at the time, "There is no free speech issue here. This is putting people's lives in danger."

Day trading. A persistent theme throughout 1999 was online day trading: why it's gambling, why small investors do better by buying and holding, and how it contributed to (*Newsweek*, ABC News) or was irrelevant to (*Time*) the state of mind that led day trader Mark Barton to shoot thirteen people and himself in Atlanta on July 27.[3] Related stories included the widely reported University of California at Davis study that showed that even experienced traders tended to perform less well when they moved from phone-based trading via a broker to trading online,[4] as well as the scare stories that most day traders lose all their money in six months, where the Securities and Exchange Commission's alert to investors merely warned that most day traders suffer severe financial losses and never recoup them. What the stories never mentioned is that day trading is a *minority* phenomenon. An August 1999 report from the North American Securities Administrators Association quoted estimates from the Electronic Traders Association that only about 4,000 to 5,000 people trade full-time through day trading brokerages.[5] However, those traders make 150,000 to 200,000 trades per day and account for nearly 15 percent of NASDAQ volume.

Overactive trading used to be a problem with unscrupulous brokers, who preyed on inexperienced investors by "churning" their portfolios. While the broker racked up commissions, your assets generally shrank. A Cornell study explained the poor performance of short-term traders: they sell their winners and pay multiple commissions plus capital gains tax.[6]

"I have no doubt this craze is only momentary. The poor economics of active day trading cannot support its sustained, widespread use," Thomas Gardner, co-founder of the financial Web site Motley Fool, told a congressional subcommittee in early 1999.[7]

Internet addiction. It's always fun to show that people who spend a lot of time online or using computers are poorly socialized, pathetic, lonely, depressed people with no lives. Kimberly S. Young and her 1998 book *Caught in the Net* played right into this sweet spot with case studies of Internet addicts, pretty much all of whom had other very serious problems such as failed marriages, alcoholism, or drug abuse before getting online. On Young's checklist for determining whether you're addicted, I score just inside the category of people who have a problem, because you get points for spending many hours online, even if it's for work, and also for forming relationships with people you meet online—like that's a *bad* thing.

These stories were particularly galling to users of the Internet. The implication is that if you are one of the millions of people who spend time online connecting with other human beings who may become real-life friends, you're pathetic. But after the August 1998 death of Diana, Princess of Wales, when thousands of people stood on line in the rain for fifteen hours to sign books of condolences that no one will ever read and cried over someone they'd never met—*that* was portrayed as a healthy release of genuine emotion. And we're supposed to be the ones having the fantasy relationships?

Internet-related depression. A Carnegie-Mellon study showed that people using the Internet for as little as a few hours a month were more depressed than they were before they got online.[8] To be fair, this was a $1.5 million study sponsored by companies like Hewlett-Packard and AT&T and carried out by scientists Robert Kraut and Sara Kiesler, who have turned out good, carefully conducted work on the nature of online interactions. In the *New York Times* story on the study, researchers, sponsoring organizations, and even the subjects all said they were surprised by the results. However, several standard elements were missing from the study, notably random selection (the subjects chosen were all teens lacking PCs and Internet access of their own), regular follow-ups (the teens' state of mind was measured only at the beginning and end of the study) and, especially, a control group. The work needs to be replicated by other researchers. However, it did appear in the peer-reviewed journal *The American Psychologist.*[9] Nonetheless, the study's conclusion—that the Internet needs to be redesigned to prevent depression—struck a lot of people as absurd, and even under the study's findings you'd have to spend an awful lot of time online to get significantly depressed.

The strange career of Matt Drudge. Matt Drudge became the poster boy for Internet stardom in 1997, when he made headlines by getting sued by White House aide Sidney Blumenthal over a story he didn't check out carefully enough before posting it on his Web site and emailing it to his estimated 60,000 readers. Although professional journalists love to despise Drudge—he's pointed to as the worst example of all that's wrong with Internet journalism—his Web site, where he maintains a complete list of links to all of America's syndicated columnists plus little search engines for the main news wires, is actually very useful.[10]

Supermodels' eggs. Shock! Horror! Designer babies! Despicable trading in human life! Someone set up a Web site to sell supermodels' eggs to would-be parents! This is a case where it's not the disreputable media we have to worry about most, it's the reputable media. The selling-supermodels'-eggs-on-the-Web story appeared first, according to Britain's wonderfully sarcastic and net-savvy *Need to Know (Now)* e-zine (*NTK* for short), in the *New York Times*, from where it made the rounds of almost every respectable print or broadcast publication. As *NTK* put it,

> A story like that is fit to print whether it's true or not, so maybe it's understandable that the *Times*' journalists didn't bother to look too closely at the RONSANGELS.COM's [the site advertising the eggs] credentials: like, for example, the fact that the site invited potential fathers to pay $24.95 a month to look at "larger pictures" of said models. Or that RONSANGELS' sister sites included eroticboxoffice.com and the Creative Nude Network. Without getting too distasteful about it, it looks like RONSANGELS' ovary play was rather more intent on re-directing sperm than distributing eggs.[11]

*

Of course, the media are not the only people reacting irrationally to the Internet. Senator Dianne Feinstein's (D-CA) instinctive reaction to the Oklahoma City bombing was: Get those bomb recipes off the Net.[12] All right, we all know that in the immediate wake of a disaster people's reactions aren't always sane—first theories of the Oklahoma City bomb involved Iraqi terrorists, a theory that evaporated as soon as you remembered that people outside the United States have barely ever heard of the place. The danger, however, is not the availability of bomb-making information *on* the Internet, but the availability of the necessary ingredients *off* the Internet. To put Feinstein's panic into context, it might be worth remembering the story of David Hahn, the New York State Boy Scout who in 1995 was caught building a breeder reactor in his mother's potting shed. Hahn assembled all the materials and information he needed without known assistance from the Net. Hackerlike, he wrote to a variety of officials and companies posing as a teacher.[13]

Hacking is also relevant to the Internet addiction story, because the concept probably began as a defense in a hacker case. In Kevin Mitnick's first trial, in 1988, his lawyer successfully argued that Mitnick was addicted to computing as a way of explaining his client's obsession with hacking into a variety of large computers. Mitnick was sentenced to a year in jail, followed by six months in a rehabilitation program modeled on Alcoholics Anonymous's twelve steps.[14] In a similar case in Britain in 1993, Paul Bedworth was acquitted after copying this defense. Not everyone bought the defense's contention that Bedworth was addicted; as security consultant Robert Schifreen quipped at the time, "I feel an addiction to bank robbing coming on."[15]

Whether it was a reasonable defense or not, some people do get obsessive about playing with computers or the Internet. In her 1995 book *Life on the Screen*, MIT psychologist Sherry Turkle examines several cases of college students who seemed addicted to online interactive fantasy games known as MUDs (for "multi-user dungeons") but in fact used (or attempted to use) them as a way of working through personal troubles. One of the students turned down social gatherings to work on the MUD where he had administrative responsibilities. In his case, however, working on the computer meant he didn't continue a lifestyle of drinking and partying that he believed was leading him into alcoholism.[16]

In 1996, New York psychologist Ivan K. Goldberg coined the term

"Internet Addiction Disorder" as a joke and wrote up a set of symptoms as a parody of *DSM-IV*, the diagnostic classification system used for psychiatric illnesses including conditions such as compulsive gambling and drug addiction.[17] Goldberg, who specializes in treating people with various types of mood disorders and runs a support Web site for people with depression,[18] extended the joke by starting an online support group for Internet addicts, sort of the equivalent of holding an AA meeting in a bar.

Ever since, joke lists of symptoms have proliferated all over the Net: stopping and checking your email on your way back to bed after getting up at 3 A.M. to go to the bathroom (done that one); trying to connect to the Internet by dialing your service provider's phone number and humming to the modem; succeeding in connecting that way. Goldberg himself has said that if there is a disorder connected with Internet overuse it would be fairer to compare it to compulsive gambling than to addiction, which implies the ingestion of a substance.

Nonetheless, the idea took root—that's the most dangerous side of hoaxes—and since then a few researchers have attempted to study Internet addiction with a view to determining how big a problem it might be. Kimberley S. Young, an assistant professor of psychology at the University of Pittsburgh and founder of the Center for Online Addiction, is the most visible of these researchers. Young's interest is clearly in finding a problem of major proportions, and she has: in a survey of 496 Internet users responding to online and offline ads for "avid Internet users," she identified 396 (157 men and 239 women) as Internet addicts. Her Web site offers personal counseling for addicts starting at $30 for an email consultation. "We had been ignoring the dark side of cyberspace," she writes in her 1998 book, apparently oblivious to the fact that easily half of all Internet coverage focuses on some kind of "dark side" of the Internet.

Young's findings sound impressive at first glance, but the study's self-selected sample population inevitably skews its results. The survey says nothing about what percentage of the world's estimated 100 million Internet users might have a problem. By contrast, Nottingham Trent University's Mark Griffiths, a specialist in non-substance addiction, says that of the thirty-five to forty cases that have come his way he would class only four as addicts. "I think Internet addiction exists," says Griffiths, "but it's a very small problem." Apart from anything else, the Internet isn't a single entity. Instead, it's a medium that supports many kinds of interactions.

He believes only the real-time facilities, like chat sessions and MUDs, can be addictive.

Another important contrast between Young's results and Griffiths's is the character of the addicts they identify. Young claims that anybody can be addicted, and her results included a high percentage of middle-aged women; Griffiths's group all fit the stereotype of the lonely adolescent male looking online for self-esteem. Not everyone who runs up huge phone bills or loses a job for wasting company time, argues Griffiths, is an addict. By analogy, he says, "Is a pathological gambler who can afford to lose a pathological gambler?" People who loses their jobs but then become self-employed, where online use is an asset, haven't necessarily suffered negative consequences.

Spending large amounts of time online does not in itself signify a problem. Are people who spend hours passively sitting in front of the TV set, read six books a week, or obsessively practice an art, sport, or musical instrument dangerously addicted? They, too, may give up social lives, decent food, physical fitness, and their sense of reality, just like people send real wedding presents to soap opera characters. In an essay examining the question of whether Internet addiction exists, clinical psychologist Storm A. King proposed this useful distinction between healthy and destructive obsessions: "A passion adds value to one's life; an addiction takes away value."[19]

Griffiths also makes the point that such an addiction may not be what it seems. The obsession could be with the computer itself, fantasy and role-playing games (as in MUDs and certain kinds of chat rooms), shopping, cybersex, contact with a particular person, or simply discovering and hoarding information. In addition, it's not immediately clear whether the person has a long-term problem or is simply reacting to the novelty of the Internet and will settle into spending less time online once that novelty wears off.

The symptoms all look the same: the person spends a lot of time sitting at the computer, to the detriment of other things. But confusion is common. In December 1998, for example, when Reuters published its "Glued to the Screen" research report, even though the report was primarily about information overload and the need to teach kids and employees information management, most of the press treated it as a story about Internet addiction. In fact, the only key findings specifically related to the Internet were the statistics that 55 percent of respondents worldwide feared that children will become information junkies, 72 percent feared their obsession will be exacerbated by the Internet, and 76 percent of U.K. respondents believed that PCs, the Internet, or information in general could become addictive to some people in the future. That is a far cry from reporting that Internet addiction is a serious problem *now*.

John Suler, a psychology professor at Rider University, comments in a paper on computer and cyberspace addiction that it's likely that much of the media hype about Internet addiction has more to do with ignorance and fear, as well as society's current obsession with addiction and recovery,[20] than it has to do with a real phenomenon. To gain acceptance for Internet addiction as a disorder, he says, research must establish two things: first, that there is a consistent, reliably diagnosed set of symptoms that constitutes the disorder; second, that the diagnosis correlates with similar elements in the histories, personalities, and future prognosis of people who are so diagnosed. "If not," he says, "where's the beef?"[21]

Young, however, is so horrified by the specter of Internet addiction that she wants college campuses to close down access to MUDs and chat rooms. Comparing the availability of these services to a college's opening a twenty-four-hour bar, she focuses on the Internet as a cause of divorces, pedophilia, and teen withdrawal, even though she admits that other factors in her case studies' lives were the primary causes of their problems. Nowhere does she consider the possibility that online contact might extend and deepen real-life relationships. What is false about Young's—and many other critics'—argument is the assumption that the Net and real life fall on opposite sides of some binary boundary. For most people on the Net, the two intermingle over time.

Certainly, Matt Drudge is an example of someone for whom the time he spent on the Internet turned into a real-life career. I first came across Drudge when he began posting copies of his then fledgling Drudge Report to a number of newsgroups, including one of my perennial favorites, *alt.showbiz.gossip*, a home for those (known as ASGers) who mix a love of trashy popular culture with a sense of irony. Drudge alienated most of the newsgroup's regulars by apparently not sticking around to read the replies to his bulletins, which were generally less interesting than the tidbits ASGers pick up regularly to prove the rule that if you get enough people together at least some of them know someone who actually knows something. But Drudge persisted. He set up a Web site. He got picked up by *HotWired*, the digital arm of *Wired* magazine,[22] and then, in June 1997, by AOL, where he was featured as "the hottest gossip before anyone else."

Hot, new gossip was not what he was known for on ASG. "He's always been known for lifting his 'exclusives' out of tabloids or the PR sheets of magazines," Ron Hogan, a long-time ASG regular and the maintainer of a site of author interviews,[23] told me in 1997. "His writing is pretty tortuous, and his obsessions tend to get weird—back in 1996, he was real hung up on the film *Babe*, for some reason." I remember those postings: long paeans of praise and some odd comments about lactating with excitement that are still joked about on ASG. "It's a great example of how shrewd PR work can get everybody talking about a decisively mediocre product," Hogan added.

Even so, Drudge was credited with being first with the news that comedian Jerry Seinfeld wanted $1 million an episode for his top-rated show's eighth year, and with breaking the broadcast media's agreed-upon silence to announce the results of the 1996 presidential election hours before the polls closed, a rule-breaking escapade that earned him a kind of wry admiration. Then in July 1997 he got into a nasty spat with *Newsweek* when he leaked details of a story the magazine was working on examining claims that President Clinton had sexually harassed a White House staffer (Drudge is rabidly right-wing). By June 1997 *Time* magazine was calling him "The Liz Smith of cyberspace."

In his August 11 Drudge Report, he claimed that then new White House aide Sidney Blumenthal had successfully covered up a past as a wife-beater. A day later, Drudge published a full retraction, saying he'd run the story without checking. Blumenthal still filed suit for $30 million, even though the Net provides what Electronic Frontier Foundation in-house counsel Mike Godwin calls "a better remedy than anywhere else, including the courts" for libel because you have the same access to the medium as the original commentator.

Drudge seems to fancy himself a latter-day Walter Winchell, even sporting a Panama hat in his publicity photos. Winchell, like the twin-terror gossip columnists from the early days of the film industry, Louella Parsons and Hedda Hopper, was so powerful that he could make or break careers. But there are major differences between Drudge's background and that of major media gossip columnists. Liz Smith, for example, worked for NBC, *Cosmopolitan*, and *Sports Illustrated* before starting her column for the *New York Daily News* in 1976. Drudge graduated from high school and worked at the CBS Studio Store and seems proud of having had no journalistic training. With the lawsuit pending, the media felt free to smugly define him as an example of cyberjournalism's lack of standards.

In a nice ironic twist, *Time* quoted Drudge as saying he was "80 percent accurate." In fact, the 80 percent figure, came from a comment he made to the Web-based magazine *Salon*, to the effect that he was 80 percent sure of the Blumenthal story and that his own biases made him want to believe the story and so not to look too closely. This quote was transformed by *Washington Post* media critic Howard Kurtz into "boasting that his information is 80 percent accurate,"[24] and from there was picked by everyone (sadly, including me), in an example of how the media cue the media.

What was odd about Drudge was the ire the press directed at him. If you listened to mainstream journalists talk, Drudge was irresponsible, unethical, and an example of the dire future that awaited us in a world with an Internet with no gatekeepers. Of course, they ignored the thousands of sites that publish accurate, useful, public-interest information that would never have gotten into mainstream publications because it didn't fit the editors' or corporate publishers' ideas. Nor do mainstream journalists often point the finger at themselves or their own organizations for inaccuracy, biased reporting, or sensationalism on any subject.

Drudge himself only benefited from the fuss. Once Blumenthal's suit made him famous, he was signed by Fox to do a weekly TV show of gossip and interviews, though this only lasted a few months.[25] Even then, people still blamed Drudge for the state of journalism. Frank Rich, writing in the *New York Times*, commented:

> How he changed the press is self-evident. The elevation of rumor and gossip to news is now ubiquitous in mainstream media; few except professional worrywarts bother to complain any more. . . . We're so inured to speculation in the name of news that it's become a constant white noise. No Matt Drudge, however incendiary his or her own "scoops" may be, could possibly shout loudly enough to be heard over the now-permanent din.[26]

Where do journalists get this kind of thing? Is it Dorothy Parker's well-known definition of nostalgia: "Nothing is more responsible for the good old days than a bad memory"? When did the financial papers ever eschew speculation? When weren't rumor and gossip published?

Remember all those 1930s movies—*Nothing Sacred, His Girl Friday, The Front Page*—about the scurrilous, underhanded, ruthless, malicious, make-it-up-and-file press? To most people, journalists rank right alongside politicians and used car salesmen. Anyone reading the British tabloids or the *National Enquirer* or watching a show like *Hard Copy* can rightfully ask exactly what journalists have to be so pompous about. Who exactly made Drudge a media star?

Drudge may have no training as a journalist, but neither, these days, do lots of professionals, particularly in the computer/Internet arena, where technical knowledge is often more badly needed than a journalism degree. He's not accurate? *Time* magazine did a lot more damage by running a 1995 cyberporn scare story that relied on a study that was later exposed as fraudulent.[27] Even though the magazine ran a full-page correction, that study is still quoted by people wanting to regulate the Net. The continuing concentration of all media into the hands of a few large corporate owners and the persistent cutting of staffing and budgets in news organizations are far more damaging to journalism than Drudge will ever be, even if he gets every story he runs out of trash cans next to the CBS store from now until the year 3000.

Meanwhile, plenty of really important Net stories have been largely ignored. For example, one of the most contentious shake-ups of 1997 to 1999 was the revamping of the domain name system or DNS (see chapter 5), when the most intimate inner workings of the Net, previously run by a handful of volunteers and a government-awarded monopoly, were turned over to a complex new corporation. The only major media outlet that I'm aware of that gave the issue regular coverage was the *New York Times*, in stories written by freelancer Jeri Clausing, many of which appeared only in the online edition of the paper. Editors generally thought the story was too boring, complicated, and arcane for mass audiences, even though the upshot was that an entirely new and important international power structure was being created.

Even *Wired* nodded on this one. The first substantial coverage it gave the DNS mess was an early 1998 piece that focused on "domain name dissident" Eugene Kashpureff and his escapades. *Wired* stories, as a fellow journalist commented at the time, tended to follow a formula: lone crazy guy with wild hair standing in a field, taking on the establishment. Kashpureff certainly fit that description, but the new DNS did not.

In the early 1990s, Netheads liked to speculate that the reason the media only ran sensationalist scare stories about the online world was that newspaper and magazine editors, publishers, and writers knew their livelihoods were under threat. Many Netheads thought that the public's ability to directly access the raw material from which news stories were made would put reporters out of business. They didn't take into account the massive amount of information people would have to wade through, and they discounted the importance of access to sources. How many phone calls can Bill Gates take?

Perhaps one reason we're always so disappointed by the media is that, like science, we expect it to produce immediate answers. Media may be like the weather, but journalism is a process of revealing truth in small chunks as they become available. Also like science, journalism is self-correcting over a long period of time. Instead of condemning the Net as being full of unreliable trash, journalists should help people to tell good source material from bad. That is, after all, one of the things we've supposedly learned to do.

2

Selling Community

Virtual communities are social aggregations that emerge from the Net when enough people carry on those public discussions long enough, with sufficient human feeling, to form webs of personal relationships in cyberspace.
                    —Howard Rheingold, *The Virtual Community*

One reason so many media folk have trouble understanding the workings of the online world is that they themselves have not really become part of it except in the shallowest sense—they have email addresses and perhaps use the Web for research. Many may not even do that; the October 1999 issue of *Quill*, the magazine published by the Society for Professional Journalists, actually ran an article debating whether email was an acceptable way of conducting interviews.[1] Obviously there are lots of times when email isn't satisfactory, but the fact that the magazine had this argument five years after the *New Yorker*'s John Seabrook exchanged email with Bill Gates for several months to get to know him better before interviewing him in person[2] tells you something about how alien the Net still is to many mainstream journalists. No one's writing articles about whether telephone conversations are acceptable instead of face-to-face interviews.

"If all cyberspace gives you is an e-mail address—a place to hang your virtual hat and chat about your hobbies," cyber rights lawyer Mike Godwin wrote in 1993, "you've been cheated."[3] He went on, "What most of us want is a place where we're known and accepted on the basis of what Martin Luther King, Jr. called 'the content of our character.'" A long-time member of the tightly knit San Francisco–based electronic conferencing system WELL, Godwin also noted that "one of the reasons the WELL . . . is such a tony address in cyberspace is that the perception of community is so strong. A few WELL users argue that, in fact, this perception is illusory, but they ignore the fact that the value of a shared hallucination is that it's shared."

Of all the mirages shimmering on the sides of the Internet bubble, "community" beckons the most powerfully. For all sorts of businesses—not just Internet service providers (ISPs) but even banks—"community" is the ultimate sticky dream of hanging onto customers. For everyone wishing for a kinder, gentler world, "community" represents the old values of unlocked doors and neighbors you can trust. From about 1997 on, every Web site that aspired to any sort of staying power sprouted a "community" link to encourage users to bond with each other. On a financial site like Motley Fool, this might mean cheering on or attacking stock picks; on news sites it meant users voted on whether media coverage of John F. Kennedy Jr.'s death was overblown or whether Microsoft was a monopoly.

Many of those blatantly commercial efforts to hook users aren't particularly compelling. They function as a sort of obligatory add-on that distinguishes commercial sites from their offline broadcast/print/sales activities, and their rather narrow agendas are set by the official material at those sites. If anything, they epitomize Godwin's comment about hobbies. The intent of these sites is much different from that of the older Net communities, where the star of the show is the relationships that form among the regulars via the many-to-many communication that really distinguishes the Net as a medium.

In a few cases, these more commercial communities seem to work, in the sense that they enhance the sites' core businesses while encouraging users to feel like more than just customers. On Amazon.com, anyone who cares to can contribute a review of any book listed on the site. While these reviews may include personal vendettas, bad taste, and even in-jokes (a hilarious review of *The Story of Ping*, a children's book about a duck named Ping, evaluates the book as if it were a manual about the eponymous UNIX utility[4]), they are often interesting to read and include a different perspective. On eBay, instead of reviewing the items for sale, buyers and sellers post feedback about each other. The auction format encourages the sites' users to get to know each other, since they bid against each other for items and become familiar with each other's buying habits, just like rival collectors of rare Japanese art might in physical-world auction houses.

Along with Amazon.com and eBay, online community designer Amy Jo Kim called Ultima Online and Slashdot the best of the newer communities on the Web. Ultima Online, a gaming site with (then) more than 100,000 registered members, uses a system of clothing and symbols on players' avatars to warn newcomers of predators who might kill them before they can get into the game.[5] Slashdot (more properly written "/.") opened in September 1997 and bills itself as "News for Nerds. Stuff that Matters."[6] It is a highly focused, intensely active geek community with a strong shared interest in technology issues, especially those affecting open-source developers and users (see chapter 7). Ten years ago, the equivalent of Slashdot was probably the collection of technically oriented newsgroups. The Web is less efficient to read, but it unifies hosting conversations, makes software available for download, and links to news stories and other related sites.

According to Kim, conversation-only sites are very hard to sustain. "You need to build a community around a central activity shared by the community members. We don't go to places or join communities just to chat or post messages, whether online or in the real world. Dialog and conversation are always incidental to the main activity."[7] People talk in restaurants or shops, for example, forming communities that would not exist without other central activities. "The notion that an online community can be solely about coming together to talk is going to be less and less successful. If the truth be told, it's an idea that's never worked very well."

Kim's statement seems to me breathlessly wrong-headed. To have conversations is exactly why a lot of people go places like cafés with their friends: the café is in most cases an interchangeable setting for the conversation, unless it's something like the Algonquin Round Table, where the location matters because participants show up unpredictably. It is true, however, that strangers typically meet over an activity in which they have common interest—which may be conversation, as it was in the Paris literary salons of the nineteenth century. However, as British journalist Andrew Brown pointed out one day on the WELL, "This is a hangout for people who like to read and write. There are not that many of us."[8] Perhaps not in comparison to the population at large; but surely the Net is large enough to support all kinds of niches.

What's special about the older, generalist conferencing systems is that a single interface and registration lead you to many different subcommunities that mix the same people in different ways. There is, as the WELL's conferencing director, Gail Williams, points out, a benefit to having this kind of multi-dimensional community:

If someone's an absolute, raving idiot in *politics*, but in *parenting* is talking about their daughter's being sick, you see a second side and have compassion. If a community's sophisticated enough to only retaliate *ad nauseam* in the *politics* conference and let the person be different in another context, then there's room for people to start becoming real to each other and not be cardboard characters.[9]

A lot has happened to online community in the fifteen-plus years since the early conversation systems were set up. In the mid 1980s, when a lot of those systems were launched, online was a novelty for most people. Like early computers, you could make a sort of blank space available and then see what people did with it. When what the early users did was talk and form human connections—as Howard Rheingold noted in *The Virtual Community*, the early online services found that there was more money to be had from selling users to each other than from selling them content[10]—it was natural to presume that the "killer application"[11] for the Net might be community.

A remarkably wide range of technologies can support community. Asynchronous messaging allows people from different time zones to participate at their own convenience. Internet Relay Chat (IRC) and the chat facilities supplied by sites like *Dilbert* or AOL require everyone to participate simultaneously. In text-based role-playing adventure game worlds (MUDs and MOOs[12]) or their newer graphical equivalents, such as Worlds Away[13] or The Palace,[14] users interact via cartoon representations of each other. Your character and any areas you've built persist, but your character is only active when you're logged in.[15] More recently, the daily Net jottings known as Weblogs or blogs have created a new mix of publishing and community by surrounding the blogs with comments from small groups of trusted readers.[16]

What's often not mentioned is the crossover among all these systems: game players may discuss the events in their worlds on Usenet or in other asynchronous forums; members of a particular service may set up a private area (or email list) in which to discuss the larger service; or people may chat privately in real-time while surveying current discussions elsewhere. The strongest communities use a mix of technologies that allow a variety of relationships, public and private.

As video and audio begin to permeate the Net, these elements will also be incorporated, but my guess is they will not be the runaway success that people may expect. Just as most people don't want picture phones at home that show them cleaning up their desks in the nude while talking, most people are likely to want control over whether their pictures go out online. On the Internet, everyone will know you're a dog if your real image accompanies you everywhere you go. Audio poses a different problem: it is very difficult in multi-party telephone conferences to be sure who's speaking at any given time and to maintain enough order for people to hear each other. One reason some European businesses have taken to using IRC is that it's easy to see who's said what and to keep a electronically searchable log of the discussion, as well as being extremely cheap to implement.

As soon as you think about the idea that community can somehow be defined by the type of technology that it runs on, you see how silly that idea has to be: as Clinton might have said, it's the people, stupid. The bigger issue is whether the community's members have real or fantasy identities. There is far more difference between adopting a persona in a role-playing game and participating in a discussion using your real name and personality than in whether the supporting technology is real-time or asynchronous.

Businesses were always involved in online community, from the WELL (particularly after Rockport millionaire Bruce Katz became sole owner in 1994)[17] to CompuServe (for a long time the only really profitable company in online services), Prodigy, and AOL. Services founded later, such as Microsoft Network (MSN) and Britain's LineOne (a joint venture among British Telecom, News International,[18] and the Mirror Group), and Virgin Net all presumed that users would want spaces in which to talk to each other. Hobbyist bulletin board systems and Usenet were the exceptions. Bulletin board systems are, of course, under the control of their owners. But on Usenet, no one's in charge, and no one can pull the plug.

Community became the latest fad among Net businesses in 1997 with the publication of *net.gain* by John Hagel III and Arthur G. Armstrong, McKinsey consultants who argue that the virtual communities the Net is uniquely capable of supporting are the future of marketing.[19] In one sense, this claim was a relief. Netheads had been saying all along that the online medium's unique many-to-many capabilities were its single biggest distinguishing characteristic. On the other hand, the proliferation of message boards debased the word. Hagel and Armstrong were long on business but short on online experience, and it showed. Most of the business folk deciding to add a community button to their Web sites are probably the same way.

This may be how Gerard van der Leun, a senior editor at *Penthouse* and co-author of *Rules of the Net: Online Operating Instructions for Human Beings*,[20] came to post a long rant in a Web-based discussion area on the subject of online community:

> Ah, I love the smell of 'community' in the morning as one organization after another burns large sacks of money in pursuit of this grail. Each one refusing, because the suits know better, to learn from hard won and long experience.[21]

Van der Leun went on to list the elements needed:

> Minds + variety + freedom + disk space + speed + time = successful online conferencing. It really is, to quote the immortal Ross Perot, "Jes' that simple." But each part of that equation is critical and trying to run cheap on any one of them dooms the whole. This has been true since the dawn ages of The Source and Parti [two of the earliest online services], and will be true until the last ding-dong of doom.

That recipe sounds simpler than it is. Disk space and speed are easy, because they can be achieved by throwing technology at the system. Speed is important because lengthy time lags while you wait for your typing to appear turns users off. Disk space allows the community to have a collective memory. A newcomer to the WELL can access the archives and read large parts of the WELL's history as it happened. CompuServe, by contrast, allocated limited disk space to each forum, and when that was reached old messages scrolled off onto company backups, never to be seen again unless there was a lawsuit. The only exceptions were threads the sysops actively archived in the forum's library of files.[22] These design decisions, though vitally important, are sometimes casually made in the interests of getting something started with the intention of refining it later. Such details can completely alter the feel of the system.

One interesting design question is how far an online world should go in emulating its offline counterpart. On Worlds Away, for example, your avatar must actually walk—literally, with cartoon legs moving and landscape scrolling by in the background—from one place to another within the world. You can get around this to some extent by shrinking yourself to a small cloud and whisking from room to room as a "ghost," useful also in allowing limited screen space to accommodate more characters. Or you can pay a token to use the teleports scattered around the world. Imposing geographical constraints pushes you into exploring the world and allows the social involvement of walking in company with others.

On the other hand, Jim Bumgardner, creator of The Palace, deliberately chose not to include gravity. "There is no attempt to mimic real world physics in The Palace. As far as I am concerned, physics basically present obstacles, and I wanted to create a world with few obstacles," says Bumgardner, explaining The Palace's dream-like feel in a paper by John Suler, a professor of psychology at Rider University.[23]

Suler believes this dream-like feel may be healthy in supplementing real life and allowing people to experiment with new ways to interact with others.[24]

> People may be attracted to such virtual environments because—like dreams—they satisfy this need for an alternative view of reality by encouraging the unconscious, primary process styles of thinking. Like dreams, they also encourage the acting out of unconscious fantasies and impulses, which may explain some of the sexuality, aggression, and imaginative role playing we see on the Internet.

That's the polite way of putting it: it would be more accurate to say, as the WELL's Gail Williams has, that "a lot of online socializing is people working out their high school angst." Part of becoming familiar with a community is discovering that it contains people you don't like. You may be able to block their messages, but you can't entirely remove them, particularly if the community blends online and offline contact. Add the moderators (the equivalent of hall monitors, perhaps) and long-term contact, and you wind up with a mix with cliques, silly fights, and rebellious behavior, all made more potent perhaps because as adults we want the revenge of going back to high school and winning. When someone invites you into their private conference, it can feel as though you have gotten that revenge.

This kind of behavior is as old as cyberspace. As the old-timers mourned the death of ASCII on CompuServe in July 1999, they reminisced about the good old days when snobs were snobs, interfaces were difficult, and the old-timers could play tricks on the newcomers. Stuff like: a newcomer comes into a forum. Old-timer sees newcomer loitering at the "OK!" prompt and SENDs the newcomer a real-time message using the required syntax, "SEND# HELLO." Newcomer doesn't know you have to type "SEND" and a number to identify who the message is for, and blithely types "HELLO" back. Result:

newcomer finds himself logged off the system and offered a chance to log back on because HELLO is a command. Snicker. OK: childish and dumb. But let's face it, a lot classier than the only prank you can manage in today's graphical interfaces, which is to ask the newcomer to give you his password.

The Palace, which Bumgardner says had three main influences (text-based MUDs, 3D virtual reality systems, and multimedia authoring systems), was meant to be both an equalizer and a slightly subversive place where people would feel free of ordinary inhibitions. Letting users design their avatars themselves rather than sticking them together out of ready-made parts as in Worlds Away was part of that freedom, as was ignoring physics. An extra element of freedom was provided by Bumgardner's decision to release the server as well as the client software people run to access The Palace. The upshot is that many Palace offshoots have sprouted, each an individually designed site with its own feel and regular clientele. Some may not please the original designers, but they create a culture around the technology.

Bumgardner assumed that people would play games, and that many would be sexual in nature. He discovered, however, that a major sources of trouble was that everyone thought they knew what inappropriate behavior was—and they all disagreed.[25] That phenomenon, too, is common to all types of online community.

Physics may create an artificial drag in cyberspace, but some human habits create other kinds of drag that can't be changed so easily. In a 1987–1988 experiment sponsored by Lucasfilms, Randy Farmer built a world known as the Habitat that attracted some two hundred people. Farmer set up an internal economy (copied by Worlds Away) that awarded users tokens every time they logged in or when they won certain kinds of contests. You could also buy and sell objects within the world. Since tokens were not scarce and a few clever users made themselves rich by taking advantage of variable pricing around the world, gradually an entirely different economy emerged, based on the unique Heads offered as prizes.[26]

Another familiar problem: some of the inhabitants began stealing other avatars' belongings and shooting them in their virtual homes. Murdered avatars lost their place in the game but weren't actually terminated. Debate split the system into equal numbers over whether it was a crime or part of the fun. The several weddings that took place in Habitat, meanwhile, showed that the designers hadn't thought through all the possibilities. Cohabitation was difficult, because the system had been programmed to allow only one account to access a particular turf. More interesting were the Habitat's attempts at self-governance. When the world elected a sheriff and then held a vote to decide what he should be allowed to do, the system's voters split again into two basic camps, one favoring anarchy, the other government.

Similar debates take place everywhere in cyberspace, as they must have in the earliest human societies. After an incident on The Palace in which a "snert" sexually harassed a female user named Quentin both by shouting obscenities at her and by using a spoofing function to put words in her mouth,[27] the newsgroup set up to discuss Palace community standards filled with debates over how much power and anonymity guests should have, how much freedom of speech/expression should be available, real versus virtual "rape," decency laws, and who should be allowed to use The Palace. While the people sponsoring decency laws and anti-pornography campaigns seem to believe that Netheads are just irresponsible goons, in fact every issue about the Net that's ever been discussed offline has been discussed with far greater thoughtfulness, depth, and intensity online.

Virtual worlds and virtual communities have different origins, but increasingly the designs of the fantasy worlds are likely to blend with the reality of the discussion systems. "The combination of virtual worlds with virtual communities . . . is the Holy Grail," says Bob Jacobson, a long-time researcher in this field.[28] "The problem is bringing together disparate disciplines and professionals who never speak with each other to work this one out."

A text-based experiment along these lines has already taken place: Amy Bruckman's MediaMOO, a text-based virtual world, was used to help professional media researchers and practitioners make contact with one another. Bruckman chose text because "with current technology, graphical virtual worlds are awkward at best. For example, no graphical system developed to date can give the user the ability to express more than a minimal range of human emotions."[29] As Bruckman goes on to say, many more people can successfully add to their characters' descriptions by writing words than by designing graphics. For myself, I note that accessing the WELL via its new Web interface always makes me feel as though I'm outside the WELL looking in, whereas using the old ASCII interface set to green letters on a black background, which feels intimate to me, gives me the sense that I am inside the WELL looking out.

The center of MediaMOO is a model of the MIT Media Lab where Bruckman was a graduate student when she created the MOO. It is surrounded by models of other buildings familiar to those who frequent the MOO, such as an Apple building that made at least one newcomer feel at home immediately.[30] It had been built by an earlier resident, an important point, particularly as commercial organizations get interested in these kinds of virtual spaces. "Many current virtual reality projects, particularly those intended for entertainment," Bruckman observes, "are like Disneyland; artists and programmers design wondrous creations for users to experience. . . . If the power of this technology is to be unleashed, users need to be the creators and not merely consumers of virtual worlds."

This is a basic principle learned from discussion areas, too. If you build too much, the first users rattle around in an empty space with which they feel no connection. Start smaller, and let the space expand as needed. The Palace, for example, was built as a mansion with many rooms, on the assumption that people would need places to talk. Many of those rooms are empty most of the time, because people prefer to congregate.

Letting users guide the design of a virtual space is important for another reason: ensuring that they're comfortable. Bumgardner's decision to give all guests the same avatar and no persistent identity would, he thought, encourage membership. Instead, he found it encouraged regulars to treat guests badly.

Linda Stone, head of the virtual worlds group at Microsoft, explained in 1997 how fine-grained the decisions can be:

> Whether or not you know that other people are present or privy to a conversation, whether you can connect an online identity to a real-world person, whether you have only a faint notion of the personalities of those around you or a vibrant and detailed impression—this is all determined by the design of the environment.[31]

Stone cited as an example a discussion about how to implement a feature allowing one user to ignore (that is, filter out) another. "Should everybody know that a person is being *ignored* by someone else? Should nobody know?" Arguments about this kind of issue, she said, often split along gender lines. "The guys might say, everybody should know. The women say that if someone is sexually harassing them they don't want them to know because they might find other ways."

But, as Stone says, in the end, "Community isn't about software, it's about people." Or, as Pavel Curtis, founder and chief wizard of LambdaMOO, told *Wired News*: "People are the killer app of the Internet."[32] Or Martin Turner, the managing director of CompuServe UK from its inception until 1998: "A good community is made by the members, the residents." Or, as van der Leun called it, "Minds." This is not really news. Two of the earliest pioneers in online community, Randy Farmer and Chip Morningstar, realized it long ago.[33] Nonetheless, engineers and media designers keep imagining that they can plan out everything in advance.

Getting the right people is the most difficult part of starting a new online community, if only because you can't get someone to code them, or at least not easily. There are exceptions to this, such as the bits of robot software some systems use to make the areas seem more populated and friendlier. Some are useful and provide help or directions in answer to questions; others just liven up the service by playing little games. They don't answer the same need as people, but they do help create a livelier, more interactive background.[34] On the other hand, people create trouble in a way that 'bots don't. "Building community is a fundamentally different activity than writing computer code," writes Peter Kollock, a sociology professor at the University of California at Los Angeles who studies online communities. "Code does not write back and code does not respond strategically to one's actions."[35]

On most systems—Usenet is the notable exception—someone out there is actually running things. This is the big difference between real life and the Net: on the Net there is always a known God and you can send Him email. Often that person is the founder, who typically ropes in a group of friends to help seed the conversation and get things rolling. On commercial systems like AOL and CompuServe, the person is a business partner who has signed a contract to run a particular content area in return for royalties based on traffic to the area.

These paid moderators, however, are merely the tip of an iceberg. Both AOL (originally founded as Quantum Link in 1984) and CompuServe were really built by the efforts of volunteers. As an area grows to thousands of messages a day, the moderators typically recruit volunteers from the most active members to help do the inevitable scut work such as making files available for download, dealing with user questions and technical problems, patrolling discussions, keeping the density of interesting stuff high, and breaking up fights. Moderators have many names, such as sysops, oracles (Worlds Away), or wizards (The Palace, LambdaMOO). My favorite term is Bruckman's: janitors. None of these are jobs for the power-mad, and on many systems the rule quickly became that anyone who wants the job probably shouldn't have it. Slashdot, home to a particularly contentious class of people, adopted an unusual scheme that involves a points system to help users cut down on noise. Slashdot appoints rotating moderators for a few days at a time with strict checks on what they are allowed to do.[36]

Anyone who's ever functioned as an online moderator knows this is a tough job. You work with all eyes on you and everyone ready to accuse you of censorship, the online equivalent of throwing someone in jail without a trial. In a commercial setting, conflict over censorship is almost inevitable, if only because most businesses running online communities want to ensure they won't be sued for libelous comments posted by the users or prosecuted if someone breaks the law. Moderators are accordingly usually contracted to ensure that users adhere to the terms of service they agreed to when they signed up, a procedure that attracts a certain amount of resistance.

In the early days of these services, when users were charged for every minute they stayed connected, some of the more successful contract owners made a very good living from their royalties, and free accounts might save volunteers hundreds of dollars a month in online charges. The more generous ones passed some of their revenue stream on to the volunteers; certainly some paid for training and other benefits. But as competition increased, services dropped their prices, cutting the contract holders' revenue. When the services went flat-rate to compete with ISPs, the economics changed entirely. Where under the royalty system a niche area could do reasonably well with a small but loyal band of devoted users, under flat-rate both the service itself and the content provider had to come up with new sources of revenue, such as selling related merchandise, or advertising. Either required a large audience, with the upshot that both services rapidly began shutting down the quirky niche areas and focusing on the mass market.

Many thriving, intense online groups have ended because the service that hosted the group decided, for one reason or another, to pull the plug. Businesses often do not value the communities they create the way their users do. When, for example, *Time* magazine moved from AOL to CompuServe in 1995, the AOL message boards, described as very lively and active by former participants, were abruptly shut down rather than being turned over to the members to run. When AOL took over Netscape in 1999, it shut down the communities that had been forming around its Netcenter portal, firing the moderators who had been working to create them.

CompuServe is a truly astonishing case. A pioneer in online community—the service's earliest forums date back to 1978—by 1999 the company was so confused after years of shrinkage and changes of management that it had completely forgotten what was good about the forums or why they were one of the service's biggest strengths. Some of the problem was old technology, since the original forum software, designed with an inscrutable ASCII interface, was not Y2K compliant. Rather than try to patch it, in July 1999, the sysops opened the last ASCII forum on CompuServe, the ASCII Test forum, to the public for an all-night vigil and then shut it down, leaving everything else to run on a machine interface that required proprietary software.[37]

Incredibly, at the very moment when everyone else was trying to figure out how to construct successful online communities, CompuServe took a successful, *profitable* system that fostered many thriving, tightly knit online groupings of loyal, "sticky" customers and systematically removed all the elements that made it work. The people who understood the business had by then moved elsewhere in a diaspora with the one benefit of freeing skilled moderators to found new communities elsewhere. CompuServe would have done better to turn itself into a consultancy and broker their expertise.

Something similar happened when the San Francisco–based ISP Hooked was bought, along with the WELL,[38] by Reebok millionaire Bruce Katz and then subsumed into Whole Earth Networks. Hooked was unusual for an ISP in that it encouraged internal community by starting its own private newsgroups and an online monthly magazine, guided by the company's owner, David Holub. Once the service was sold, however, these efforts died away.

Says early Hooker Mimi Kahn:

There is still a small Hooker community that hangs out on a privately-owned message board—pretty much the same people who used to hang around in the Hooked internal newsgroups. Sometimes we still get together in RealTime. Some of them have become genuine, RealLife friends. It was a close-knit group that evolved there.[39]

All such changes are hard on community spirit—it's exceptionally difficult to take a community that's thriving in one location on a particular technology and move it to an entirely different location that involves completely different technology. Persistence of location and technology, however, is rarely mentioned on anyone's list of what it takes to keep an online community successful. Neither van der Leun nor Kollock list it as a criterion. Kollock comes closest when he says, "In my book it's a success if you still have a viable community after a decade."

Even IRC, the most ephemeral of the kinds of interaction you can have over the Net, has well-established, reliably available channels, one thing that distinguishes it from AOL chat. Emma Reardon-Smith, an IRC channel operator, says, "It's extremely difficult to have a community on AOL because it's difficult to join the same channel twice—you can't arrange to meet in a specific room." This is a consequence of AOL's software design, which limits AOL chat rooms to twenty-three people (the limits on IRC channels, if any, are imposed by the channel operators). You can, of course, set up a private chat room and invite only your friends, but then you lose the spontaneous remixing of people that is so much a part of any community, online or off—and, as Lawrence Lessig points out in his book *Code and Other Laws of Cyberspace*, the twenty-three-person limit disables users from staging any effective kind of live mass protest.[40] If you were building a virtual community as an adjunct to government, the existence or absence of those limits is the difference between a democracy and a police state.

In February 1996, users on Worlds Away got so riled over delays in getting private spaces ("turfs") that they staged a sit-in. Fed up with many delays from Worlds Away's then owner, Fujitsu, avatars filled the locales where new users first arrive in the world, standing and chanting, "No turfs, no peace . . ." (the words scroll up above the game's window)—while paying per-minute online charges. To Kollock, that protest was a sign of Worlds Away's success as a community. "The simple fact that they had a protest speaks volumes about the space—the commitment and collective action."

The list of elements Kollock thinks necessary for the success of online communities, whether they're text or graphical, is more formal than van der Leun's: persistent identity, ongoing interaction, a sense of history, a sense of group boundaries, user-created rules for sharing resources, mechanisms for resolving conflicts, an internal economy and monetary system, the ability to change and modify the environment, and a moderate amount of risk.

Almost immediately, you can come up with counter-examples for most of these criteria. Aside from some MUDS and Worlds Away, few systems have an internal economy or monetary system—and for many it would be wholly inappropriate—though you could argue that people create their own internal barter economy of information, whereby users help those who help them back. Many systems don't allow users to change or modify much. On CompuServe, for example, only forum owners can create chat rooms or start message sections, and the rules for each forum are laid down by its owner. Worlds Away can't be modified either. Users can rent turfs, which they can decorate as they wish, but they can't trek out into the jungle and build a house or extend the landscape.

Some of the elements on Kollock's and van der Leun's lists map more closely to each other than it appears at first, for example disk space, which enables the sense of history. Kollock's user-created rules and van der Leun's freedom also boil down to letting users develop their own set of community standards, a major point of contention between Net communities and governments (and regarded with great trepidation by most businesses).

The WELL's ethos was like this. "It was part of the design to let people play as much as possible without violating each other's privacy," says Gail Williams, the WELL's conferencing manager, going on to say that this basic design decision, carried out in both software and rule-making, gave the WELL its essential character.

By contrast, LambdaMOO was not originally run this way, but in 1992 its owner and founder, Xerox PARC researcher Pavel Curtis, decided it was time to stop making decisions on behalf of the fledgling community he'd founded with a few friends two years earlier. In an open letter, he announced that in future the wizards would merely carry out the community's instructions and manage the technical infra-structure.[41] What evolved from that was a system of petitions and ballots that have made an interesting experiment in Internet governance (those familiar with LambdaMOO's experience could probably have predicted the DNS mess discussed in chapter 5).

LambdaMOO struggled through some difficult moments, most notably the "rape" Julian Dibbell wrote about for the *Village Voice* in 1996. Yet those are the moments that make community. Writing about a later decision not to "toad" (that is, terminate) one of the more irritating inhabitants of LambdaMOO, Dibbell wrote, "The MOO had grown, not just in size but in its soul. . . . LambdaMOO itself, somehow, somewhere along the path from its genesis in the mind of Pavel Curtis to its luminescence in the minds of thousands, had gotten a life."[42]

One issue that Kollock brings up, however, is vital but not often discussed: size matters. If a community's size falls below a certain threshold, participation plummets to zero; if it's too big, the intimate community feeling tends to suffer and the group splinters into cliquish groups, becoming vulnerable to bad behavior that is more controllable when the community is smaller.[43]

This is no different in fantasy worlds. "Because virtual reality is inhabited by real people, it does not provide an escape from real people and real problems," wrote Rebecca Spainhower in a paper on virtual communities and real problems. "The most frequent MOO problems, and the ones with potentially the most catastrophic results, stem from population growth, harassment of users, and guest characters."[44]

No one has yet worked out what the optimum size is for an online community—and membership figures don't tell the whole story. Generally, 80 to 90 percent of the members of any given area never post. For most people most of the time, the Net is a passive experience rather than the active experience everyone assumed it would be in the early days. Even those users who do participate actively do so unevenly.

One big factor not on either list is offline connections. These come ready-made in some professionally oriented online communities, in that people may work for the same employers or be familiar with each other's work. Apple Fellow Steve Cisler, who has written extensively about online community, likes to stress the importance of the online/offline mix:

> I grew up on the WELL and was there a bit before Howard Rheingold, so I know much of what can happen in an online environment with rich discourse. It is certainly happening elsewhere, but I think you need sustained physical contact to have a real community, and in many cases proximity. I think the online tools can help solve some of the problems of geographic communities, and I think that parties and conferences can in the real world can help online affinity groups grow stronger.[45]

This may be altogether more effort than most businesses other than Tupperware want to put into online community. It's the kind of thing that has to be sustained by the members' own desire to meet. The problem is that the stronger the bonds between the people grow the less the hosting business matters, as in the Hooked case. As Hagel and Armstrong admitted in their book, businesses will have to change a lot culturally to use community as a marketing tool—they'll have to welcome competitors' products and allow criticism of their own products, for instance. Online users demand freedom, but most businesses like to control everything.

The question remains what makes a community successful, depending how you define the term. Is the WELL unsuccessful because it has "only" 10,000 members, or successful because it's survived technical crises, the opening up of the Internet, and two changes of owner? Is Usenet unsuccessful because it's overrun with a lot of junk and bad behavior, or successful because conversations among hundreds of thousands of people have thrived there for two decades despite the noise? It's fashionable to dismiss Usenet, but it's the one online construction that no one can shut down: that single fact makes it the town square.

To Amazon.com and eBay, doubtless success means that the community aspects of their sites enhance their core businesses by encouraging repeat sales and building an atmosphere of trust that makes customers feel as if they are part owners. In a support group for breast cancer sufferers, success may mean simply providing enough information and shared experience to help people cope with what's happening to them. In the vertical communities everyone seems to want to build now, success may mean that everyone has a useful resource for help with professional technical questions.

It seems to me shallow to define the success of a community by its numbers, the measure that the commercial services use when they shut down areas that are "underperforming." That is imposing the values of the mass entertainment industry on a new medium whose strength is, if anything, its ability to fill niches. If it were up to me, I'd say that an online community's success is measured by the degree to which it develops a sense of autonomy and ownership.

The trouble is that humans can make community out of anything, whether it's the solitary act of reading a book or the more gregarious one of going to a football game. People can imbue plain ASCII characters with enough meaning to grieve their passing. Perhaps, there-

fore, the reason doing online community is hard is not that it's difficult to get humans to engage with each other, but that it's too easy: if
humans can make a gesture of mutual trust, as two did in the virtual
world Worlds Away (now Avaterra) by briefly holding each other's
cartoon heads at an imaginary wedding that existed only as pictures
on monitors around the world,[46] any shared hallucination of community is possible.

3

Who Owns the Net?

> It took about 20 minutes to convince the Secret Service that it was
> OK to let Jon into the [White House] dining room—and I must
> admit that all the blue suits who normally populate that dining
> room were staring over. They normally think of themselves as quite
> important people, and Jon with his sandals and pony tail and beard
> and so on was not quite the style of the place. But I remember
> thinking at the time that in a town where people worry a lot about
> what history will think, that there was nobody else in that dining
> room that history is going to remember, except Jon Postel.
>   —Ira Magaziner, at Jon Postel's funeral

On a sunny southern California November day in 1998,
several hundred people turned up at an auditorium on the University of
Southern California campus to remember Jon Postel.[1] The service,
filled with live chamber music and the world's most famous geeks,
ended with a eulogy by Postel's brother, who reminded the audience of
Postel's love of rock-climbing.

> If you hike in the Sierras or and climb a pass or a summit where Jon
> might have climbed, touch a rock that he might have touched and say, "I
> was there." In the distant future, when every coffee maker and vacuum
> cleaner has its own IP address and Jon's a mere footnote, remember this
> time and, say, "I was there." In the memory of Jon Postel!

Then Postel's family and the other invited speakers (including then
White House aide Ira Magaziner) launched paper airplanes at the audience. I still have one that landed near me: I was there.

Postel was a member of the first and most important online community: the technical community (as distinct from a committee) that created the standards that define the Internet. As a collection of Internet
pioneers put it in a brief account of the history involved:

The Internet is as much a collection of communities as a collection of technologies, and its success is largely attributable to both satisfying basic community needs as well as utilizing the community in an effective way to push the infrastructure forward.[2]

If an online community is truly successful when its "residents" come to feel that they own the place, the technical community was exceptional in that in a very real sense it actually *did* own the place if anyone did. Postel was the first individual member of the Internet Society, a founding member of the Internet Architecture Board (remaining on the board until his death), custodian of the *.us* domain, and, most importantly, editor-in-chief of the series of Requests for Comments (RFCs)[3] that define the standards that form the technical underpinnings of the Internet going all the way back to 1969 and the beginnings of the ARPAnet.

Probably few outside the geek elite knew who Postel was before he died, though afterwards even some non-U.S. newspapers called him the "God of the Internet."[4] Postel, as speakers like Magaziner made plain at his memorial service, was there at most of the important moments in the development of the Internet.

People think of the Net as anarchic, particularly in its early days, but at heart its structure was tightly controlled by a relatively small group of engineers. This group was a meritocracy that would allow anyone in who was capable of making a technical contribution the others would accept as beneficial. The system relied on the circulation of the documents known as RFCs. There are literally thousands of RFCs (so far) covering everything from the formatting of email headers to the secure version of the Web protocol, HTTP. Most are not standards, but discussion documents or explanations of anything from technical matters to the functioning of Internet organizations. Postel's nearly thirty years of work, for example, was memorialized in RFC2555, published on the thirtieth anniversary of the publication of RFC1, "Host Software." Anyone who wants to understand the technical underpinnings of the Internet, the process by which they were created, or the experimental efforts that failed can trace (or even re-create) all of the Net's design through these documents. Probably no human invention has ever had such careful, detailed documentation of its progress and deployment; on the other hand, probably no human invention has ever been such a lengthy collaborative effort of so many disparate individuals and organizations. It is clear now that it would have been impossible to collaborate so effectively over such a long period of time without superb documentation.

Postel was so necessary that if he hadn't existed someone would have had to invent him. Besides editing the series of RFCs, he made many technical contributions to such Internet fundamentals as Simple Mail Transfer Protocol (SMTP, involved in sending just about every email message), File Transfer Protocol (FTP, used for transferring files), Telnet (which allows you to log onto remote computers as if you were attached to them directly) . . . the list goes on and on. The process by which RFCs were created and modified and the standards they laid out and implemented was and is a model of cooperation: if something was valuable, it was widely adopted.

Even in the United States, RFCs represented a new and much-criticized way of working at the time. Like any online community, the technical community's discussions of the proposed documents were heated and inflammatory. It required courage as well as technical smarts to write and release an RFC. In that heated atmosphere, telecommunications professor Dave Farber's comments about Postel are even more remarkable: "Jon never argued with people. I never remember him raising his voice. He would just look at you until you understood his point of view."[5]

Steve Crocker, author of RFC1, explains in RFC2555 that one reason the documents were called Requests for Comments was to emphasize the fact that the initial Network Working Group was informal and was opening a dialogue rather than asserting control.

> At the time [thirty years before, when writing RFC1], I believed the notes were temporary and the entire series would die off in a year or so once the network was running. Thanks to the spectacular efforts of the entire community and the perseverance and dedication of Jon Postel, Joyce Reynolds and their crew, the humble series of Requests for Comments evolved and thrived. It became the mainstay for sharing technical designs in the Internet community and the archetype for other communities as well.[6]

Some future sociologist will get a lengthy doctoral dissertation out of comparing the process revealed by the RFCs to the institutional standards process used to create a competing European standard for public networking known as Open Systems Interconnection (OSI). OSI took years to produce via the more usual process of extensive research followed by lengthy meetings of official standards bodies. Within Europe, OSI had officially been adopted as a standard for connecting heterogeneous computer networks. But while OSI's seven layers of protocols were being developed, Vinton Cerf, then working at the Defense Advanced Research Projects Agency (DARPA)—now a senior vice-president at MCI Worldcom—and Robert E. Kahn wrote the protocols known as TCP/IP, for Transmission Control Protocol/Internet Protocol (RFCs 793 and 791, respectively). People found TCP/IP useful and began connecting their computers. By the early 1990s TCP/IP was integrated into almost every network operating system, so that anyone who had a local area network also had the capacity to hook to the growing Internet. Once the Web came along and people began piling onto the Net by the hundreds of thousands, OSI died. The network externalities (or network effects) beloved of information age economists, whereby the value of a network increases logarithmically in relation to the number of people connected to it, took over.[7]

That, anyway, is the mythological version in which can-do American know-how beats out the Old World dinosaur. The overwhelming visibility of American companies, culture, and individuals on the Net lead people both inside and outside the United States to think of the Net as American. This view, whose wrong-headedness will become increasingly obvious through the early years of the twenty-first century, leads to some extremely silly comments, the most notorious of which came during debates on the future of the domain name system, when Congressman Chip Pickering (R-Mississippi) claimed that Americans invented the Net and shouldn't give away control to other nations. In fact, at the same time that ARPAnet was being developed as a test bed, networking experiments were proceeding in Europe and some of the key ideas that went into designing the Internet came from people outside the United States. Alex Mackenzie, who worked at Bolt, Beranek, and Newman, the company that built the first ARPAnet nodes, believes it could all have happened much faster, since a protocol was agreed by the International Network Working Group (INWG) as early as 1976 but not adopted by the ARPAnet.

According to Janet Abbate in *Inventing the Internet*, it all goes back to the different ideas the United States and the United Kingdom had about time-sharing, the technique developed to give multiple users the illusion that their terminals were all in sole control of the mainframes they were using. Briton Donald Davies, then at the National Physical Laboratory (NPL), who had become interested in time-sharing, wanted to cut the soaring telephone costs inherent in the terminals' having become increasingly remote from the computers to which they were attached.

Computers use open telephone connections inefficiently because they send data in bursts and the silences in between are meaningless to the machines. Accordingly, Davies came up with the idea of adapting telegraph-style message switching to make maximum use of the open connection by sending a continuous stream of data "packets" that would be switched by specialized computers according to the instructions carried in the packet header, a sort of envelope. When Davies presented his ideas in March 1966, however, he discovered that American Paul Baran had come up with the same idea three years earlier—not to maximize access to a scarce resource but to build a network that would survive a bomb outage. Davies had an additional motive behind his dream of creating a national packet-switched data network: to ensure that the United States did not dominate computer technology. Although Davies set up a small experimental network in the NPL in 1967, his idea of a national network for commercial use didn't materialize. Struggles for funding severely limited what he could do, compared to what was achieved in the United States.[8] As Abbate notes, whereas NPL was a civilian government laboratory with a modest budget in a country where the Post Office owned all communications, ARPA was part of a huge multi-billion-dollar defense complex with a mandate to pursue advanced technical projects.[9]

Although the Post Office (now split into the Royal Mail and British Telecom) eventually developed data networking services under the leadership of the NPL's Roger Scantlebury, when it adopted packet-switching it used a system based on the ARPAnet. Abbate makes the point that packet-switching in fact was a communications revolution—but one spawned by computer scientists because telecommunications experts couldn't imagine in the 1960s that it would be possible to deploy dozens of computers to do switching, given that the computers of the time were large, expensive, and slow. Davies, however, got the last word by coming up with the term "packet."

Plans to build the Internet were drafted by the INWG, which was formed in 1972 and included researchers from the United States, the United Kingdom, Switzerland, and France's research Cyclades network. Cyclades began in 1972 with funding from the French government and was designed by researchers Louis Pouzin and Herbert Zimmerman. According to Mackenzie, one of the members of the INWG, the French network was built with an unorthodox idea. Instead of relying on the network to provide perfect, constant connections and deliver packets in the same order in which they were sent, Cyclades relied on a host protocol that did nothing more than ensure reliable connections. The packets didn't need to arrive all at the same time or in the same order; error-correction meant that whatever order the packets arrived in they could be reassembled correctly, and that if some were lost or missing the host protocol could request retransmission. This self-repairing design that presumes the network is unreliable is one of the most important ideas that makes the Internet work—and it came from France, not the United States. According to Cerf, "We began doing concurrent implementations at Stanford, BBN, and University College London. . . . So effort at developing the Internet protocols was international from the beginning."[10]

One key experiment took place at Britain's NPL. Researchers examined whether it would be preferable to run different host protocols on different computers and translate between them, or whether it was more efficient for them all to run the same host protocol. As you might expect, running the same protocol proved faster even though it meant the deployment troubles of replacing existing host protocols. This, too, was built into TCP, in part because it was a design more likely to scale successfully as the network grew. Even OSI, the abandoned European networking protocol, had a big influence on network design. Its seven-layer model gave networking researchers a way to think about the protocols they were developing.[11] A geek joke T-shirt even plays on that model, placing an extra politics layer above the technical seven.

Americans certainly jumped onto the Net faster than the rest of the world—but then, Americans usually jump on new technology faster than anyone else. One notable exception is wireless telephony, which has been much better developed in Europe and as a consequence has achieved much higher penetration, to the point where sending short text messages from cellphone to cellphone became a teen craze in 1999. But even if it were true that the United States invented all of the existing Internet, it would still be absurd to presume that any single nation can own the Net. If we went by which country was first to deploy things, Japan would be demanding royalties on every fax machine, and if we went by who set international standards, Britain would own time.[12]

Once the Internet got started, the telecommunications costs that plagued Davies became a problem for everyone else, substantially slowing online penetration outside of North America. In Britain in 1984, the only legal source of modems was British Telecom, which charged three or four times the U.S. price. Similarly, per-minute telephone pricing for even local calls made it much more expensive for anyone outside North America to finance an online habit, especially bearing in mind that at the time pricing for online services was itself expensive ($22.95 an hour for CompuServe forums, for example), with fat telecommunications surcharges as well. When Microsoft Network (MSN) launched in 1995 it cost twice as much to access in Europe as it did in the United States.

Even as late as early 2000, telecommunications costs made it expensive to use the Web outside North America. Few could afford to stay connected for long periods, even though people upgrade their modems much more quickly to take advantage of higher speeds. Users outside North American therefore have learned to prefer systems that support offline reader software to automate connections and minimize online time. Companies like AOL have to take these differences into account, knowing that the average amount of time a non-U.S. user will spend online per month is a fraction that of a comparable U.S. user. Until flat-rate, high-speed services like Asymmetric Digital Subscriber Link (ADSL)[13] and cable modems become widespread in Europe, Web-based conferencing systems that dole out one message at a time will simply be too slow and expensive to use. Even then, people used to the efficiency of threaded offline readers will find them too cumbersome to trouble with. A smart business that hopes for an international audience would design its conferencing system with a Web interface—but behind it a standard Usenet server, so that the rest of the world could access it using commonly available Usenet offline reader software. In early 2000, surveys still showed that telecommunications costs were slowing down the development of electronic commerce in Europe—maybe the one incentive that finally unlocks the flat-rate cabinet.

In addition, the costs for ISPs are higher outside the United States. ISPs do make some savings in non-U.S. markets—the high cost of telephone calls means that users log off sooner, so a larger customer base requires less capacity than a comparable U.S. one. But the cost of equipment is typically higher. In Britain the rule for estimating the price of a particular piece of computer hardware or software is to take the dollar price and stick a pound sign in front of it, a markup of 40 to 60 percent. Many other countries are more expensive.

Telecommunications also take a bigger bite because the cost of leased line connections to the United States is higher than the reverse connections. Worse, ISPs have claimed, because typically other countries thought it more important to hook to the United States than vice versa, the cost of those international connections fell disproportionately on the rest of the world.

In 1996, for example, Mike Rogers, then the general manager of products and services for Demon Internet, pointed out that "international cabling is not going to come down in raw price. The only way it's going to get cheaper is when the U.S. sees a need to be connected to Europe. Europe is the poor cousin, so we pay."[14] At the time, Rogers figured a T1 (that is, 1.5 megabits per second) line in the United States cost roughly the same as a 64-kilobit leased line in the British town of Dorking. New Zealand is also expensive, paying three times U.S. costs, according to a 1997 report in which the New Zealand Ministry of Commerce compared New Zealand prices to Australia, Sweden, the United Kingdom, and the U.S. state of Colorado.[15]

In 1995, an ADMedia report calculated that telecommunications costs in the United States were one-eighth those in the European Union.[16] European prices have come down a great deal since then because of deregulation, but even so the difference is enough that in 1998 the Paris-based Web-hosting firm FranceNet serving the French market announced it would set up a server center in California, claiming it would improve performance even for European users.[17] An accompanying diagram shows clearly the U.S.-centric pattern of backbone connections and cites the experience of the Swedish company Telia that routing European traffic via the United States, though technically inefficient, is cheaper.

Things get worse as you move out of the developed world. For one thing, the accounting practices in use in international calling make calls even more expensive in, for example, Africa—exactly where the charges are least affordable. In a talk at the 1999 Computers, Freedom, and Privacy conference, Tracy Cohen laid out the problems of wiring Africa and estimated the cost of Internet access in some places reached $10 an hour.

This contrasts with OECD figures which estimated recently that 20 hours of Internet access in the U.S. costs $29, including phone and provider fees. Although European charges are more ($74 in Germany, $52 in France, $65 in Britain, and $53 in Italy) all of these countries have per capita incomes which are ten to one hundred times greater than the African average.[18]

The American digital divide aside, the gist is clear. The United States was the source of some but not all of the earliest ideas behind the Internet, and the U.S. government was the source of funding for the most important early U.S. nodes, as well as much of the research that went into creating and developing computers—something the large libertarian community of Silicon Valley often forgets, as Paulina Borsook has pointed out.[19] But the Internet is the aggregation of all those other networks: Britain's Joint Academic Network (JANET), set up in 1984 to link fifty academic and research institutions and now serving two hundred organizations including libraries, schools, and museums; the European EUNet; the burgeoning networks now being built in China, Africa, and Latin America. Only Americans could imagine that the Internet is American—though the dementia that it is possible for a single nation or group of nations to control the Net seems to be a shared one.

The international character of the Net's design and its ability to expand like a disparate set of bacterial colonies growing together in the same Petri dish are among the things that are exceptional about the Internet. Certainly, it did not have to be designed the way it was. The decision to publish all proposals and work in an open, collaborative way proved exceptionally effective, in part because it ensured that no one controlled the standard, freeing the network for competition and innovation. Later developments, such as the World-Wide Web and the open-source software movement, have copied this style of working, which owes its character more to science than to business.

Someone who sits on many standards committees in Europe once explained the attraction to me by saying that participating in the endless meetings that were involved was "a chance to change a very large world by a very small amount." Standards roil passions for all sorts of reasons. For large commercial companies—IBM in the 1970s, Microsoft in the 1990s—proprietary standards are a way of locking in customers. In Europe in the 1980s, open standards (that is, UNIX) was a way of keeping IBM in check. For small companies, open standards make it possible for them to compete.

In today's commercial Internet, companies do not embrace openness equally. Microsoft has been accused many times of seeking to change standards to make them proprietary, whereas other companies seek to establish technology they've invented (such as Sun's Java) as open standards so they'll be widely accepted. Nonetheless, a big cultural shift has taken place in this area. At the Association for Computing Machinery's Policy '98 conference, an engineer with long experience commented that in the early days of the Internet, if anyone had promoted a solution to a particular problem on the grounds that it was good for his company, he'd have been shouted off the stage; now that sort of thing is commonplace.

As Abbate points out in her book *Inventing the Internet*, although technical standards are typically thought of as socially neutral and rather dull, the fact that people get so worked up over them shows they're anything but.[20] Nowhere is this clearer than in the battles to create a new domain name system. When the domain name system was first created—as an RFC—the social and commercial significance of domain names had yet to develop. Now, as we look forward to a world in which perhaps even toasters will have their own domains, we are still guessing how best to design a system that will survive the strangest that humanity can throw at it. It's taking an entire organization to carry on from Postel's years of stewardship. The Internet Corporation for Assigned Names and Numbers persists in speaking of its new functions as purely technical. A lot of other people, however, believe that what's at stake is nothing less than Internet ownership and governance.

4

The Heart of the Net

Blessed be he who would govern the Internet, for he shall run out
of asbestos underwear.   —Wendy M. Grossman

One of Jon Postel's most significant contributions to the Internet's development was running the domain name system (DNS) from the time he and Information Sciences Institute colleague Paul Mockapetris wrote the original RFCs defining it until his unexpected death in late 1998. Looking back from the vantage point of the rampant international success that the Internet has become, it's astonishing to realize how much power was concentrated in his hands simply because he was there and willing to do the work, and how much, even in late 1999 when electronic commerce was generating billions of dollars, still depended on volunteers with computers under their desks. This became clearer as efforts to change the domain name system proceeded. It would have happened in any case. The U.S. government, which provided minimal funding for Postel's management work, wanted to get out of running the Internet, and part of that effort meant professionalizing what passes for Net governance—control over the Net's technical underpinnings.

Essentially, the domain name system is a human-friendly interface to the dotted clumps of numbers that routing computers understand. One domain I use, *skeptic.demon.co.uk*, for example, stands for the number 158.152.8.200. You could certainly remember that if you had to—if, say, it were the combination to unlock the safe in which you kept a million dollars' worth of gold bars, or if it were your best friend's phone number. But committing more than a few of these to memory is for the sort of person who likes to do memory tricks at parties.

For a computer, the dots separate the numbers into hierarchies, just like the names of Usenet newsgroups.[1] IP Numbers are handed out to Internet service providers in blocks, and routers understand, for example, that all of 158.152.* goes to *demon.co.uk*, and the servers belonging to Britain's Demon Internet route the traffic more precisely by examining the right-most clumps. Allocating these numbers and ensuring that the blocks don't become fragmented (which would slow the Net down considerably because of the processing time that would take inside the routers) is an important technical function that's divided up among several agencies worldwide. Until the 1998 creation of the Internet Corporation for Assigned Names and Numbers (ICANN), the process was overseen by the Internet Assigned Numbers Authority, managed by Jon Postel.

The DNS was put in place in 1983, when the original system of maintaining and updating daily a simple text file called *hosts.txt* became unwieldy. Each new organization coming online chooses a domain name that identifies it to network users. In a name like *nyupress.nyu.edu*, *.edu* is the broadest category, called a top-level domain. The *nyu* is a second-level domain, and it's the part the organization registers when it picks its name. The *nyupress* part is a third-level domain, and is really just the name of a machine on the network belonging to *nyu.edu*. It can be changed, added, or eliminated at the system administrator's will; it does not need to be formally registered.

Top-level domains come in two types, generic top-level domains (gTLDs) and country code domains. The country code domains are the two-letter country codes set by the International Standards Organization (ISO): *.fr* for France, *.za* for South Africa, *.uk* for United Kingdom,[2] and so on. Within most, though not all, of those domains, second-level domains perform the same kind of human sorting function that the gTLDs do. So you'll have *.org.uk* for a British charity, or *.com.au* for an Australian business. Under that structure, the domain people register when they set up online is the third-level domain—the *demon* in *demon.co.uk*. Although it's rarely used, because most U.S. organizations prefer gTLDs, there is a *.us* domain, with subdivisions according to city and state; a number of schools use these.

Throughout the 1990s, the number of gTLDs remained small, all of them short and intended for specific purposes: *.com* (commercial organizations), *.org* (non-profits) *.net* (Internet service providers and staff, but not customers), *.edu* (universities and educational institutions), *.gov* (government departments), *.mil* (military), and *.int* (international organizations such as the World Health Organization or the International Telecommunications Union).

What's amusing about this structure is that at the same time that everyone was saying that the Net knows no frontiers they were applying geographical divisions to it. In one way, it makes sense. The Net's management had to be divided up somehow, and geography is an obvious way of delineating responsibility. But by the mid 1990s it had become obvious that the pioneers were right. This thoughtfully structured system was stable through the stampede online except for one thing: almost everyone wants to be in *.com*. Snobbery won out over logic.[3] As of January 4, 2000, *.com* had nearly 7.7 million registrations, roughly seven times as many as the second most popular TLD on the list, *.net*, at 1.17 million. Germany's *.de* is third, with some 870,000; *.uk*, with 757,000, beats out *.org* by only a thousand.[4]

American businesses all joined *.com* because it was the domain intended for commercial organizations. Non-U.S. businesses picked *.com* because they thought it made them sound large, international, and appealing to American audiences. Conversely, large American businesses with overseas subsidiaries also register under ISO domains—such as *microsoft.co.uk*—so they'll sound local.

Collisions abound. For example, *prince.com* has been used since 1995 by a British computer supplier, to the resentment of the American sporting goods company, which after a failed court case finally had to settle for *princetennis.com*. Had the United States followed the rest of the world's rules, this wouldn't have happened because American companies would sit in something like *.com.us*, and *.com* would be reserved for multinationals. The underutilization of *.us* is a shame: *acme.ithaca.ny.com.us* is long but perfectly clear after a minute's getting used to the syntax, and it leaves room for *acme.ithaca.mn.com.us*.

Around 1995, the DNS began to get crowded. Not only did every company want to be in *.com*, but they all wanted short, memorable names that related to their business.[5] Conflicts like the Prince situation became common, partly because a lot of businesses have the same or similar names, and partly because a lot of them compete in selling the same sorts of things. There may be many drugstores named Acme in the real world, but there can be only one *acme.com* and one *drugstore.com*. With this kind of pressure, the consensus by the mid 1990s was that the DNS needed to be revamped to create more "good" domain names.

There was another problem: Network Solutions (NSI). In the process of commercializing the Internet, the U.S. government managed to create a monopoly by awarding the contract to register domain names in *.com*, *.net*, and *.org* from 1993 to 1998 to this then small Virginia-based computer consultancy; it compounded its error by agreeing in 1995 to allow the company to charge fees. NSI began charging $50 a year for domain name registrations that September. A portion of the money went into a fund for improving the infrastructure of the Internet (scrapped in April 1998, at $45.5 million). A subsidiary of Science Applications International Corporation, NSI went public in 1997 even though, with its contract due to expire in March 1998, it had an uncertain future. The company was eventually bought by Internet trust services specialist Verisign in March 2000.

People on the Net reacted to the registration fee pretty much as though someone had suddenly started charging them to breathe, but worse were the complaints that began to surface about NSI. The company announced in June 1995 that it would suspend domains that were challenged on trademark grounds and wait for a court decision, a method that many people felt risked unfairly penalizing companies operating in good faith. NSI tended to favor American companies. The British Prince found itself suddenly cut off after marketing the address, for example, because the American Prince pointed to its federal trademark. Other policies, such as billing new registrants after sixty days, made it easy for people to engage in hostile practices such as "cybersquatting"—that is, registering the name of a major company or product with no intention of using it and then demanding a large sum to give it up to the company in question.

Two years later, when renewals came due, there were complaints about inadequate billing procedures when a number of companies (including British Telecom) found their domains shut down "for non-payment." Technical problems surfaced when, in an alarming incident in 1997, large chunks of the domain name system were wiped out for most of a twenty-four-hour period when a database update was bungled.

This incident is important to understanding the kinds of technical decisions that were at stake in the efforts to revamp the DNS. The mappings of domain names to those computer-readable numbers are held in a database to which each new name is added as it's registered. The database is held at NSI and is transferred daily to the baker's dozen of computers worldwide known as root servers, from where it propagates to the Internet's many routers. It was one of these nightly "zone transfers" that failed, and the root servers were neither able to revert to their old copy of the database nor use the new one. Much criticism was aimed at NSI for not having put systems in place to catch and rectify this kind of failure.

Even if NSI had been a perfect guardian of the DNS, however, a lot of people would still have been uncomfortable with its monopoly over the global domain name "space." By late 1996, companies were springing up to handle worldwide domain name registrations, figuring that comprehensive registration was a valuable service, given that each registry had a different set of regulations. But even if there was competition at the reseller level, the database was under NSI's control, and it was the sole registry for *.com*, *.net*, and *.org*. By 1999, 40 percent of the registrations in those three TLDs were from non-U.S. organizations, and there were a million new registrations a year in *.com*.[6] There was, in other words, competition among registrars but not among registries. There was also a lot of money involved. NSI had more than $93 million in revenues in 1998.[7]

Postel began publishing suggestions for revamping the DNS in 1994. By late 1995, a few people you might call domain name dissidents who felt the existing system was too rigid began experimenting with alternative domain naming systems (on the Net disputes lead not only to more disputes but to action).

One of these was known as eDNS (for "enhanced DNS").[8] Set up by Karl Denninger, founder of the Chicago-based ISP MCSNet, eDNS aimed to foster competition among top-level domains by creating new ones that filled obvious needs and encouraging people to modify their domain name servers to incorporate the extra TLDs.[9] Some of eDNS's suggestions make considerable sense: *.k12*, for example, for material aimed at children, or *.biz*, for general business use. But this project never really gained wide acceptance.[10]

Another was an outfit known as AlterNIC, an obvious play on "alternative" and NIC, as in the InterNIC, the main "network information center" where you could look up domain names and their registrants.[11] Run by a network administrator named Eugene Kashpureff, AlterNIC also used pre-sorted domain names. Implementing names such as *.xxx* (for sex-related domains), AlterNIC, like eDNS, found only a small audience. There was some logic to both proposals, and had they come earlier in the Net's history when the people flooding online were still technically oriented, they might have succeeded. By 1996, however, new registrants tended to be people and businesses who were more likely to follow the most obvious path. In many ways, it's a pity. For example, rather than relying on filtering software, it would be a lot simpler to block or allow specific domains, which would be possible if everyone could be relied upon to follow such a system. The problem is that it's simplistic. You can't put everything in *.k12* that a teenager might need for term paper research, for example. The big issue, though, is that someone would have to police these domains to ensure that they were not misused. This is one function everyone involved with registrations is anxious to avoid, for all kinds of reasons, from the amount of work to the legal liability to the implicit role as an Internet censor.[12]

Kashpureff himself provided an example of the difficulty of getting people to conform to rules when, in July 1997, he suddenly rerouted traffic intended for the InterNIC to his own AlterNIC. No real damage was done. People just saw his page for a few seconds and then were routed on to their original intended destinations. Kashpureff himself was tracked down by the FBI in Canada and pleaded guilty to charges of computer fraud. According to the online news service *C/Net*,[13] Kashpureff apologized publicly for his actions, although he also said (earlier) that he was glad to have publicized the controversy over the domain name system. A year later, in August 1998, the Defense Advanced Research Projects Agency (DARPA) announced it had awarded a $1.4 million contract jointly to Network Associates and the Internet Software Consortium to secure the DNS to make this type of "spoofing" impossible;[14] the system wasn't quite ready in July 1999 when a similar incident hit NSI again, this time rerouting traffic destined for three of its sites (*networksolutions.com*, *netsol.com*, and *dotpeople.com*) to the sites of two organizations set up as part of the efforts to revamp the DNS, ICANN and CORE.[15]

A third dissident DNS effort was fielded by Paul Garrin and his company pgMedia, now known as Name Space. In March 1997 Garrin petitioned NSI to add some three hundred new gTLDs to the existing three. When the company's request was refused, pgMedia filed an antitrust suit against NSI and the organization that awarded it the monopoly, the National Science Foundation.[16] While appeals against the court's ruling that NSI had immunity under its contract from the NSF were still proceeding, in 1999 Name Space had been accepted as a testbed registrar under the plan that was finally adopted. Kashpureff, despite his April 1998 write-up in *Wired*, was essentially a sideshow.[17]

With or without these ideas, everyone except NSI agreed that one of the biggest issues in revamping the DNS was creating competition in domain name registration. With this in mind, along with the need to accommodate the possible billions more registrations to come, several of the organizations traditionally involved in creating new standards and technology got together to create a design for the future. These included the Internet Society, Postel's Internet Assigned Numbers Authority, and the Internet Engineering Task Force, plus other nongovernmental organizations such as the International Telecommunications Union, and the World Intellectual Property Organization. Trying to navigate your way through the interrelationships of these organizations, each of which has its own commonly used abbreviation (in order, ISOC, IANA, IETF, ITU, and WIPO), and the committees and documents they spawned is like playing one of those awful Scrabble games where your opponent gets all the good letters.

The most important committee they set up to discuss the matter was the International Ad-Hoc Committee (IAHC). The IAHC came up with a plan in February 1997, and throughout that year the alphabet soup committee seemed to believe it would be able to agree upon, implement, test, and roll out the plan by March 1998, when NSI's contract with the NSF was due to expire. The plan was known unharmoniously as "The Generic Top Level Domain Memorandum of Understanding," abbreviated in a way only an engineer could love: gTLD-MoU. As soon as it was proposed, the IAHC disbanded in favor of the new committee specified in the memorandum, the Interim Policy Oversight Committee (iPOC), which included some of the same people.

The plan had several prongs.[18] First, the memorandum was to be deposited with the ITU, which would circulate it to public and private organizations for signature and help implement it. Four committees were to be set up under the gTLD-MoU: a council of registrars (CORE), to be established as a Swiss association; a policy oversight committee; a policy advisory body with membership open to any signatory and whose function would be to make recommendations to the policy oversight committee; and administrative domain name challenge panels, which would handle disputes over trademark infringements in the registration of second-level domains, and whose decisions were to be binding on CORE members. The procedures for creating the panels and bringing challenges before them were to be administered by WIPO. Finally, seven new gTLDs were to be created immediately, to be followed by many more once the success of the new arrangements had been evaluated and modified as needed. The one technical challenge was the creation of a distributed, shared database so that new registrations could be entered immediately by any registrar on a first-come, first-served basis.

The IAHC made several assumptions, first and foremost that the domain name space is a public resource and that its administration is a public policy issue. They believed, further, that the new system should be market-oriented and self-regulating, and also obviously assumed that any hope of convincing people to use *.us* was lost. NSI would become one of many competing registrars, and the database of domain names would belong, if it belonged to anyone, to the whole Internet.

Once written, the memorandum was circulated by the ITU to public and private organizations for signing, a reasonable way of seeking a consensus. They didn't get it, although a number of organizations did sign it, including Digital Equipment Corporation, a variety of smaller ISPs from around the world, Telecom Italia, and Bell Canada. None of the biggest names—IBM, Microsoft, AT&T, British Telecom, AOL, major governments—showed up on the list.

By 1997, however, when the plan was first being publicly proposed, NSI was somewhat resistant to giving up its monopoly. A Web page called "Internet Domain Name System: Myths and Facts" presented NSI's view of the situation.[19] The company denied there was any crisis over the availability of domain names; claimed its registration services were cheap compared to other "top" registries; claimed it had made a "significant investment" in marketing to make the *.com* gTLD a sought-after "brand"; and claimed it had invested millions in developing the infrastructure to run domain name registrations. The document noted that NSI had registered 1.3 million names (with only twenty-six lawsuits!).

While it's safe to say now that there wasn't actually a crisis in 1997, since two years later people were still finding names to register, it was still true that many of the good names were taken. NSI correctly stated that the rules under which domain names were formed gave wide latitude. However, saying this meant there were a "virtually infinite" 37^{22} possible domain names was nonsense. Yes, it's perfectly possible, mathematically, to have a domain name like *ewotyghww087skbyew.com*, but how would you remember it, let alone market it? People want names that are short and easy to remember, even if the words aren't necessarily familiar, or words that are familiar even if they aren't short. Things like *wired.com, cnet.com,* or *outthewazoo.com,* or even (as a sporting goods site showed in 1999) *fogdog.com.* Even allowing for cybersquatting, the number of available "good" names had undoubtedly shrunk substantially, even by 1997. In 1999, *Wired News* writer Declan McCullagh surveyed the dictionary and concluded that "the *.com* versions of nearly all popular words have been taken. Of 25,500 standard dictionary words we checked, only 1,760 were free."[20]

Others who complained about the plan included the Association for Interactive Media,[21] a Washington-based trade association for business on the Internet, now a subsidiary of the Direct Marketing Organization, which called it a "coup" and a "hostile takeover" by the IAHC. It added that the proposed structure amounted to a "world government for the Internet" and claimed that the plan would fragment the Internet and stop email and Web services from working reliably.[22]

Still, many of the other complaints were legitimate. Most complained that the old guard Netizens had consulted each other and their lawyers but had excluded the Internet's many newer stakeholders, such as ISPs, commercial online services, consumers, electronic commerce companies, content providers, and many others. The structure proposed in the memorandum did not automatically grant committee seats to any of these groups, and with no process proposed for elections, it was difficult to see how the group could become broadly representative or to whom it would be accountable.

The planners were confident about their scheme, though. Former ISOC president Don Heath, who chaired the IAHC during its deliberations, and Bob Shaw, who represented the ITU, both laughed comfortably when asked about the complaints and discounted their importance.[23] According to them, the proposals had been circulated widely for comments, and the newer stakeholders had the same chance to comment as everyone else. It was true that some parts of the plan were modified in response to protest. Besides the change from *.store* to *.shop,* the memorandum dropped the lottery scheme for choosing registrars proposed by the IAHC.

But the most cogent criticism, which showed up first in a posting to University of Pennsylvania professor Dave Farber's "Interesting People" list, came in the summer of 1997 from Donna Hoffman, a professor in marketing at the Owen Graduate School of Management at Vanderbilt University.[24] Hoffman asked the most important question.

> What's the problem? That we hate Network Solutions? That we're running out of names? That we need to update the gTLDs because they no longer reflect the nature of the Internet? What is the goal? What are the criteria? I just want to make sure that it's not just lawyers and technologists.

Her point was that each one of those questions might have a different answer, and that chances were that none of those answers would be the IAHC proposals. If the problem is NSI, open registration to competition. If the problem is running out of names, make more. But that could mean anything from creating new gTLDs to developing the largely unused *.us* domain or demanding that businesses use third-level domains to distinguish their products instead of second-level ones, say, registering, *titanic.paramount.com* instead of *titanicmovie.com*. How you create new gTLDs also depends on defining the problem. If users need a predictable structure for domain names so that the "namespace," as it had started being called by then, as a whole creates an automatic directory service, the answer would be something different again—perhaps something more similar to eDNS and AlterNIC.

Hoffman's own concern was at least partly the needs of electronic commerce, her specialty.

> I think it's my role to argue that the commercial voice has not been heard. I have a broader concern, which is that this whole process left out, pretty much ignored, all but just a few stakeholders, so it's not really a surprise that the solution is so weak. They didn't lay out criteria that had to be addressed, and didn't identify the constituents or their needs, so no wonder the solution is stupid and everyone is upset about it.

The biggest fuss: everyone hated the seven new names, *.firm*, *.web*, *.shop*, *.rec*, *.arts*, *.info*, and *.nom*. If it is not entirely obvious to you which companies would go under which one of these gTLDs, you're merely displaying the same confusion as everyone else. The only one that's clear is the most obscure of the seven, *.nom*, a sop to the French, intended for personal domains. If you're a legal firm that sells will-making services via a questionnaire over the Web, sells law books, and also maintains a free online library of basic legal information, are you a *firm*, a *.shop*, or a *.info*? Do you want to hand out email addresses in *.web*? If you're Microsoft will you let someone else have *microsoft.arts*?

Clearly, you're going to register your name in all of them to keep others out, something the Anti-Cybersquatting Consumer Protection Act (see chapter 8) does not protect consumers against, and that defeats the purpose of creating more names in the first place. This was part of Hoffman's argument: "The categories should be mutually exclusive and exhaustive, but also flexible enough to accommodate evolution tomorrow, and that's hard, because no one knows how it will evolve."[25]

We know the Net is continuing to grow at an amazing pace, particularly outside the United States, where there's a lot of catching up to do. We know—or think we know—that a lot of commercial transactions, particularly business-to-business, will move online over the coming decade. We also know that someone or something has to run the DNS and allocate Internet numbers, because for the foreseeable future more and more are going to be needed. This means any new system needs maximum flexibility.

The other controversy over the IAHC proposals concerned moving arbitration for domain name challenges outside the United States. (Significantly, the British Prince's win took place in a British court.) From the fuss that ensued, you'd have thought someone had proposed to move the Statue of Liberty to Geneva. The fact is that, as we saw in chapter 4, the Internet was built by everyone who is part of it and incorporates the ideas and efforts of many researchers worldwide. Claiming otherwise is the worst kind of chauvinistic nonsense.

Nonetheless, the U.S. government recognized that it had a special responsibility in trying to hand off what was essentially Internet governance, and once it became obvious that the controversy wasn't dying down, it put out a request for comments in July 1997. A year later, it published a discussion green paper and finally a white paper proposing the creation of what is now known as ICANN to coordinate the technical functions of handing out both IP numbers and domain names.[26] In many ways, the proposals aren't all that different from the IAHC's plan. Both create a massively complicated new oversight body with subcommittees and advisory panels; both seek to open the domain name business to competition and to create new names. However, ICANN was intended to be set up as an accountable body—its interim directors were supposed to create the organizational structure and then disband in favor of an elected group.

The white paper was published in July 1998, and ICANN was incorporated in September. Postel died a couple of months later, and from the testimony he gave before a couple of congressional subcommittees that October he seems to have believed that the Internet community had, incredibly, succeeded in its first effort at self-governance by creating a non-profit organization that could work by the consensus of the community it served. He was very specific about what ICANN was intended to do:

> This process was never intended to create an entity that would be a "monolithic structure for Internet governance," to use the White Paper's language. Rather, and again using the White Paper's language, we sought to create "a stable process to address the narrow issues of management and administration of Internet names and numbers on an ongoing basis."

It was, he noted, "hard to overstate how difficult even this limited assignment has proven to be."[27]

Postel never found out the half of it. In the year following his death, setting up ICANN turned into a protracted and messy squabble. Like the IAHC plan before it, ICANN was criticized for lack of accountability, secrecy (its first meetings were closed), power-grabbing (especially when the interim board members asked for their terms to be extended an extra year), and staging a "coup." Like NSI before it, ICANN faced complaints about its funding. People balked at the interim board's first proposal, charging $1 per registered domain name. David Post, a professor of law at Temple University, who with University of Pennsylvania telecommunications professor David Farber and University of Miami law professor A. Michael Froomkin set up the ICANN Watch site,[28] called it "taxation without representation."[29] In late August 1999, ICANN announced it would seek $2 million in funding from a variety of corporate sources,[30] only months later confirming reports in the *New York Times* that it was out of money.[31] No one seemed to question this, even though in public policy terms it might make sense to consider whether a non-profit corporation charged with managing technical issues should be funded by private interests rather than by the Net as a whole. NSI, meanwhile, committed several tactical blunders that cost it a lot of support, such as withdrawing the InterNIC, the network information center that pre-dated NSI's involvement in domain names (it was maintained by the research institute SRI until 1993), and claiming that the entire database of domain names was its intellectual property. It was a surprising misstep given that its new CEO, Jim Rutt, was a long-time WELL user and Nethead, a point he played on in testimony before Congress while simultaneously deleting almost every message he had ever posted to the WELL. Had it played the situation more cleverly, NSI could very possibly have won the public relations battle. ICANN, whose name was associated in many people's minds with government and bureaucracy, attracted almost immediate paranoia.

One reason—and this is a thread running through all the domain name disputes—is the intense suspicion of government that seems to be endemic among technogeeks, a tendency writer Paulina Borsook summed up as "Cyberselfish" in a 1997 essay for *Mother Jones* magazine and later dubbed technolibertarianism.[32] British journalist Andrew Brown likened the DNS disputes to Robert A. Heinlein's science fiction and its rough, tough, solitary heroes.[33] ICANN itself attributed the ill-will to an orchestrated campaign by NSI.

At the end of September 1999, however, ICANN, the Department of Commerce, and NSI announced that they had reached a tentative agreement. Everyone was now going to be friends. NSI would guarantee public access to the domain name database via the "WHOIS" search facility as long, as all the other registrars were required to give everyone access to the whole database; the InterNIC would be reinstated with links to all the other registrars; NSI would participate in funding ICANN; and NSI would recognize ICANN and become an accredited registrar.

It's interesting that all of the debates surrounded the naming system, even though ICANN was also being given responsibility for handing out IP numbers. Numbers are, if anything, more important than names, since without an IP number assigned to your machine you can't hook to the Net at all.[34] But the business of IP numbers doesn't invoke trademarks; it's an extremely technical matter handled by ISPs in negotiation with their number authority, and it's not an area in which anyone was making money before ICANN was created.

In any event, few seem to believe that ICANN will restrict itself to the purely technical matters it was founded to address; they think that ultimately this is really about Internet governance. When Internet specialist Gordon Cook, who has tracked the domain name disputes in detail in his *Cook Report on Internet*, writes, "We are at war for the future of the Internet," he is being overdramatic, but there is still a germ of truth in what he's saying.[35]

People were probably unfair to the engineers who worked on the first effort at revamping the structure, who were simply operating in the time-honored manner of seeing a problem and trying to fix it. Where they failed was in not understanding how much the Internet had changed and how many new interests felt they now owned the place. More than that, money had changed everything. For most people, the Net and its development are no longer more important than their own companies. There are exceptions, of course, such as Web creator Tim Berners-Lee and his World Wide Web Consortium. It remains to be seen if ICANN will be one of them.

So far, it doesn't seem to be. ICANN came in for a lot of criticism for favoring large business interests when it commissioned a report on the subject from the World Intellectual Property Organization that came down heavily on the side of favoring trademark holders in domain name disputes.[36] The domain name system under Postel was traditionally first-come, first-served. Under this way of thinking, trademarks shouldn't come into it unless someone is actually claiming to be a company they're not. I think it's right for people to want the populist Net to survive, and part of that is the ethic that says that if you didn't "get with" the Net early enough to secure your name in *.com* and someone else got it first, tough noogies. In any case, if protecting trademarks is that important, it shouldn't be difficult to create a carefully policed trademark gTLD, among other possibilities. The United Kingdom's national registry, Nominet, did something exactly like this in creating the *.plc.uk* and *.ltd.uk* domains; to register in either, you must produce copies of the documents registering your business with the Companies House, the United Kingdom's center for business registration.

Businesses, of course, won't necessarily like any of this—almost no one chooses to register in *.plc.uk* or *.ltd.uk*. So what should be a series of technical questions keep relentlessly morphing into larger ones of intellectual property rights and public policy.

The major issue of the next few years is going to be the future of the two-hundred-odd country code TLDs, managed under contracts awarded by Postel according to criteria he laid out in RFC1591.[37] These arrangements vary widely, from the United Kingdom's mutually owned Nominet to volunteer academics with their country's root server sitting under their desks. In a few cases, such as the Kingdom of Tonga (*.to*), the root server is a computer sitting in San Francisco and producing revenue selling domain names to foreigners who value them more than the country itself does. Nothing in international law so far requires countries to be tied to these TLDs. One concern is therefore that ICANN might try to abuse its power by imposing unacceptable conditions on the country-code contract-holders. Similarly, some people worry about its control over the root servers, especially since any centralized organization could take it upon itself—or give in to pressure—to implement censorship in the form of content controls.

Practically speaking, it's the smaller countries whose autonomy is at risk from any abuse of power ICANN might attempt. A country like, say, France isn't going to be much impressed with any regulations ICANN might seek to impose on how domains may be registered within its code, and it's easy to imagine the governmental squabble and massive publicity that would follow quickly if ICANN cut off the entirety of *.fr* from the Net.

Gordon Cook, whose *Cook Report on Internet* tracked the DNS mess for several years, has been one of the more dramatic critics, but also one of the more meticulous ones, laying out every detail he's been able to discover of the backroom machinations behind the stew of organizations. The way he tells it, the whole thing is a carefully plotted coup by Vinton Cerf and a few other members of the old guard, bent on power.

It isn't easy to weigh this material, aside from rather obvious absurdities like his calling claiming the database of domain names as a public resource "socialist." For one thing, decisions about the technical structure of the Internet have, for the most part, always been made by people who knew each other. The big change is the secrecy. Accusations that the Internet was run by a cabal are as old as . . . well, the Internet. Hence the *alt.usenet.cabal* FAQ, which is posted monthly even now to *news.admin.** newsgroups and begins, "There is no cabal. If you are invited to join the cabal . . ."[38]

What's scaring people—or what should be scaring them—is the threat that the Internet will become regulated the way broadcasting is. In radio and television, the excuse was the scarcity of resources in the form of available spectrum. By saying that domain names are a scarce resource that needs to be tightly controlled, we risk setting up an authority that has all the power over the Net that we have so far been able to argue that governments lack. ICANN through the end of 1999 showed little accountability. When it did open its meetings, the minutes show only lists of motions passed without dissent, suggesting that all the discussions must have taken place elsewhere. The ICANN Web site shows no give-and-take between the interim board members and the community whose consensus they claim to have achieved. Even the British and U.S. governments, during the years they spent trying to convince everyone that key escrow was a good idea, *really*, routinely published the dissenting views they collected.

The Internet can only perceive censorship as damage and route around it (in John Gilmore's famous phrase)—if there is an alternative route. Given the current structure of the DNS, that's not possible. For everyone to be able to reach everyone else, somewhere there must be a centralized authority that maintains the database.

Or must there? Did the groups revamping the DNS just not think imaginatively enough? Postel thought it would be possible to create an unlimited number of gTLDs—the original seven proposed by the IAHC were meant to be just the first of an eventual hundred and fifty. Dissident groups like the AlterNIC and eDNS also proposed many more gTLDs. But all these proposals have in common the assumption that there will be one "A" root server that holds the ultimate authoritative copy of the domain name database. More recently, the SuperRoot project has questioned even that. Could we not have a series of "A" root servers that trade information as peers?[39]

What is intriguing is that all of the proposed ways of revamping the DNS focus on political and administrative structures rather than technical ones. The change from *hosts.txt* to the 1983 DNS was much more fundamental. Yet without the benefit of knowing how fast the Internet would expand or how many people would ultimately use it, its designers did a pretty good job. The system scaled well, in engineering parlance, in the sense that adding millions of unexpected users did not break it. But only technically. Like many computer systems, the DNS was ruined by the users.

ICANN should take its cue from the W3C. It should publish its proposed standard agreements with registrars as if they were technical standards, allow comments, and alter the agreements accordingly. It should restrict its activities to the technical functions it keeps saying it was set up to manage, and it should resist all pressure to get into other areas. If ICANN represents the Net's attempt to govern itself, then it needs to be much more obviously of and for the Net. If, instead, it's a government-backed organization for managing day-to-day technical details that the government would much rather not handle itself, then its authority should be clearly descended from the government and clearly limited.

Three years into the public part of the dispute, at a press briefing in London, ICANN representatives said that in 2000 they would begin considering the question of whether or not to create new gTLDs. First, however, they said they would have to figure out exactly what the guiding principle behind the creation of those names should be—exactly the problem Donna Hoffman criticized the IAHC for not having thought through in 1997. Interim CEO Michael Roberts noted that he'd been surprised by the most obvious bit of advice imaginable, which came to ICANN from University of California at Berkeley professor Hal Varian: that ICANN should pick the system that is simplest from the point of view of the user.

As things stand, we can still create a system that is ludicrously over-complicated, absurdly expensive, dangerously controllable, and dissatisfying to everyone. Of course, the original system largely depended on one guy—Postel—and placed a dangerous amount of power in his hands. Postel could, had he gone nuts one day, have taken down the whole Internet. Everyone trusted him not to, in part because he earned that trust by being a responsible, disinterested, and reliable steward for more than twenty-five years, and in part because "that's how it's always been done." Sometime around 2030, maybe ICANN will enjoy that kind of trust.

5

A Thousand Points of Failure

Buy ten backhoes.

—Simson Garfinkel, *Fifty Ways to Kill the Net*

"How many bombs would it take to bring the Net down, and where would you drop them?" This is the kind of question that can silence a room full of Netheads, and so it did at a panel presented at the 1998 Computers, Freedom, and Privacy (CFP98) conference in Austin, Texas. This is a group—Netheads, lawyers, hackers, cryptographers, net.activists, and journalists—that needs no reminding that the Net was designed to withstand precisely that: bomb outages.

"Zero" was the consensus of network security specialists Matt Blaze and Steve Bellovin. Both are net.heroes even though they work as researchers specializing in network security for AT&T, surely one of the most hated organizations in the early days of the Net. Blaze came to fame for cracking the Clipper Chip and Bellovin for being one of the three 1979 graduate-student inventors of Usenet.[1] Bellovin is a member of the Internet Engineering Task Force and the Internet Architecture Board.

"Zero" is not good news, because it turns out there are far more effective ways of crippling the Net, whether by malice or by accident.

This is one of those areas that's very difficult to write about without falling into sensationalist scare stories or anti-Net hype. Of course there are risks in making the Net a basic infrastructure. There are risks in all parts of life, and security risks should not be a reason not to use the Net. Equally, security risks should not become a reason to regulate the Net. The point of highlighting risks is that we should pay more attention to what we are doing in increasing our reliance on the Internet than we have in deploying computer systems generally. As the ten years of work that went into averting a Y2K crisis made plain, we are trusting even life-critical systems to computers whose workings no one understands any more. On the other hand, people have been predicting the imminent death of the Net since before the first email message was sent, and it's important to keep some perspective: adaptable humans keep improving the Net's infrastructure, though sometimes not as quickly as might be ideal.

Peter Dawe, the founder of Pipex, Britain's first commercial ISP, listed in a 1994 interview some of the "ten thousand" things that could kill the Internet.[2] Video and audio were among his concerns, particularly video, which he thought would swamp the Internet's switching capacity. At the time, the Web was just taking off, and it really wasn't clear whether academic institutions would continue to finance making large amounts of information available. Given enough traffic, it seemed possible that the load of visitors could rapidly increase beyond anything the universities could reasonably be expected to want to finance. Other fears of the time included the worry that routers would run out of address space, or that ads would drive everyone away.

In 1996, Bob Metcalfe, the founder of the networking company 3Com, predicted the Net would start collapsing of its own weight and volume in the coming year, suffering the equivalent of a series of brownouts. A few services did suffer outages—notably AOL and its twenty-two-hour marathon—but the Net itself survived, and Metcalfe literally had to eat his words at the sixth World Wide Web conference in early 1997.[3] It was some of these outages that exercised Blaze and Bellovin on their CFP panel—the ones that really could take out the Net by using the simple fact that although the Net was built to withstand a bomb it was not built to be suspicious: the computers that direct traffic all trust each other. The Internet was designed to share information. It was not designed to be secure, and in the academic research world it began in, it didn't need to be: it made perfect sense to build a network based on trust.

The two domain name server incidents mentioned in chapter 4 were part of the impetus for this panel. On July 16, 1997, a large chunk of the Net was cut off when Network Solutions bungled a domain name system database update, allowing a corrupted version of the file to be propagated to the world's dozen or so root servers, so that large parts of the Net couldn't find each other. The failed update was widely criticized at the time as an example of poor design. A database of such critical importance should be designed so that it automatically checks its integrity after an update and can roll back to the last previous working version. Criticism continued when Network Solutions later said it was a human error—a system administrator had ignored alarm warnings. The corrupted file was replaced after only about four hours, but the damage took many more hours to correct completely.

Two days later, Eugene Kashpureff, the "domain name dissident" behind the renegade AlterNIC service, diverted traffic intended for Network Solutions' Web site to his own using a technique called "spoofing."[4]

Web spoofing was not a new idea: it had been described in a 1996 paper by Princeton University's Edward Felten and others[5] and even then was being used by a few legitimate services such as The Anonymizer,[6] a service designed to protect privacy by hiding user details as you browse the Web. The idea is similar to that of bogus cash machines, which appear to accept your card and PIN normally but in fact copy the information to create a duplicate. Both this kind of attack and Web spoofing rely on the idea that experienced users react to familiar cues without looking too closely. In Web spoofing, the attacker inserts his Web server in between the victim and the rest of the Web, so that all traffic goes through the attacker's site and is controlled by the attacker. Initiating the attack may be as simple as rewriting a few commonly followed URLs on a Web page to go via the attacker's site. The attacker's Web server retrieves all the pages requested, but rewrites the links on those pages to divert via the attacker's site. As long as the user doesn't examine details such as the status line of his browser window or the source code of the document, the diversion will probably remain unnoticed. A more sophisticated attacker can eliminate even those cues by using a Java program to replace the user's own menu bar and status line. By this means, the attacker can retain copies of any personal information the victim sends—user names, passwords, credit card details—even if it's typed into secure forms.

"We do not know of a fully satisfactory long-term solution to this problem," Felten and his colleagues conclude, although they recommend that secure connections (when personal information is most at risk) should include a clear indication of who is at the other end of the connection—company names, rather than URLs.

Kashpureff's goals were not so complicated or sinister: he merely wanted to protest NSI's monopoly of the domain name system. Nonetheless, don't try this at home: Kashpureff went on to face federal wire and computer fraud charges.

The one person who did get away with diverting the Net's traffic was the eminently trustworthy Jon Postel. For about ten days starting in late January 1998, he quietly rerouted the Net by instructing the administrators of about half of the world's dozen root servers to get their updates from him rather than directly from Network Solutions, the company that manages the assignment of addresses within *.com*, *.net*, and *.org*. Postel said afterward that it was a test in preparation for the revamping of the domain name system.[7] Because Postel *was* Postel, the people operating the root servers obeyed the instructions, and no one doubted that he had the right and ability to do what he did, given his special position with respect to the Internet and the domain name system. It's difficult to imagine that any one person will have as much power—or as much of others' trust—in future.

Even so, as ICANN takes over these functions, the vulnerability is largely the same: centralized authority provides a wonderful target for the malicious, as Bellovin went on to point out that day at CFP. "I live in fear that somebody with a malicious bent of mind will notice these accidents and say, 'Gee, I could do that, too,'" he said in recounting some of these incidents. The biggest dangers seem to be the kinds of attacks Blaze and Bellovin were talking about, where the Internet's own infrastructure of trust is turned against it.

For example: routers trust each other. They believe what they're told by other routers, and they depend on having access to accurate information matching numbered addresses to named domains, which information is stored in about a dozen root servers worldwide. If a misconfigured router in a small company convinces its upstream ISP that it's the best route to much of the rest of the Internet, the upstream ISP's router will act on this information and pass it on to other routers. When this happened in 1998, it took hours for all parts of the system to stabilize, even though the misconfigured link was shut down in half an hour. "What if somebody did that deliberately from a few different points?" wondered Bellovin. "This could be a massive denial-of-service attack on the Net—or an eavesdropping attack."

Denial-of-service attacks form a large category of problems of different types, from mail-bombing someone to tying up their Net connection with useless probes. Essentially, it means that the person under attack can't use their connection or their server for its intended purpose. In a mail-bomb attack, someone sends megabytes of mail messages, clogging up the mail server or (in some cases) email box so that legitimate email can't get in or out. (It's tempting—but not quite fair—to say that the 1.5Mb useless attached word-processed files PR people send out instead of plain text press releases are like this.)

All of these attacks are possible, in a sense, because on the Net all computers are equal. As Blaze put it, "The vulnerabilities of the Net arise from the fact that powerful access to the structure of the Net is available to everyone on the Net, and second of all, every machine on the Net can be controlled, to some extent, remotely by any other machine on the Net." Your $19.95 a month enables you, if you are knowledgeable and malicious, to send false packets of data to the routers and reprogram them. This puts the Net in danger from everything from software bugs to human error, mechanical failure, or deliberate damage—an issue that is going to loom larger as always-on broadband connections like ADSL and cable modems reach the mainstream. Security experts like Chris Rouland, a broadband specialist with Internet Security Systems, have begun warning that broadband access, coupled with the ready availability of cracking tools on the Net and the lack of ethics training for kids, will empower a new generation of teenaged crackers.

Or, as London-based networking consultant David Morton, who participated in British Telecom's ADSL year-long trial, put it when talking about the many cracking attempts he logged on his network, "This is forty to fifty kids over the space of a week that have nothing better to do than try to crack into a server where there's nothing interesting anyway. It's going to be an enormous problem."

Much of the Internet's functioning has also always depended on voluntary good citizenship. The Internet protocols are designed so that end points on the Net—a company's network or an individual machine—behave in ways that are best for the network as a whole. For example, if a packet fails to get through, the sending machine assumes that the problem is network congestion and waits longer and longer to try again rather than clog the Net by trying continuously until the data gets through. "Right now, all the vendors of software that run these protocols distribute well-behaved software that does this global optimization," said Blaze. "But a vendor could do well on its own benchmarks by behaving in ways that are very bad for the Net at large."

Bellovin had a better strategy for bringing the Net to its knees: "My favorite way is to introduce a new killer application. The Web almost took down the Net." He was only half joking, as anyone knows who tried to download the Starr report right after its release. In that case there was a simple solution: because the document was static and issued by the government and therefore public, it was a relatively simple matter for news media sites and individuals to make mirror copies, thereby relieving the pressure on the original site.

Some alterations to the Net's technical underpinnings could fix a lot of the potential for spoofing routers. The domain name system could be secured by using cryptography for authentication. According to Blaze, "The protocols for doing secure DNS—that is, making the DNS less vulnerable to forged data giving misleading DNS responses—exist. Those protocols are there, there's software to do it, it's just a matter of getting them deployed."

Upgrading the IP protocols would help, too. The specification for IPv6, the new version of the Internet protocols, was finished in the summer of 1995, but by the end of 1999 it still had not gone into wide use, even though the rollout had been announced and the problems it was designed to solve persisted, especially the risk that the Internet would run out of address numbers to assign.

As Blaze noted, "The hard part is designing new, good, robust protocols, and that's non-trivial, particularly new, good, robust protocols that scale. The much, much harder part is deploying them on the scale of the Internet and getting people to actually run them." In fact, secure Internet protocols were designed about ten years ago, and there is software available to run them. "If everyone in the room could convince a million of their friends to run it, the Net would be a lot safer."

One difficulty is that as the Net has been commercialized, it has developed many more single points of failures and has become much less diverse, as security writer Simson Garfinkel pointed out in 1997. He estimated, for example, that 80 to 90 percent of the Net's routers were made by Cisco Systems.[8]

The greatest threat to Net security in 1999, virus attacks, played on this monocultural, cloned-sheep type of weakness. Melissa, for example, played on the fact that a large percentage of email users now use Microsoft's Outlook Express. Using the standard file name, location, and format of Outlook's address book, the virus emailed copies of itself to the first fifty email addresses it found with a subject line saying "Important Message From" and a familiar name. The recipients typically looked at the email, saw it was from a colleague, thought it might be important, and clicked to open the attached document, thereby setting off another round. In this case, the virus's successful spread depended on two population stereotypes: first, that many users all have the same software installed in standard ways; second, that humans instinctively trust people they know. In that sense, the virus might better have been called an impersonator, the harbinger of worse such security risks to come. The irony is that after years of patiently explaining to every new-comer who arrived online that the "Good Times Virus" was just a hoax[9] and that viruses cannot infect anything from pure text email messages, Microsoft turned email into a more devastating danger than a hacker attack by making attachments easy to use, decode, and run. Even the network administrators who heard the news, downloaded the necessary patches, and secured their mail servers before work started on that fateful Friday weren't exempt: they wound up spending the whole day explaining to their companies' directors why they didn't have to shut down the server.

The big new security issue for the early 2000s is likely to be related to broadband. The problem with always-on connections is that most mass-market computers have no security built in, and what has not oc-curred to most people is that if you can reach the Net 24/7, the Net can reach you. Most of the attacks David Morton logged during the ADSL trial were cracking attempts of dreary mediocrity in which someone who's downloaded Back Orifice[10] used it to probe standard holes that many consumers may not understand are vulnerable.

This is one area where Microsoft is at least partly to blame. Secu-rity was not a completely unknown field even in the early days of DOS. One reason Linux has done well, aside from its (lack of) price, is that its UNIX-like design emulates the security control found in UNIX, rather than that in DOS/Windows. While you can get into endless religious debates about whether Java or Active-X should be allowed to reach down into your PC and run programs, the fact is that the ability to lock away chunks of data and protect them from being tampered with or found just isn't there on millions of mass-market PCs. Even worse, the standardized directory structure many programs impose on you—you have to get instructions from an ex-pert on how to remove the standard "My Documents" directory, for example[11]—make most PCs sitting ducks for attacks if someone can figure out how to access them.

The existence of tens of millions of mostly identical machines, each with its own static IP address, is going to precipitate a new set of risks. Apart from the privacy issue of whether "they" can monitor your every

Net foray, we are talking about something close to Orwell's night-mares: instead of a world where the central historical record could be changed untraceably, we may end up with one where collective history is largely unalterable but our personal history as expressed in our computer data is vulnerable.

All is not lost, of course. Consumer-level firewalls are beginning to appear on the market, and the companies offering ADSL are beginning to think more carefully about security requirements. It seems as though one reason they've been so slow to think about this is that several of the phone companies imagined that what people would want ADSL for is video on demand. Shocking but true: no one cares about video on demand but everyone wants to be hooked to the Internet.

Other 1999 incidents were just examples of human stupidity, like the college system administrator who, in November 1999, decided to block all of *.uk* because a single spam message had come from a *.uk* domain. Yes. The sysadmin cut off a whole country until someone pointed out to him what he'd done. One presumes the problem was simple ignorance. If the Marx Brothers were making *Duck Soup* now, is this how Fredonia would start the war?

6

The Empire Strikes Back

Is a talking paperclip all we have to show for over half a century
of computer science research?   —"McKing" on Slashdot

On November 5, 1999, U.S. District Court Judge Thomas
Penfield Jackson released his "Finding of Fact" in the long-running Department of Justice (DoJ) antitrust case against Microsoft.[1] The case
was still a long way from assessing penalties, and everyone knew there
would be an appeal. But Jackson's assessment—followed in April 2000
by a decisive guilty verdict against Microsoft—was one that most com-
mentators felt would stand on appeal, and it was a firm first step down
the road to acknowledging what most people in the industry said privately they believed, though few wanted to go on the record: Microsoft
is a bully.[2]

Microsoft CEO Bill Gates responded by saying that he believed the
company competed "vigorously and fairly" and that "we respectfully
disagree with a number of the Court's findings."[3]

The history of antitrust cases is interesting and varied, but the cases
fall into two general types. The first is a traditional monopoly where a
particular company is accused of monopolizing an industry or having a
very large percentage of market share. This is what happened with
IBM, in the case ending with a consent decree signed in 1956. As a
remedy, the company was ordered to sell as well as rent its mainframes
and to license its patents to other manufacturers. IBM was investigated
again 1969–1982 with a view to breaking it up. The investigation was
dropped by the Reagan administration, but insiders note that it substantially changed the company's culture. The best-known antitrust
case in recent years is, of course, the 1984 break-up of AT&T, whose
monopoly over the local loop allowed it to control the long distance
business.

In the second type of antitrust case, a single company controls a large percentage of one market and seeks to control a large percentage of a second, when the output of the first is necessary for the second. The movie industry before 1948, when the studios were ordered to divest themselves of movie theater chains, is an example. Movie theaters simply couldn't exist without the movies the studios produced. Standard Oil, similarly, used its control over the supply chain to require independent dealers in petroleum products to sign exclusive contracts.

It's arguable that Microsoft fits both types of case. It dominates many of the markets it competes in, owning 90 percent of the operating systems market for desktop computers and a similar percentage of the market for office productivity software. Its dominance in operating systems also gives it unique control over what applications work well with those operating systems.

Microsoft "got Net" on December 7, 1995, when Bill Gates called his troops together and announced a massive change of plan, having finally become convinced that if the company didn't embrace the Internet it would go the way IBM did when the PC came along.

"Essentially, Microsoft's plan is to leverage its dominance of the PC market—in which it holds a more than 80 percent share—by building Internet hooks into its complete product line," *Internet World* noted at the time. "By bundling a host of Internet functions into Windows 95, Windows NT, and Windows applications, Microsoft's goal is to give users Internet capability while keeping them within the Microsoft product fold, with its continuous cycle of upgrades."[4]

It didn't take long for Microsoft to make its Net presence felt. By mid-1996, *Time* was talking about the war over the soul of the Internet, and the so-called "browser wars" between Microsoft and Netscape were fully underway.[5]

Microsoft had already attempted—and failed—to take over the online services business by creating its new MSN as a proprietary service to be bundled with Windows 95. It failed largely because MSN merely emulated the older big successes, CompuServe, Prodigy, and AOL (then number three) by ignoring Internet standards. When Microsoft's plans became known, AOL and CompuServe complained that it was unfair competition if Microsoft could promote its service as part of Windows when they couldn't. In a consent decree finally approved by Judge Jackson in August 1995, days before Windows 95 was due for its worldwide midnight launch, Microsoft agreed to give AOL icon space on the Windows desktop, to stop some of its licensing practices,[6] and to stop tying products together.

It was this consent decree that the DoJ claimed Microsoft had violated when, in 1997, it hauled the company back into court demanding an attention-getting fine of $1 million a day. This sounds like a lot, but if you did the math, Microsoft had enough cash in the bank to pay the fine every day for twenty-seven years. Microsoft, the DoJ claimed, had violated the decree by tying together Windows 95 and Internet Explorer.

In other words, the center of all the fuss was a Web browser.

At the time, the notion that such a small, apparently fringe product as a Web browser could be the subject of a major antitrust action seemed laughable to most people. Where was the DoJ when Microsoft was taking over the office productivity software business and knocking out Borland, Lotus, and WordPerfect? Netscape had gone public with a market capitalization of $3.1 billion. On the day Gates announced his conversion Netscape had $81 million in sales, six hundred employees, and 90 percent of the browser "market," if you could call it that given that most people got their browsers for free, either from their ISPs or by downloading test, or beta, versions. Microsoft codified the free price, though, by distributing Internet Explorer free to businesses as well as individuals, which Netscape hadn't done. This was Netscape's worst nightmare. Web browsers and servers were its only products, and its funding came entirely from what sales of those products it could make coupled with the money it had raised from venture capitalists in its initial public offering (IPO). Competing against a company with more or less infinite funding for any project it cares to take on and a large amount of control over 90 percent of the market's computers is never likely to be a winner.

Once Microsoft attacked the browser market, both Netscape's market share and its stock price slid quickly. Netscape was the original Internet bubble stock that launched a thousand IPOs in its own image. It opened for trading in the summer of 1996 and popped from $27 to $71 its first day out, peaking at just under $80 a share the following January before beginning the halting slide downwards to acquisition by AOL in February 1998 at just over $30 a share.[7] By September 1999, according to surveys of Web sites, the free server Apache still had 55.5

percent of the market, with Microsoft number two at 22 percent, and Netscape vanishing at 7.51 percent.[8] In late 1999, *Business Week* estimated that Microsoft had 64 percent of the browser market.[9]

The computer industry moves fast, and antitrust cases move slowly. The May 1998 decision came too late to save Netscape. At that point, Netscape played its only possible remaining card and made its flagship browser free of charge to everyone, hoping the browser would encourage consumers to try Netscape's chargeable server software. At the same time, Netscape made a more interesting and complex decision, to release the source code for its flagship browser, in the hope that the thousands of talented programmers worldwide who used it would write add-ons and new features for it that would help keep the browser at the cutting edge.

"It's hard to know what the future might have held for Netscape in a normal competitive environment, though given its dramatic initial successes, I have no doubt the sky was the limit," wrote company founder Jim Clark in his 1999 book, by way of explaining why he began looking for a buyer for Netscape as early as 1997.[10]

This was not the view of Charles H. Ferguson, the founder of Vermeer Technologies, whose Web page authoring product is now better known as Microsoft Front Page. Describing Netscape CEO Jim Barksdale as "arrogant, ignorant of technology, distracted by politics and glamour," and arguing that Front Page was the swing vote in the browser wars, Ferguson writes, "It became clear to me that, even playing fair, Microsoft would kill Netscape, and I was sure Microsoft wouldn't play fair."[11]

AOL's buying Netscape didn't bring much comfort to those who feared monopoly—or oligopoly—control. For one thing, no one knew at first what AOL's plans would be regarding the browser. AOL, which itself is despised by plenty of Net old-timers,[12] made it plain that its primary interest in the company had to do with Netscape's portal, the home page that every copy of the software loaded automatically on start-up.[13] Users could change that setup, but just as they tended to stick with Internet Explorer if it shipped pre-installed on their systems, they tended not to change their browsers' home page. In other words, by 1998 the business had changed again, and large aggregates of users visiting the same pages were more valuable to companies like AOL, Yahoo!, and Amazon.com than the software they used to make those visits.

AOL, like Microsoft, is committed to proprietary software. AOL as a system eschews Internet standards almost entirely, the sole exception being the TCP/IP protocols that connect users to the service, which do allow you to operate your AOL connection as a standard ISP connection. Within AOL, the graphics, display technology, message boards, and email are all based on proprietary software. There's a business reason for this and for AOL's failure to use Internet standard email, which would give its users many more software choices: if AOL keeps you under its control, it can make money from showing you ads. So the news that the two most important Web browsers were now both going to be in the hands of large companies dedicated to proprietary software outweighed anything that might have seemed good about the arrangement.

The years 1995 to 1997 had seen Microsoft invest widely. Besides its nuclear arms race against Netscape to bloat browser software, it set up the Web-based literary magazine *Slate* and local listings services *Sidewalk*, terrifying the competing startup Citysearch. It invested $1 billion in Comcast, the fourth-largest cable company in the United States. It developed Web- and TV-based content in partnership with the American network NBC. It bought the television-based Internet access service WebTV. Finally, it continued to push its lackluster Microsoft Network. On top of that it increased research spending by opening its first non-U.S. facility in Cambridge, England, handed $150 million to Apple (in exchange for including Internet Explorer on the Mac desktop), bought the video streaming company VXtreme, and handed $45 million to language specialist Lernout and Hauspie.

Over that same period, Microsoft increased the number of desktop and network computing areas in which it's dominant. It has 86 percent of the desktop operating system market; 87 percent of office suites (Lotus has 6 percent, Corel 4.7 percent); and 39.8 percent of units shipped in 1996 in network operating systems, slightly ahead of Novell and UNIX. Plenty of Microsoft competitors have fallen by the wayside as the company has achieved those numbers, while many formerly successful third-party products have lost out as their functions have been subsumed into the operating system. The rare competitor that has succeeded is Intuit, whose Quicken product still outsells Microsoft's competing Money.[14]

Meanwhile, it also got into electronic commerce with sites like Carpoint and travel retailer Expedia. It couldn't even let the market for *free* email go by: when Hotmail launched on July 4, 1996, and amassed six million users within a year, Microsoft bought the company (in 1997) for $400 million worth of Microsoft stock. The actual price was not revealed, but the SEC filing showed it as 2,769,148 shares. (Yes. Microsoft paid $400 million to give away an email service, but only on paper. Such is the logic of the Internet business.)[15]

The company is just as important in the market areas it hasn't entered. Just about any new company filing for an IPO notes in its SEC filing under "risks" the possibility that Microsoft could enter its market and hurt its business. One example is Openwave (formerly known as Phone.com), which makes a microbrowser for cellphones and sells a license to use it and its server suite to network operators and phone manufacturers. Microsoft was not known to be interested in cellphones at the time, though it had a cut-down version of Windows (CE) for palmtops that was not competing particularly effectively against rivals such as Psion's EPOC and 3Com's Palm. Within six months of Phone.com's IPO, Microsoft signed a deal with Ericsson to create a microbrowser, and analysts were beginning to talk about a replay of the browser wars in the wireless world.[16]

Nonetheless, the $1 million fine that got all the headlines was never imposed. Microsoft objected (of course) to Judge Jackson's ruling that it had to stop requiring computer manufacturers to bundle Windows 95 and Internet Explorer. In its court filing on the subject, Microsoft claimed:

> By directing Microsoft to license to computer manufacturers a version of Windows 95 that does not include Internet Explorer, the district court has forced Microsoft to license an operating system that is plainly deficient and that Microsoft should not be required to have associated with its name.

This was, of course, the same software that Microsoft promoted so tirelessly in August 1995.

Nonetheless, under pressure not only from the DoJ but also threats of antitrust investigations in the European Union and Japan, in February 1998, Microsoft signed an agreement allowing computer makers the freedom to install Windows 95 without Internet Explorer. That same month, the Appeals court ruled that the injunction should not apply to Windows 98, and the operating system upgrade shipped.

The court agreement was cautiously welcomed by Microsoft critics such as Consumer Project on Technology director James Love: "The current dispute in the US is important but extremely narrow, as were the recent two settlements in the EC," he said. "What the EC and the US—and possibly Japan—need to do is bring a far broader suit against Microsoft and seek much broader remedies. The model we have been most interested in is the conduct rules imposed on IBM to open up the interoperability of its mainframes."

In the 1984 EC ruling to which Love refers, IBM agreed to share information and provide assistance to competitors marketing interoperable hardware and software. Something similar could be done with Microsoft now, forcing the company to reveal details of file formats and other information that would make it easier for outside developers to write interoperable programs, and requiring the company to support open protocols and standards.

In fact, the ruling made little difference in the end. Instead, three months later the Department of Justice, twenty U.S. states, and the District of Columbia filed a new antitrust suit alleging Microsoft had abused its market power. Supporting documentation submitted by the DoJ came not only from Netscape but also Compaq and Gateway. These cases were consolidated and heard by Judge Jackson throughout 1999, culminating in his November 1999 "Finding of Fact."

There were a variety of issues concerning Microsoft besides the antitrust case, most of which were ignored. Over Christmas 1997, for example, while the Bill Gates Personal Wealth Clock[17] ticked past $38.6778 billion, the Washington state legislature was considering a bill allowing companies to withdraw time-and-a-half for overtime for software developers earning more than $27.63 an hour. One of the chief beneficiaries would be Microsoft, which around then announced a 53 percent increase in profits; the company was the largest member of the bill-backing Washington Software and Digital Media Alliance.

A second case, which did get some press attention, was Sun's suit against Microsoft, filed in early 1998. The suit alleged that Microsoft had made changes to its version of Java that compromised the standard Sun had worked to create since its announcement in May 1995.

Java is a system made up of four components: a programming language, a virtual "machine" that runs on a piece of hardware and provides an environment in which Java programs ("applets") can run without change from any other type of hardware, a set of libraries that Java programs can draw on for standard routines, and a Java compiler. Any device that can run a virtual machine and has a set of the libraries installed should be able to run any Java program without alteration. Compare this to the Windows world, where a copy of Word for Windows cannot possibly run on an Apple Mac, or a program written for Windows 95/98 may not run on Windows NT,[18] and it's easy to see why Microsoft might have been alarmed.

In the court case, Sun claimed that Microsoft was introducing changes to its version of Java that made it no longer fully compatible with the standards set by Sun. The first rulings in the case, in late 1998, granted a preliminary injunction in Sun's favor; however, the ruling was suspended on appeal in August 1999.[19]

Stories that Microsoft changes standards in order to lock customers into its own implementation abound, so the only really surprising thing to most people was that the antitrust case hadn't started ten years earlier and focused on the applications market. Instead, it took the development of the Net and, according to Michael Lewis's *The New New Thing*, a push from Netscape founder Jim Clark to focus the government's mind on Microsoft's business practices.[20]

To be fair to Microsoft, this is not a story with white and black hats where in which Netscape gets to play the injured innocent. In fact, it's more like the beginning of the Marx Brothers movie *A Night at the Opera*, where Groucho, finding the bad-guy tenor beating up on Harpo, asks, "Hey, you big bully, why are you beating up on that little bully?" Like Microsoft, Netscape added non-standard extensions to its browser's support of HTML and probably would have behaved much like Microsoft if it had had the size and clout. And Netscape itself was founded with the intention of killing off a competitor—Mosaic, the browser the Netscape team wrote as students in Illinois.[21]

In fact, the primary losers in the browser wars were the many browsers that previously populated the Net. Before the buzz about Netscape and Internet Explorer, the Web was full of browsers in progress: Cello, WinWeb, OmniWeb, Mosaic, and especially the still widely used, text-based Lynx. Most of these ceased being developed and fell too far behind to catch up after Netscape and then Internet Explorer came along, in part because of the extra extensions both insisted on creating without waiting for the World Wide Web consortium's unified standard. Whereas in the past any site would work in any browser, the competition between Microsoft and Netscape required Web designers to test their sites extensively on several versions of each browser.

Many commercial sites decided not to bother beyond the two most common browsers, locking out other browsers rather than using lowest-common-denominator designs that would display universally. I preferred Cello, for example, to either commercial contender, but I finally had to give up using it when forms became a way of life on the Web. The only new browser anyone talked about after the big two came along was Opera.[22] First developed in 1994 as an in-house browser for the Norwegian telecommunications company Telenor and publicly released in 1996, Opera made a lean antidote (it would run on an old 386!) to the bloat that began afflicting browser software after the Netscape–Microsoft fight began.

In other words, Bill Gates had a point when he claimed that Microsoft didn't do anything other companies didn't do. "Everybody plays rough in Silicon Valley," Daniel Lyons wrote in *Forbes* in December 1998. "They bundle weak products with bestsellers, give away freebies, bad-mouth rivals, and use standards and alliances to favor friends and punish foes."[23] Even so, power changes everything. The same moves by a smaller industry player are no less unethical, but they are less damaging to the others in the business. The real losers, of course, are consumers.

For all these reasons, it made sense for the DoJ to look ahead at Microsoft's impact on the Internet. Judge Jackson's "Finding of Fact" pulled together the many strands of evidence and made sense of them as a pattern whereby Microsoft sought to protect what the ruling called "the applications barrier to entry." Any software that made Microsoft's operating systems less necessary—by giving application developers a way of creating software that would run on most machines but not rely on Windows—was challenged in one way or another. In some challenges, Microsoft fielded a competing product (as in the Netscape case); in others it altered standards so as to lock developers and customers into Microsoft's software (as Sun alleges it did with Java), imposed contractual restrictions (as in several cases detailed in the ruling, including that of Compaq), or made simple threats (such as the threat to cease developing MacOffice if Apple wouldn't promote Internet Explorer and exclude Netscape).[24]

All these apparently disparate things posed a danger that attracted Microsoft's attention. Even Intel, whose chips couple with Microsoft's operating systems to give a PC its essential character and behavior, was shown in the "Finding of Fact" to have come under fire from Microsoft when it wrote software to make certain types of multimedia programming easier.

The Web and Java posed the biggest challenge, however. The hype of 1995 promoted the idea that the Web would kill Microsoft by making information available on any platform.[25] As long as there was a browser available—and Netscape was deliberately building browsers for everything it could think of—users would have access to the Web. Java opened the potential for users to run mini-applications ("applets") across the Net on any machine. A major idea of the time, for example, was that instead of buying a desktop publishing program and a CD-ROM full of six hundred fonts you don't need so you could use just one of them on, say, a Christmas card, you might access a design site across the Web to create your Christmas card, paying a much smaller fee for one-time use.

All this matters because the biggest selling point for Microsoft Windows isn't the company that produces it or the (debatable) quality of the software, it's the number of applications written for that operating system. Most people, after all, do not buy computers because they're "your plastic pal who's fun to be with."[26] They buy computers in order to use them to play games, balance a checkbook, or publish a magazine. The bigger the base of software available for a particular type of machine, the more valuable it is to anyone buying it.

If Microsoft were solely an operating system vendor, its interests would be different. Instead of subsuming functions such as browser software or housekeeping utilities into its operating system, it would want to get as many outside companies as possible to integrate with it. There's no doubt that Microsoft needs competition and outside ideas. DR-DOS pushed the company to add much-needed features to MS-DOS; the Mac pushed it into developing graphical interfaces; Netscape woke it up to the Internet. "Name one product innovation that Microsoft has generated," Sun CEO Scott McNealy challenged London journalists in October 1999. "Name one game that was not bought or stolen."[27]

There are plenty of reasons to worry about the future of the Net if Microsoft comes to dominate it. If most people are using a single company's software for both client and server,[28] we've taken a step toward turning the Internet into a proprietary system, as developers change to take advantage of the most common software. In such a system, the company that owns the browser and server combination could easily cripple its competitors by making subtle but incompatible changes to its technology. People are right to fear this outcome, given the developments we've already seen.[29]

Consumer advocate Ralph Nader and economist James Love, both part of the Consumer Project on Technology, summed up the situation in 1997:

> Some say Microsoft is a blessing because it has given us inexpensive software and made it easier for consumers to share and exchange documents and data. . . . However, we should recall that low-priced consumer software was pioneered by Borland and other software companies and that the Internet has vastly enhanced the sharing of data on a system that was designed to be open and competitive. . . .
>
> But in every field where Microsoft has gained overwhelming dominance, there has been a dramatic decline in innovation. . . . If Microsoft monopolizes the user interface for the Internet, it can bias the selection of content and services, which will create new opportunities for Microsoft to partner with various industry sectors, while rendering Internet commerce less competitive, thus harming consumers. Apart from economic considerations, we believe society is harmed by excessive concentrations of power.[30]

You could argue—and a lot of folks frustrated by today's Internet might agree—that a single proprietary system might work better than the present standards-driven open network with its delays and confusions. People seem to like the security of having a single organization to blame when something goes wrong with technology, a reason sometimes given to explain why people are slow to adopt free software. This ability is more apparent than real, however: in one of his many papers on open-source software, free software hacker Eric S. Raymond makes the point that many software licenses disclaim even merchantability, so the "somebody to sue" idea is an illusion.[31]

But often in the computer industry growth and innovation have followed open standards that have broadened the number of minds working on a given problem. IBM's market, for example, increased after the European Community required it to share information and help competitors market interoperable hardware and software. Similarly, the amazing success of the IBM PC design over better contenders such as the Apple Mac is typically attributed to IBM's decision to license the architecture, opening the way for other companies to make compatible hardware and increasing the incentive for programmers to create software for the machines. IBM's own size and clout didn't hurt, of course, but it's widely held that Apple's failure to license its operating system condemned it to remain a marginal player.

In the wake of the "Finding of Fact," Microsoft's newer rivals displayed optimism that the market could open up for them. "What Judge Jackson's ruling creates is a leveling of the playing field," Robert Young, CEO of the Linux company Red Hat, told CNBC the Monday after the ruling. "There's no doubt to anyone who's been in this industry as long as I have that Microsoft has played very aggressively. All the stories that are coming out are true. They're things that people in this industry have lived for the last decade." Unlike a lot of people, Young did not want to see the company broken up. Instead, "I'd like to see them policed. Otherwise, the owner of that monopoly can do difficult things to his competitors."

It was a surprising reaction, given the fact that much of the technical community seem to distrust government to extreme. Microsoft is no exception: outside the tech world, what got a lot of people about the antitrust action was the arrogance of Microsoft's response. His Billness, as Gates is often known online in Britain, seemed at first to dismiss the government's power to call his company to account, and, once the case went to court, engaged in hair-splitting and delaying tactics on a par with President Clinton's uncertainty over what "is" is.[32] Intel, by comparison, when faced with an antitrust action, cooperated quietly and reached a settlement comparatively quickly.[33]

As an example, when Judge Jackson imposed a temporary order against Microsoft prohibiting it from requiring computer manufacturers to bundle Internet Explorer with Windows 95, the company offered computer manufacturers the unpalatable choice of making Windows 95 inoperable by deleting Internet Explorer or installing Windows 95 as originally released, without any of the interim updates and fixes. In a classic courtroom moment, Judge Jackson decided to try removing Internet Explorer for himself via the Add/Remove Software button and found the process quite simple. It was only then that Microsoft revealed that Add/Remove takes out only twenty of more than two hundred files (and 66Mb) making up Internet Explorer (nice to know what happened to all that disk space). Microsoft won its appeal on that point, accusing the court of "unprecedented judicial intrusion into basic product design."

Technical smarts and resentment against big government seem to be a common mix. One characteristic of this mindset is an apparently complete inability to believe that governments ever do anything useful. "The whole premise of antitrust law is wrong," Raymond told *Salon*'s Andrew Leonard after the "Finding of Fact" was released. "Governments don't break up monopolies, markets do. Governments create monopolies."[34] Useless, perhaps, to say that the market can't handle the problem if the power balance is weighted too much toward one player, or to point out, as Leonard does, that the free availability of the operating system UNIX, developed at AT&T, was due to a 1956 court decision barring the telephone company from selling equipment unrelated to its core business, though he hastens to add that code-sharing existed before UNIX's development.

As the court case winds on through appeals and findings of law, what happens to Microsoft will be the question. Do we police the company? Block its expansion into new markets? Force it to release the Windows source code? Break up the company up?[35] Meanwhile, the first suit against Microsoft didn't take long to materialize—the state of California filed suit within a couple of weeks over the pricing of Windows 95, which the "Finding of Fact" showed had been set unnecessarily high. Private suits were expected over other points.

The most interesting possibility is probably opening the Windows source code. There are flaws to this remedy—primarily that the code is so huge that it would take programmers a long time to read and understand it—but it might do the most to create a truly level playing field and would almost certainly improve the quality of what is, by traditional standards, very flaky and insecure software. To most people, it's counterintuitive that software could possibly be better developed by a motley band of volunteers than by a tightly organized major corporation. But this is the central claim of those for whom free—that is, open-source—software is not only a philosophy but a lifestyle and a culture. Judge Jackson dismissed Microsoft's claim that Linux was a credible competitor to Windows, despite the so-called Halloween memoranda, internal Microsoft email naming Linux as a dangerous competitor.[36] If Microsoft is less certain Linux can be dismissed so blithely, it has good reasons: it's been fighting the hacker community its whole life and ought, of anyone, to understand the power of free software.

7

Free Speech, Not Free Beer

> If fifty—can you imagine, fifty people a day—walk in and sing a
> bar of "Alice's Restaurant" and walk out, they'll think it's a move-
> ment. And friends, it is a movement, the Alice's Restaurant Mas-
> sacree of movements.   —Arlo Guthrie, "Alice's Restaurant"

Back to the future. As the lights spun out of the Eiffel Tower
on Millennium Eve, the hot operating system was a clone of the hot operating system of the 1960s. How retro can you get?

The operating system is known as Linux, and its single most famous
distinguishing characteristic from Microsoft's Windows is: it's free.

Taking first things first, free software is not shareware, nor is it necessarily free of charge. The key to distinguishing among these several
types is how they are copyrighted.

Commercial software typically comes with a license that gives you
the right to run the software, but prohibits you from modifying it in
any substantial way. You can change the colors on your Windows desktop or install a program that replaces the desktop with a different one,
but you can't legally go inside the software and rewrite it to make it
faster or connect to your Furby via infrared. Even if you could do this
legally, you can't do it practically because you don't have access to the
source code.[1]

The company that writes the software may, however, publish an application programming interface (API) that allows third parties to develop additional modules that can be plugged in. Publishing APIs allows programs to interoperate—such as plug-ins for Web browsers like
Real Audio. One API that's been a particular bone of contention is the
cryptographic API (CAPI), intended to circumvent the export controls
on strong cryptography by exporting software with a hole in it so that
users outside the United States could install the cryptography module

of their choice; the U.S. government scotched this plan by declaring that CAPI, too, was regulated software under the International Traffic in Arms Regulations (ITAR). When the Bureau of Export Administration and the Department of Commerce announced in September 1999 that cryptography regulation was going to be lifted, it specifically excluded CAPI from the thaw, leading many to wonder if the easing of restrictions was going to be more apparent than real.[2]

Shareware is less different from commercial software than it sounds, and it usually comes with a similar license. The big difference is in how it's distributed: you can pick up a copy of shareware for free, or just for the cost of the medium (CD-ROM, floppy disk, Internet connection) it's distributed on. After a specified amount of time to evaluate the software (usually thirty days or a specified number of runs), you are asked, nagged, or required to pay for the software if you want to continue using it. Redistribution is usually unlimited, except for the proviso that the distribution set not be changed in any way. Like commercial software, shareware is typically written with a prohibition that users will not attempt to hack into it and change it. (I mean hack in the old sense, of course—that is, taking something apart to understand how it works and then making it do things its creator never thought of.)[3]

Freeware is free of charge, but, like shareware, usually remains under the control of the program's author. Free software in the sense I'm using it here, however, is software whose source code is published—what's more recently come to be known as "open-source" software. Some truly important software falls into this category, including the four most important pieces that help make the Internet work: BIND (for Berkeley Internet Name Daemon), Sendmail, Perl, and Apache. These, are, respectively, the software that resolves domain names into IP addresses, the most commonly used email routing software, the most popular scripting language, and the top Web server. All are, as Eric S. Raymond says, supremely reliable because umpteen thousand hackers have been banging on the code for a decade or two knocking all the bugs out of it.[4]

One of the best-known pieces of open-source software is PGP (for "Pretty Good Privacy"), a cryptography program that was released onto the Net in 1991 to head off threats that the U.S. government would make the domestic use of strong cryptography illegal. PGP's being open-source was important for several reasons: first, it ensured the software's survival if anything happened to its original developer;

second, it enabled peer review, so that the software's credibility could be assured.[5]

The terms "free software" and "open-source" are more different than they sound. They indicate a split in the ranks of the programmers who work on these projects, though the two sides of this schism have more in common than either has with anyone else. Nonetheless, the difference is real.

For a piece of software to be officially either free or open-source, it isn't enough simply to distribute the source code. The Open Source Initiative (OSI),[6] set up in 1998 to promote open-source software, has an official definition that lists a number of additional criteria: free redistribution; the freedom to modify or use the code in derivative works; no conditions attached to the distribution that discriminate against particular people or groups of people or specific fields of endeavor.[7] In other words, if I write a program to track the rankings in professional tennis and I want to call it open-source under the OSI definition, not only must I distribute the source code along with the compiled version, but I must allow others to redistribute it or fix it, and I can't make conditions that fans can use it but professional sports organizations such as *Sports Illustrated* and the Women's Tennis Association have to pay for it. Nor can I require that the program be distributed only with other open-source software can't be part of a commercial Web site running copyrighted material.

The philosophy behind this was not invented by the Open Source Institute; it existed even before personal computers were a mainstream product. In his 1984 book *Hackers*, Steven Levy tells the story of the artificial intelligence (AI) lab at MIT, where everything was shared. Computers were rare back then, but at the time software was generally free—it either came with the hardware or you wrote it yourself.

This ethic began to collide with commercial software in 1977, when Microsoft founders Bill Gates and Paul Allen came back from Albuquerque with their first commercial software, a version of BASIC[8] and some utilities for the primordial personal computer, MITS Altair. After a demonstration of the first version of BASIC at a Palo Alto hotel, a copy of the paper tape the program was stored on was taken, copied, and distributed widely, visibly cutting into the revenues for BASIC. The nineteen-year-old Gates then wrote his famous "Open Letter to Hobbyists," which was published in a number of hacker newsletters: "Who can afford to do professional work for nothing? What hobbyist can put

3-man years [*sic*] into programming, finding all bugs, documenting his product and distribute for free? . . . Most directly, the thing you do is theft."[9]

The letter caused huge controversy at the time, and not just because Gates called the hobbyists thieves.[10] The view that software was something written professionally that should be paid for was alien to this particular culture, which comprised most of the people passionately interested in computers at the time (and if you weren't passionately interested, you probably had nothing to do with them). But even then things were beginning to change: as they grew older, the hackers in Levy's book fanned out across the country, many of them to California, where their engineering skills helped them build machines and turn their inventive genius to commercial uses for large companies like Hewlett-Packard or for start-ups.

Free software didn't become an identifiable movement until the late 1990s when Linux awareness began percolating into the mainstream, but if it had a founding date it might have been 1984, when AI lab survivor Richard Stallman set up the GNU Project with the avowed intention of creating a complete system of free software.

Described by Levy as "the last true hacker," Stallman traces his commitment to software freedom to his days as a student at MIT. The computer known as the Incompatible Timesharing System at the AI lab was used by two incompatible groups of people: hackers whose primary interest was in getting the computer to do new and wonderful things, and graduate students and other official users, whose primary interest was getting their work done. Despite their differences, these two groups managed to coexist and share both the computer and its software, granting each other free access. The AI lab itself was an environment where everyone shared software and had complete access to each other's systems—a genuine anarchy in the sense that the no-holds-barred structure relied on absolute faith in people. When I interviewed him, Stallman said he was also enormously impressed by a decision made by the Harvard computer lab, which he visited regularly.

> One of their guys wrote a utility program that he was selling as a proprietary package, and he offered Harvard a free copy, and they said no. They said they were an educational institution, and their goal was to teach students about operating systems and programs, and they wouldn't install anything unless they could put up the source code for the students to study. I was impressed with the policy, that they were setting an example that they

would rather do without the software than accept it under terms which conflicted with their mission.

Later, he says, the lab was forced to change its policy because Digital Equipment Corporation stopped releasing the code for the timesharing system they were using. "They weren't determined enough to write their own."[11]

Stallman's way of thinking has a lot in common with that of the academic researchers who founded the Internet. One reason the Net has grown as rapidly as it has is that the standards are open and the protocols are free. While you can spend a lot of money setting up servers to handle Internet connections using commercial software if you want to, you can also set up a very cheap group of machines using free software that is, as its devotees say, more reliable, more secure, better understood, and supported by a worldwide community of people, many of whom take individual responsibility for their bit of the overall system. The culture surrounding the RFCs that define the many Internet standards (see chapter 4) is very like the culture surrounding free/open-source software.

There is another tributary to this story, however: the operating system UNIX. UNIX began life as free software by court mandate; it was developed at AT&T in the 1960s, and because AT&T was prohibited from selling it, the company gave the operating system away to academic departments, where a generation of programmers worked on it, extending it and, in some cases, turning it into a commercial product. Microsoft, for example, licensed UNIX as early as the late 1970s, porting it to PCs under the name Xenix.[12] UNIX was an important operating system in European government departments, where it was seen as an "open system" that would keep large computer installations from being locked into proprietary systems, especially those of IBM, the dominant manufacturer of the time. One consequence of the number of different organizations working on it, especially given AT&T's new-found interest in protecting its software after the court-mandated break-up, was that UNIX diverged ("forked" in hackerspeak) into distinct "flavors" that persist today, from Microsoft's Xenix to NeXTstep, the operating system sold by the company Steve Jobs founded between Apple and Pixar.[13]

UNIX, in the words of British computer consultant Liam Proven, is "about as user-friendly as a cornered rat."[14] However, just as Windows put a pretty face on the black void of DOS, there are graphical front-ends for UNIX (including NeXTStep) that make it less terrifying, and even a Windows emulator to let the truly determined have their UNIX and eat their Windows software, too. Because the system has been around for so long, it's well understood and documented, and there is a huge community of programmers and engineers who understand how to make it reliable and, importantly, secure.

GNU, Stallman's project, was intended to be UNIX-like, but the name stands, recursively, for "GNU's not UNIX." There are other UNIX-like free operating systems, but part of the point of GNU was that it was intended to be a completely clean clone. That is, it would contain none of the copyrighted source code that made up the many versions of UNIX. Another free UNIX-like operating system, FreeBSD,[15] ran into troubles in 1993 when AT&T's UNIX System Laboratories sued, claiming the developers had violated the company's copyright on UNIX by copying some of the code. Nothing like that should be possible with GNU. By the early 1990s, large chunks of the GNU system had been written, some of them by Stallman personally.[16]

More important than its software was the GNU Project's General Public License (GPL), a template for software licenses that retains rights for the creators (mostly so other people can't claim them) but makes modification and redistribution free—like the OSI definition. GNU software is "copyleft," rather than copyright, meaning that it's distributed under the GPL, which itself, also recursively, is given away to anyone who wants a copy.[17]

Linux[18] got its start in 1993, when a Swedish-speaking Finnish computer science student named Linus Torvalds got interested in writing a UNIX kernel.[19] In operating system terms, a kernel is like the heart: it's the innermost chunk of program code that hooks everything together and makes the hardware work. Once his kernel was written, he uploaded it to the Net, and others began downloading it, trying it, studying it, and helping debug it. Torvalds, now working for the California company Transmeta, still "owns" Linux in the sense that he oversees and coordinates its development.

An operating system needs more than a kernel, just as a human body needs more than a heart. By 1993, GNU had a lot of the elements ready for a complete operating system—except they didn't have a kernel. They were working on one, but by the end of 1999 it still wasn't finished. A so-called Linux distribution (such as Red Hat) is therefore really the Linux kernel, plus a bunch of GNU programs (drivers, utilities, and other bits of software), plus contributions from a number of other sources.

Stallman insists therefore that it would be more accurate to refer to Linux as GNU-Linux;[20] he figures that about 28 percent of most distributions of Linux are actually GNU. There are, of course, many other contributors to a typical distribution. Whatever you call it, by late 1999 estimates were that there were 20 million Linux users worldwide.[21] By any reasonable standard, that's a success.

Part of this success is fueled by hatred of Microsoft (memories of the "Open Letter" die hard), just as some of Microsoft's and, especially, Apple's early success was fueled by loathing of IBM. To be fair, there are plenty of good reasons to despise Microsoft software. For one thing, it crashes: even a user of Microsoft's most reliable operating system, Windows NT, considers herself lucky if she only has to reboot her computer once every ten days or so (I made it twenty-three days once, but it was really gluey by the end). Devotees say a Linux box will run continuously for a year or more, reliably turning over and working away. Microsoft software consumes hardware resources as if they were limitless; Linux will run on much less hardware, so not only is the software cheaper but the resources it demands are cheaper, too. A small British ISP, for example, explained to me that when they hit a certain size—about two or three hundred users—the saving was enormous in switching to a Linux machine as a mail server, especially because Linux scaled better than the other choice (Windows NT) and would serve them longer as well as costing less up front.

These are points of pride in the open-source movement. "The real point of the exercise is to develop the best software possible," Raymond told *Fast Company* in November 1999. "And in most of the ways that matter, the open-source model is more disciplined and more rigorous than the traditional approach to creating software. The open-source model gets you better software."[22] The reason, he says, is that "when people are frustrated with their work environments—when they don't trust the institutions they work for—it is virtually impossible for them to do great work." This kind of frustration is generally thought to be the reason that "Easter Eggs" have proliferated. These hidden routines inside software packages, which may be complex and ornate— there was a flight simulator hidden inside one version of Microsoft

Excel, for example—can be entertaining, but they are also a sign of poor quality control on the part of software companies.

As Raymond goes on to say, open-source contributors do get tangible rewards for their efforts and the reputations they establish; in addition, the most successful projects are run by the kind of people other people want to work for and help. "It's no coincidence that Linus Torvalds is a nice guy who makes people want to help him; it's no coincidence that I'm an extrovert who likes to 'work the room.' . . . To build a development community, you need to attract people by interesting them in what you're doing."

The point about whether the software should be called Linux or GNU-Linux is important to relatively few; it's the kind of internecine argument that arises in subcultures that have become large and established enough for passion to flow freely. It's too easy to paint it as a personality clash. The argument is not about Stallman versus Raymond (or the Free Software Foundation founder against the Open Source Initiative founder), but about whether it's moral to own software. Stallman holds that it's not—but he's not the only one, as out-of-step with today's business world as that seems. Even those extremists who believe that the ownership of information is a threat to civil liberties, however, are not against business and do not claim that hackers get nothing in return for their efforts.[23]

For some in the open-source movement, freedom is more important than the quality of the software itself. Stallman, who is at the idealistic extreme of this way of thinking, has said he would use free software even if it wasn't as good as the commercial alternative, and even if it required more effort to program and manage.[24] As Andrew Leonard wrote in *Salon*, "His stance makes some factions of the burgeoning 'open source' community uncomfortable—so uncomfortable, in fact, that the very choice of the name 'open source' demonstrates an attempt to distance those factions from the unsavory radicalism of Richard Stallman." However, he concludes, "If the pragmatists of the open source cause sacrifice him [Stallman] to make free software safe for business, it seems to me, they risk losing their movement's soul."[25]

There's a good reason for their discomfort: most people aren't willing to give up ease of use for their principles, and pragmatism requires accepting that. When you talk to Stallman you get the feeling that this hurts him. More practical hackers may feel that in order to sell the world—especially the business world—on the value of free software, it's important to stress advantages such as price and reliability.

But for Stallman, the point is to keep from being fenced in—or from fencing other people out. You get the impression that the restrictions that apply to commercial software that won't allow you to look under the hood and fix a bug or add a useful utility feel to him like prison bars. It's not a feeling I have about software, but a reasonable analogy for an average consumer might be that a condition of watching TV was that you weren't allowed to show it to anyone else. Or, for an American, perhaps it would be akin to the discovery that in Britain you can't really loan anyone else your car because insurance policies typically specify a single driver for a specific car.

Raymond has claimed that the open-source movement doesn't reject Stallman's ideals, just his rhetoric.[26] In a rebuttal posted to Slashdot on his behalf,[27] however, Stallman disagreed, saying, "'Open source' was designed not to raise the point that users deserve freedom." Describing the situation as "like two political parties within our community," Stallman concluded, "We disagree on the basic principles, but agree on most practical recommendations. We work together on many specific projects."[28]

In person, Stallman has a habit a number of journalists have remarked upon in print of examining his hair closely for split ends while you're talking to him. When I asked if I should print that, he said, "Well, I hope you won't, because the only reason you would do it is to humiliate me. And then people won't listen to what I have to say because they'll think I'm weird."[29]

Stallman *is* weird, by most people's standards. Not that this is a bad thing or even unusual. Lots of creatively obsessed people are weird by most people's standards. So what? What's probably harder for him to accept is that he may be too weird for his own movement of geeks, especially now that success seems within reach. Remember the people skills Raymond said were needed.[30]

Judging from the kinds of things that get said, especially in the press, about geeks, most people think anyone intimately involved with technology pays very little attention to what its negative uses or consequences might be. Despite the mad, arrogant scientist of popular myth, it's notable that the people who invented the Net and hack away at improving its underpinnings are intensely thoughtful about what they do. In his "How to Be a Hacker FAQ," for example, Raymond advises anyone who wants to be a hacker to learn to write well. He doesn't mean programming languages, he means English.[31]

This is not a new trend. In the 1970s, Tracy Kidder noted that the developers working on Data General's Eclipse MV/800 computer debated the same consequences of widespread computing power that we argue about now with respect to the Internet: revolution, privacy, the nature of intelligence, and the "machining" of humans.[32]

Raymond's own articles are as impressive a set of metaphorical and practical ruminations on technology as any, and the phenomenon is visible over and over again. In his most famous piece, "The Cathedral and the Bazaar," Raymond compares software development in the commercial (the rigidly controlled hierarchical cathedral) and open-source (the anarchic, open, and egalitarian bazaar) worlds and analyzes the model he believes serves open-source development best.[33] He argues, for example, that it's important to have users and treat them as co-developers; software developers should release new versions of the code early and often, thereby keeping the user base interested and rewarded. While even Microsoft does this—there must have been millions of beta testers for Windows 95—the significant difference is that Microsoft isn't enlisting its users in understanding and solving the problems that surface with its code.[34] By contrast, Raymond has what he calls "Linus's Law": "given enough eyes, all bugs are shallow."

The key difference between the time when the GNU Project was launched and when Linux began is that Linux's developers could use the Internet to enlist users to test the system. In a very real sense, the open-source software movement—at least, as a worldwide phenomenon that can challenge the top commercial software companies—is one of the first shakeups made possible by the Internet. As Raymond says, "Linus [Torvalds] was the first person who learned how to play by the new rules that pervasive Internet made possible."

The key is that the Internet enables cooperative working and communication and can, under the right conditions, foster community. The way the Internet's standards were developed taught us plenty of lessons about building reliable software in a cooperative fashion. But just as there are debates about whether or not software can be owned, there are debates about the nature of the currency circulating in the open-source movement's "gift economy" (as Raymond calls it).

Many, if not most, hackers gain some reward: they work at least in part for credit and to enhance their reputation. If you are only a hacker if other people call you one,[35] then being a visible contributor to a collaborative project is the only way your reputation can grow enough for you to reach that status. There are, fortunately, plenty of projects to go around.[36]

For many Linux programmers, working on the joint effort provides not just enjoyment, but a little bit of immortality. For one such developer I interviewed for the *Daily Telegraph*, this was literally true: he had an inoperable brain tumor at age thirty-three, and he considered his open-source email program his legacy.

Patrick Caulfield, a software developer who "for fun" spends his spare time working on networking protocols and bits of the kernel for Linux, says, "I take a sort of parental pride in the thing. The sorts of stuff I do are very self-enclosed and they only have me working on it, so it really is my little baby. I'm really driven to fix it because you don't want things wrong with your software."

Users sitting on hold waiting for technical support from some major commercial company would love to have such personal involvement from the developers. It brings back the early days of Britain's Demon Internet, when calls to technical support would reach a technical staffer who resolved your problem by poring over the source code and debugging it in real time.

Most non-technical people who have tried to install Linux burst into fits of giggles at the suggestion that it's a genuine competitor to Microsoft, an idea that's been promulgated by a sensationalist press and a major software company who would like to convince the Department of Justice that it is not a monopoly. Linux can be made prettyish by covering it up with a graphical interface. But underneath, it's still a clone of a 1960s operating system—green ASCII characters on a black screen, computing as God meant it to be—so that learning to use its arcane commands is difficult, but it gives in return the ability to intimately control the machine.

Caulfield put it well when he complained, "We're seeing the dumbing down of all sorts of things now." Cars: lots of pieces that used to be openly accessible to tinkerers are now sealed units that cost far more to replace and can't be taken apart and rebuilt. Computers: the 1990s have turned the most versatile machine ever invented into infinitely repeating identical robots. A manufacturer is prohibited by the terms of its contract with Microsoft from adding anything between starting up the BIOS and loading Windows, and from adding or changing anything that appears on the Windows desktop. Where do you want to go today? Somewhere different? Not allowed. The lack of printed documentation with machines makes it less and less possible to know what's on your hard drive, whether it's essential or can be deleted to free up space, or how to make the software do anything you want it to.

Since Linux (or GNU-Linux) became famous, the open-source movement has gotten several boosts that have made the media start taking it seriously. One was the release in early 1998 of the source code to Netscape. However, by early 2000 the project (now known as Mozilla) was still in beta.[37] Another was several well-publicized security holes in Windows.

In the meantime, however, parts of the movement had gone commercial. This sounds like a contradiction, but it's not. First of all, if you "think free software, not free beer" (one of Stallman's lines), it's obvious that you're allowed to sell software. These are people who understand that technical support and services have value that can be charged for even if the software itself is distributed for free. Plenty of people who espouse the open ethic of free software make a living from doing so—from John Gilmore, who founded Cygnus Services to sell services around GNU software, to Stallman himself, who makes his living making speeches about it.

Late 1999, however, saw something new, when Red Hat, distributor of the best-known and supposedly most user-friendly Linux distribution, went public. Much dissent ensued, and Slashdot filled up with rants from Linux hackers who found themselves shut out of the Red Hat IPO. They were being denied shares because Securities and Exchange Commission (SEC) rules intended to protect inexperienced investors from the volatility of IPOs. The problem was settled, sort of— some lied as necessary to pass the profile test required by the broker managing the flotation, while others turned away in disgust. But the tension between commercial values and the values of the open-source world remains, and it's not clear how the two will co-exist, especially when, a few months after Red Hat's IPO, the company announced it was using its then wildly successful stock to acquire Cygnus Services.[38] Combining the two companies meant that the largest single pool of Linux hackers would be under the control of a single company. Most believed the movement could survive such a concentration of talent.[39]

Nor is it clear whether Red Hat (or VA Linux, which went public shortly after Red Hat) can a create a profitable business. The company's plan, according to its SEC filings, was to make Linux as commonly available and usable a product as Windows, plus to make money by selling services. Certainly, Sun Microsystems has made a good living out of giving software away: it deliberately chose to make its Java an open standard and says it has a more liberal software license than even GNU.

But few have ever competed directly with Microsoft and lived to talk about it afterwards. On top of that, as the many critiques of "The Cathedral and the Bazaar" make clear, open-source development doesn't work for every kind of software.

Raymond himself figures that the bazaar approach works best for improving and developing projects that already exist in at least some form. You need a starting point, however flawed. In the case of Linux, UNIX was that starting point. In addition, because the type of hacker Raymond is talking about is attracted to interesting problems, which should, in the hacker rule, "only be solved once," there are boring but necessary types of software that may never get written using this approach. Or, as Clay Shirky, a professor of new media at Hunter College, has put it, "Unloved software can't be built using Open Source methods."[40]

Unloved software: like large accounting systems, perhaps, or the umpteen millionth revamping of a printer driver. Windows is unloved, but in a different way. As long as its source code remains closed and visible only to Microserfs,[41] hackers hate it. But if Microsoft ever, by court order or free will, released the source code, the Net would clog to a standstill while every programmer in the world downloaded the code, if only so they could finally prove that Microsoft's programming is as sloppy as they've always believed it is.

There's an additional problem: software developers tend to fail to understand how difficult their programs really are to use. How to get a community of people to whom a command like `tr -d "\015" <file­name.dos >filename.unix` is intuitive to write a program that's as easy to use as a cash machine may well be an insoluble problem in computer science.

Even so, the free/open-source software way of thinking has already produced the Internet and the World Wide Web, which took off in part because the "View Source" option built into Web browsers allowed users to see how a particular page was constructed and copy the design and code if they wanted to. As Shirky points out in an article about the Web's development, it would have been simple for either Tim Berners-

Lee, the British physicist who invented the Web, or successive browser writers to treat "View Source" as a private debugging option. "Instead, with this unprecedented transparency of the HTML itself, we got an enormous increase in the speed of design development."[42]

Many, maybe most, of the people who use the Web probably have never noticed "View Source." But this was a deliberate decision on the part of Berners-Lee, whose original vision was of a Web that not only allowed his physics department at CERN to share documents, but would allow people to start writing a page in a second window, copying across whatever material or links they wanted from the main display window. It was Berners-Lee, not Netscape's Marc Andreessen, who wrote the first graphical browser, but because it ran on a NeXT machine, few people saw it. According to Berners-Lee, the editing and authoring functionality got left out of Andreessen's version (first Mosaic and then Netscape) because it was just too difficult to program in Windows.[43] "View Source" arguably makes the Web one of the largest collaborative learning experiments ever launched.

The Web enables other such experiments, such as the rebirth of hardware hacking. One of the worst things about the 1990s in terms of computing is that computers were turned into impenetrable boxes. "Make the computer system invisible," Donald Norman wrote in his 1988 classic book, *The Psychology of Everyday Things*,[44] inspiring a generation of human factors specialists and usability experts. Linux hackers are from the opposite end of computing: they want intimate control, not graphics.

It's hard to disagree with Raymond's criticisms of the world according to today's commercial software companies. There's a folklore theorem that 60 to 75 percent of conventional software projects are either never completed or rejected by their intended users. As Raymond notes:

> We are entitled to wonder what, if anything, the tremendous overhead of conventionally managed development is actually buying us. Whatever it is certainly doesn't include reliable execution by deadline, or on budget, or to all features of the specification; it's a rare "managed" project that meets even one of these goals, let alone all three. It also does not appear to be ability to adapt to changes in technology and economic context during the project lifetime, either; the open-source community has proven far more effective on that score (as one can readily verify by comparing the thirty-year history of the Internet with the short half-lives of proprietary networking technologies.[45]

Even if Red Hat succeeds in making Linux usable to the mass market—the company's stated intention—it's not clear whether the pattern that developed after the mid 1980s at MIT, where one-time pure hackers dispersed and turned pro, will prevail here, too. Is it really possible for a community to coalesce permanently around a free software project when large sums of money start rolling into some parts of that community? The answer may be the same as what's happened on the Internet at large: at least parts of the community of hacker volunteers will survive as long as they feel their efforts are necessary and are not exploited. I don't buy the argument that no one ever behaves altruistically—though the ones who do are not the people who are rewarded with all the credit—but I do believe that long-term effort has to give a volunteer some reward, whether it's new skills, the personal satisfaction of making something work, or other people's gratitude and respect. It's very hard for anyone to remain motivated when lots of other people are making major amounts of money from your efforts but you are not. If all the Linux movement succeeds in doing is building a credible challenge to Microsoft, even if that eventually becomes a commercial product, they will have done the world a service. The movement itself, however, would regard such an outcome as a major cultural failure.

The free software movement stands as an alternative to a world where corporate funding is taking over academic research labs and every use of intellectual property, no matter how small, becomes chargeable. The fact that the MacArthur Foundation gave Stallman one of its "Genius" awards is an important reminder that it is essential to have alternatives, not just to commercial software, but to the intellectual property regime under which it functions.

8

The Innocent Pleasure
of Reading

Mister, you can conquer the air, but the birds will lose their wonder and the clouds will reek of gasoline.
                    —Clarence Darrow, during the Scopes "Monkey" trial

The free/open-source software movement's concerns about
what kinds of rights people should be allowed over the software they
use are just one piece of a much larger conflict that is popping up in
every area of business and society: where should we draw the line between what can and cannot be sold or owned? Businesses depend increasingly for financial success on intellectual property rather than producing widgets. However, individuals and academic researchers under-
standably resent losing access to resources they think of as personal or
public. Boundary disputes seem a logical consequence, just as in England huntsmen and walkers have spent decades battling to retain cen-
turies-old rights-of-way across cultivated land.
    You would assume, for example, that you own your own DNA. But
one consequence of the Human Genome Project is that the funding institutions want to patent the genes their researchers sequence. Proponents of gene patenting, notably those in industry, warn that funds for
research could dry up if companies can't patent the genes they find and
profit from the research they've paid for. Opponents (echoing the open-
source movement) argue that locking off genes by patenting them—
particularly when what's patented are marked-off sequences whose
function is unclear—will limit scientists' access and make research and
new treatments more expensive and uncertain (you might have to conduct extra research to ensure that you weren't straying into someone
else's patented territory).

Iceland's population of roughly 275,000 is one of the most homogeneous populations on the planet because of repeated disease and famine and the low levels of immigration. On top of that, the island has kept detailed genealogical records, some going back as far as the Vikings. Swiss pharmaceutical company Roche Holding has granted a project known as Decode Genetics some $200 million to study the island's genetic makeup. Iceland's Ministry of Health is still deciding whether to approve the project, which has profound privacy consequences. According to *Wired News*, "If the project is approved, Roche and Decode Genetics could effectively own the genes of the entire island nation."[1]

You might also assume that thousand-year-old farming traditions such as the practice of saving seed to plant next year's crops or sharing seed with your neighbors could never be challenged. But producers of genetically modified crops such as herbicide-resistant corn are claiming that these traditional farming practices, when applied to their modified plants, constitute "seed piracy" and infringe upon their intellectual property rights. Monsanto, for example, was granted a patent in 1996 for (bacterial) genes the company uses to modify plants so they are insect-resistant.[2] Recently, it has started requiring farmers to sign contracts promising not to save seed, and demanding five-figure royalty payments from those who do.[3]

Finally, you might think that simple facts such as basketball scores or natural phenomena such as mathematical principles couldn't be copyrighted or patented. But there have been attempts to claim copyright on sports scores, and underneath the dispute over free software lies a two-decade battle over whether algorithms and software techniques should be patentable. If electricity were discovered today, the discoverer would patent it—and in as broad terms as possible, so that anyone getting a shock from sliding too smoothly across a carpet in winter could be sued for infringement.

In short, a whole world of information previously thought of as beyond ownership is becoming privatized. This has been called "copyright maximalism" by Pamela Samuelson, professor of information management and of law at the University of California at Berkeley, and a 1997 winner of the MacArthur Foundation Genius award for her work on the future of intellectual property rights.

For what follows, it's important to understand the difference between copyright and patent. You cannot copyright an idea, only the expression of an idea. I may have a brilliant idea for a novel about a small band of drop-outs of various types who spend their lives traveling from one place to another to experience every available total eclipse, but I can't copyright any of it until I've created the characters, invented the plot, and written it all down. By contrast, a patent protects ideas that can be turned into actual products. I can't patent my idea for a novel, but I might be able to patent a design for a machine that would take my idea and turn it into a novel. Drug companies patent the new compounds scientists painstakingly derive in their research labs to give them time to recover their research costs before other companies are allowed to compete by copying the compound, whose formula they can of course obtain through chemical analysis.

What copyrights and patents have in common is that they are intended to encourage creators of intellectual property to work creatively by giving them time in which they, exclusively, can exploit their creations. Claims accepted by the U.S. Patent Office are good for twenty years, so that the patents on the fundamental algorithms for public-key cryptography, taken out in 1978 and held by RSA Data Security, have recently expired, opening the algorithms up for use by anyone who's interested.[4]

The length of copyright has been extended several times Until 1978, it was twenty-eight years, renewable for another twenty-eight. It was then extended to the author's life plus fifty years, and finally to life plus seventy. This last extension was part of the international harmonization efforts in creating the European Union. It was thought unfair to disenfranchise a group of authors (and, probably more important in lobbying terms, publishers) by taking away revenue, so everyone upped the term to match Germany's life plus seventy. Richard Stallman's reply to this: that it was apparently all right to disenfranchise readers instead.[5]

There are additional differences in patent and copyright rules worldwide and complexities of international agreements governing who recognizes whose protections. The Berne Convention governs copyright, and signatories honor each other's registrations. Patents, however, require multiple filings in different countries, and the rules are different enough that your application may be accepted in one country and not in another. The patent on the RSA algorithm, for example, was valid in the United States but not in Europe because before the European patent was granted the algorithm had been described and published in *Scientific American*,[6] violating European, but not U.S., rules. This kind of issue doesn't concern individuals very much, but it can have a major impact on businesses' adoption of a particular technology.

It wasn't until the 1980s that U.S. patents were awarded for processes (such as a series of steps in a software program or a business method) as opposed to devices (such as a new type of hard disk). Software was typically copyrighted until 1981 (as it still is in Europe), when a Supreme Court decision known as *Diamond v. Diehr* allowed the inclusion of a software program in a process for manufacturing rubber. The Patent Office interpreted this decision liberally. In 1993, the Patent Office awarded a patent to Compton's New Media that was so broad that it covered basically all of multimedia.[7] Other contentious patents cover such fundamental techniques as displaying a blinking cursor on screen. In a hearing held in Silicon Valley in 1994, the overwhelming majority of programmers and executives from well-known companies like Adobe and Oracle called for the elimination of software patents. By 1995, the Patent Office had reexamined the Compton's claim and rejected it.

But the problem persists, in part because of the volume of applications the Patent Office staff must cope with, and in part because it is so difficult to trace who first used a particular idea in a software program. One consequence is a great deal of wasted effort. Another is a great deal of wasted time and money in the form of lots of suits that help no one and can cost the companies involved millions of dollars, whether they win or lose. By 2000, the chart of who was suing whom among Internet companies was almost as complex as the worldwide map of the network itself.

The story of E-data is a classic example of how old patents can suddenly jump up and bite the developers of new technology. In 1996, this small company claimed patent rights in the broadest terms in electronic transactions. The original patent was granted in 1984, when an individual named Charles C. Freeny, Jr., came up with an idea for transferring information from a remote computer to an "information manufacturing machine" at a point-of-sale location. Freeny did not foresee the Internet (even though it was beginning to take shape), and in 1989 he sold the patent for about $100,000 to a since-bankrupted company called Aveda Corporation. E-data acquired the patent in 1994 for about $300,000 and began licensing it to IBM and Adobe. It also announced suits against a variety of companies, including CompuServe,

Intuit, WaldenBooks, and Ziff-Davis.[8] The judge in the case ruled that the Freeny patent did not apply to Internet transactions; an appeal is still pending.

Expectations are that we will see many more such cases: some 11,500 software patents were issued in 1997 alone.[9] By now, the only thing that's surprising is that no one has patented the process of getting something patented. Revising public policy is one solution to this mess. More importantly, the Patent Office needs time, staff, and technical expertise to come to grips with the new technology.[10]

A much more public and bitter debate is happening in the copyright area, with rights-holders campaigning vigorously for tougher laws. What most people don't understand, however, is how much ground we've already lost.

According to Samuelson, in general U.S. copyright law has avoided regulating private non-commercial activities. The U.S. Supreme Court seemed to support this when it decided in the Sony Betamax case that non-commercial, home-use recording of material broadcast over the public airwaves was a fair use of copyrighted material.[11] Because of this bias, she says, it made sense for copyright law to remain the province of industry experts: they were the only people affected. The new laws of the 1990s, however, extend the regulation of copyright into the private arena. Unfortunately, few if any organizations exist to defend the public interest because they've never been needed before. Until the Net came along, individuals did not have the worldwide reach of a printing press or a TV antenna. New organizations such as the Digital Future Coalition, a group of thirty-nine public and private organizations arguing in favor of the extension of fair use into the digital environment, are beginning to appear to defend consumers' interests.[12]

Samuelson believes such pressure is essential.

> The public is more likely to respect an expanded scope of rights for authors in cyberspace if representatives of user interests have participated in negotiations about expansion of those rights and have been persuaded that the expansion is in the public interest. Without widespread public acceptance for a broader scope of rights, it will be difficult, if not impossible, to enforce those rights without costly and intrusive efforts.[13]

This is exactly what we're seeing now in the battles between the entertainment industries and the Net over MP3 music and software to crack DVD codes.

Arguments over what the correct balance should be between rewarding rights-holders via copyright and giving the public access to information are nothing new. In 1841, for example, in a House of Commons debate over the extension of copyright from twenty-eight to sixty years, the Irish peer Lord Thomas Babbington Macauley called copyright "a private tax on the innocent pleasure of reading" and "a tax on readers for the purpose of giving a bounty to writers" that should not be allowed to last a day longer than necessary for the purpose of remunerating authors just enough to keep them in business. Since then, copyright and patent restrictions have only been extended.

The 1990s saw many initiatives to increase copyright owners' control. The No Electronic Theft (NET) Act, the Digital Millennium Copyright Act (DMCA), and the Anti-Cybersquatting Consumer Protection Act were the ones that made it into law, though a variety of other proposals either didn't make it into law or were incorporated into later legislation. In late 1996 the nongovernmental World Intellectual Property Organization (WIPO) began planning a treaty to create intellectual property rights in the compilations of facts and other material held in databases. The treaty as originally written would have prohibited the extraction, use, or reuse of significant portions of databases in all media for a period of fifteen to twenty-five years from compilation, to be extended each time the database was revised.

Opponents warned at the time that the proposals could severely restrict the reporting and use of sports statistics, as well as stock prices, weather data, train schedules, data from scientific research, and other facts that had been considered public domain in the United States. The National Basketball Association had already sued AOL over the service's real-time coverage of its games' scores and statistics, claiming it was a form of "broadcast" that infringed on the NBA's property rights.

In fact, the strongest push for the WIPO treaty came from the United States, where the Database Investment and Intellectual Property Antipiracy Act was introduced into Congress in May 1996.[14] That act proposed protection of rights in databases for twenty-five years and made damages to database owners' rights in excess of $10,000 in any one-year period a criminal offense punishable by up to $25,000 in fines and five years in jail. Simultaneously, the European Parliament and the Council of the European Union had adopted a directive on the legal protection of databases (96/9/EC) that harmonized copyright protection and also created specific rights for the makers of databases for a period of fifteen years. Member states were required to implement the directive in national legislation by January 1, 1998.

This is despite the fact that some forms of databases—notably the British telephone directory and the database of postcodes—were already copyrighted.[15] These particular databases could not be copyrighted in the United States, under the court decision *Feist Publications, Inc. v. Rural Telephone Service Corp.*, which held that for a database to be copyrighted there had to be some real work involved in creating it beyond just ordering the entries alphabetically. The example of the British telephone directory is a good one, because although lots of people wanted to put it online as early as the late 1980s, except for a few minority services,[16] British Telecom's telephone directory didn't become available online until 1999.[17]

Attempts to create rights in databases continued into 1999 with competing bills, H.R. 1858 (The Consumer and Investors Access to Information Act) and H.R. 354 (The Collections of Information Antipiracy Act). Of the two, H.R. 1858 won a measure of support from organizations such as the Digital Future Coalition, the American Association of Law Libraries, and a variety of companies such as MCI Worldcom, Yahoo!, and AT&T. The bill's focus on piracy, its application only to databases created after the bill's enactment, and its narrower provisions (which allow users to work with the information contained in databases to create new information) were all considered preferable to the broader and more restrictive clauses of H.R. 354.

Meanwhile, Congress was also giving attention to "anti-piracy" measures. On December 17, 1997, President Clinton signed into law the No Electronic Theft Act (H.R. 2265),[18] which makes it a federal crime to distribute or possess illegal electronic copies of copyrighted material valued over $2,500, even when there's no profit involved. The bill defines three levels of violations, depending on the value of the copyrighted work and the number of past offenses; possession of ten or more illegal electronic copies could land you with up to five years in prison and a $250,000 fine. As University of Pennsylvania telecommunications professor Dave Farber put it at the time, "You'd be better off going out and shooting somebody. The penalty is less."[19]

Farber is one of those people whose name keeps reappearing wherever you look in the world of Net policy. He runs one of the most useful, noise-free electronic mailing lists for anyone interested in Net-related issues, "Interesting People."[20] He is one of the three professors behind the ICANN Watch project (see chapter 4), which is pushing the new corporation to become more open and accountable. He was one of the government's twelve witnesses testifying in the Microsoft antitrust trial. And in January 2000 he began a stint as the chief technologist for the Federal Communications Commission. He was also one of the leading signatories on a letter sent to President Clinton by the Association for Computing Machinery (ACM), the American professional body for computer scientists, asking that he veto the bill.

The ACM's objections focused on the consequences for science, arguing that the bill could damage communication and information sharing among scientists because it lacked traditional fair-use exemptions, such as allowing libraries and academic institutions to make copies, quoting for purposes of review or criticism, and first-sale, the principle that allows you to loan out or sell secondhand the book you bought. The NET Act's genesis may explain why its provisions are so one-sided. It was inspired by the 1994 dismissal of charges against Massachusetts Institute of Technology student David LaMacchia,[21] who was accused of allowing the piracy of more than $1 million in business and entertainment software from a bulletin board system he ran on MIT's system. LaMacchia's attorneys successfully argued that he did not profit from the site and that he himself did not upload, download, or use the software available, which was supplied and retrieved by others over whom he had no control, and that existing U.S. law did not cover this situation. The NET Act changed those omissions, unfortunately opening the way for ISPs to become censors out of fear of liability, a prediction made by the Digital Future Coalition, among others.

The biggest legislative battle was over the Digital Millennium Copyright Act,[22] which finally passed in October 1998 after more than a year of dickering over a variety of proposals, some of which were subsumed into the bill.[23] The DMCA began life as an implementation of two WIPO treaties, one concerning copyright and the other concerning performances and phonograms. One of the more contentious clauses prohibits making or selling devices or services that circumvent technological schemes used by copyright owners to prevent unauthorized access to or copying of their works. The act specifies that these circumventing devices or services must be primarily designed or produced primarily for that purpose, have little other commercially significant purpose or use, or be marketed for the purpose. An extra clause requires all VCRs to be designed to include Macrovision, a technology designed to prevent the unauthorized copying of analog videocassettes and certain types of analog signals (though rights-holders may not apply this type of technology to free television or basic and extended basic tier broadcasts). The impact of these restrictions, particularly on encryption research, is to be assessed on an ongoing basis. Exemptions were added covering non-profit libraries, archives, and educational institutions; reverse engineering;[24] encryption research (which would be killed by a blanket prohibition on cryptanalysis); protection of minors; personal privacy; and security testing. Other clauses of the act protect copyright management information and provide for civil and criminal penalties—up to a $500,000 fine or five years in prison for a first offense, though libraries, archives, and educational institutions are exempt from criminal liability. The act also includes limitations on liability for online service providers in the areas of transitory communications, system caching, users' storage of information, directories, and search tools.

(It may seem incredible that the temporary copies created in your computer's memory when you browse the Net, or stored in a cache on your ISP's servers in order to speed up access, could be considered copyright infringements, but these kinds of copies were the subject of a European dispute through most of 1999. Rights-holders maintain that they should have the right to prohibit the caching of their material, while ISPs insist they should have the right to adopt whatever technology makes the Net work most efficiently. Caching, a scheme under which ISPs store copies of popular and often-requested Web pages to cut down on network traffic, is one of those technologies. For some ISPs it also cuts costs by limiting the amount of bandwidth they need. But caching can cost rights-holders money, too, as they lose hits—which translate into advertising dollars—when users are served up pages from an ISP's cache rather than the rights-holder's own servers. The ability to block caching is already embedded in HTML, the system of coding used to create Web pages, and the most likely solution is that ISPs will be allowed to cache as long as they don't ignore those instructions if they are present. So for the moment everyone will get most of what they want.)

Although most of the DMCA's provisions are significantly better than the ones that appeared in many earlier versions of the bill, there were still late-stage objections. ACM president Barbara Simons, still worried, said, "If, instead of attempting to outlaw technologies and devices, Congress had chosen to outlaw behavior that intentionally infringes on intellectual property rights, we would not have to worry about unintended consequences of the legislation."[25]

You can see her point. On the one hand, deciding whether a particular technology has been invented specifically for the purpose of circumventing copy-protection schemes is going to be difficult. On the other, we already have laws against mass-producing pirated copies of copyrighted material. These provisions imply a kind of technology worship—the belief that everything can be fixed by doctoring the technology. This kind of thinking has embedded copy protection into minidisc players: you can dub a CD track onto a minidisc, but the player will prevent you from copying from that minidisc copy. Did it occur to no one that you might record your own minidiscs and want to make copies? The technology, crippled to benefit rights-holders, robs ordinary individuals of the right to create and copy their own work.

This may be the wave of the future. Xerox PARC's Mark Stefik works on trusted systems that would make it possible to finely divide rights, so you could buy, say, reading rights for an article on the Net, but not downloading and printing rights. In his well-known essay "Letting Loose the Light," Stefik insists that such trusted systems will unlock creativity and make it easier for users to be honest and creators to make a living, even if new methods of digital distribution eliminate middlemen.[26]

The claim that the lack of effective online copy protection is deterring rights-holders from putting a lot of material online is a common one. Samuelson disagreed as early as 1996. Not only was there plenty of material online, at least some of it supported by other sources of revenue such as advertising, she argued, but there were plenty of other problems holding up online distribution, such as lack of bandwidth, the difficulties of creating content databases, the lack of a micropayments system that might make it possible to sell small pieces of content for tiny amounts of money, and the lack of a functioning business model by which content owners could make money from publishing in cyberspace.

Certainly, history is full of examples of inventions that happened not because some company took the risk of funding them but because some individual was grabbed by an idea that wouldn't let go. Plenty had their ideas rejected multiple times before they were eventually turned into the ubiquitous items we see today, from the Depression-era games of Scrabble and Monopoly to the map of the London Underground.

Even so, it's now clear that at least in some cases—notably the music, television, and movie industries—fear of losing control is working as a powerful deterrent to putting material online.

While in every other area of online business companies new and old are practically suing each other to get "first-mover" advantage, the music industry has delayed distributing music online while it works out a copy-protection scheme known as the Secure Digital Music Initiative (SDMI) and lobbies various governments for tighter copyright protection. The specification for MP3—industry shorthand for the compression standard MPEG 2 Layer 3, which takes the fat files that make up audio CDs and squunches them down (with some loss of quality) into smaller files for storage and retrieval across the Internet—was finished in 1992. Two sites, MusicMaker and MP3.com, both 1999 IPOs, came online in 1997 and specialize in, respectively, custom CD compilations and independent artists; by mid 1998, "MP3" had passed "sex" as the Net's most popular keyword search term. Searching for MP3 files in 1998 and 1999 was a lot like searching for pornography was a year or two earlier: half the sites so crowded you couldn't get in, abundant copyright violations, and lots of dead links because someone had been forced to take their site down. In 1999 the music industry went after pirated MP3 copies of commercial music and got a lot of it removed but, aside from a limited set of downloads on a few ecommerce sites, eschewed official digital distribution. One exception was rapper Chuck D, who began leading the way online in 1998 by releasing songs in MP3 format.[27] Another was the Grateful Dead (of course), whose surviving band members began giving away outtakes from their new album in February 1999.[28]

This is another cases where the futurists and Net pioneers who gleefully predicted that the digital era would make it impossible to protect intellectual property rights may have brought vengeance. "The Net will kill copyright" was one of those ideas that got bandied around a lot in the early 1990s as a number of the more visible pundits—including John Perry Barlow[29] and Esther Dyson[30]—insisted that the key to the future was not going to be selling or guarding intellectual property but giving away intellectual property and selling instead personal appearances or services built around the intellectual property. One of the commonly cited examples: the Grateful Dead, who became a cultural phenomenon by allowing free taping at their concerts as long as you didn't sell the tapes, and reaped the rewards from their own merchandising. More recently one could cite the open-source software movement.

If you set out to invent a medium that would make it incredibly easy to copy perfectly and distribute widely someone else's intellectual property, it's true that digital media and the Net are exactly what you would invent. Just ask humorist Dave Barry, whose column about the exploding whale on an Oregon beach has cycled around the Net so endlessly that it's in the *alt.folklore.urban* FAQ,[31] and the author is said to receive copies regularly suggesting he write about the incident.

The Net also makes it obvious how many misconceptions people have about copyright. Lots of people think that it's OK to redistribute copyrighted material as long as they attach a copyright notice (wrong); that the freedom of speech protections enshrined in the First Amendment give them permission to copy anything they want (copyright is written into the Constitution[32]); or that the fact that the material was placed on the Net by its owner gives implicit permission to copy and redistribute it (wrong again).

On the other hand, you see just as laughable misconceptions coming from some legal types panicked about protecting their copyrights. Britain's Copyright Licensing Authority, for example, in 1999 released a set of guidelines it wanted taught in schools that suggested that anyone printing out a Web page should first contact the site's Webmaster for permission. Whoever wrote that had no idea what a burden that would be to a major site with millions of pages. It was once fashionable to imagine that printing out pages would be a minority pastime. Now, *Wired News* and *Salon* have print buttons because they learned what we all already knew, that reading long articles on a computer screen isn't that much fun, and when it's a really good article you want to save a copy.

Limiting printing, though, is probably the kind of regime that large rights-holders would endorse. The owner of a site called Totalnews, for example, found himself in hot water with a number of large publishers, including London's *Times*, when he set up a search engine to return stories from those services, with full credit to the publisher. The problem was that the material appeared in his frames, rather than on the companies' pages,[33] so the big publishers lost both control over the material's appearance and the money-making opportunity to display ads around it.

In 1998, there was a fad among large companies to prohibit linking to their sites without permission, which makes about as much sense as demanding that no one talk about your TV ads. What was bugging them, of course, was the possibility that someone might put a link to their site in a context they didn't like—criticism, say, or ridicule, or a claim that might create liability for the company. But what is the Web if you can't link freely?

But then, people are still fighting over photocopying. In 1989, publishers successfully sued Kinko's over photocopying articles and book chapters distributed in course packs and used in lieu of textbooks. True, there is a visible connection between this type of copying and a loss of royalties, but what the practice shows is that the publishing industry is too expensive, inflexible, and rigid to answer the market's real needs, something online traders of MP3 music files are beginning to say about a music industry that requires you to buy a CD with twelve songs you don't like in order to get the two you really want. Textbooks *are* expensive. Does it make sense to require students to buy the whole book if all you really want them to read is one chapter?

The Net and electronic media bring with them the possibility of customizing selections. We're seeing the beginnings of this now with initiatives for just-in-time printing. Books need never go completely out of print.

Those lobbying for tighter restrictions on copyright lard their rhetoric with references to the authors and creators who must profit from their work or starve. The starving part is certainly true: probably 90 percent of writers never make a living, just as 90 percent of the members of Actors' Equity are unemployed at any given time. But the notion that authors or artists own their work is increasingly far from the truth. The 1990s saw a major copyright grab on the part of publishers, costing authors the right to resell their work in other markets. Unlike staff writers, who trade the rights in their work for salaries, paid sick leave, paid vacations, benefits, and so on, freelance writers often depended on such resale rights to make a living. The advent of CD-ROMs, electronic databases, online commercial services (both retail like CompuServe and professional like Lexis/Nexus), and finally the Internet and the Web convinced publishers that their back catalogues were worth real money if "repurposed" in these new media. A few publishers offered payments for these new reuses of freelancers' work, but most demanded all rights in perpetuity, and a few simply went ahead and republished even though they didn't own the rights.

Jonathan Tasini, the president of the National Writers Union, took a host of famous publications to court, leading with the *New York Times*, over the reuse of freelance material in electronic databases. The district court ruled in 1997 that these electronic databases constituted simply a different "version" of the publications under the copyright law. However, Tasini won (to most people, logically) on appeal.[34]

Similarly, the major record companies made millions off songs written by artists who sold their copyrights in the early days without understanding what that meant. Meanwhile, you have to get clearance to quote a few lines from a song lyric in cases where fair use would cover poetry. In Hollywood, as movies become dolls, computer games, books, and TV shows, people panic about supplying so much as a photograph of an employee who worked on a particular film without the permission of the studio that owns the film. The same is beginning to be true of high-tech toys. After Tiger released the Furby, it was almost impossible to get permission to talk officially to the people who worked on it.

Movie studios, major publishers, and toy manufacturers have tramped all over the Net with remarkable gracelessness and stupidity, given that the people they're hounding are (a) customers, (b) future customers, and (c) fans. Mattel started going after anyone using the name "Barbie" (Australia—outdoor cooking—shrimp?). Movie studios threatened fan sites that publish pictures, sounds, and fan fiction using established characters from TV series and films. As *60 Minutes* reported in December 1997, McDonald's efforts to shut down a small restaurant by the same name in a remote Scottish glen didn't thrill either the restaurant's owner or the ancestral head of the McDonald clan, who seemed to feel that perhaps he should have been consulted before the family name and a large chunk of Scotland acquired a pickle and French fries on the side.

Many of the same copyright holders who are lobbying Congress to tighten the existing copyright laws in the name of protecting creators and authors are at the same time doing their best to subvert decades of established profit-sharing. Obviously, they believe that there will be vast profits in them thar hills, someday. While there's no doubt at least some of these guys will lose their shirts in online media—how many failed online ventures has Rupert Murdoch invested in now?[35]—they don't ask creators to help them invest in the new media with an eye to negotiating fair terms once the business models become clear. There is certainly a valid argument to be had over whether artists are right to expect royalties and further payments when their creations are reused.[36] But copyright holders aren't engaging in this debate either. They just want it all.

There are essentially four possibilities for managing the future of intellectual property rights: social, legislative, technological, and contractual. If you accept Samuelson's view of the past, it seems clear that what we've had is a mix of social (applying to private, non-commercial transactions) and legislative (applying to industry). While copyright holders have been trying to extend legislative control (a slow process), the technological and contractual areas have progressed rapidly.

Technological solutions, of which Stefik's work is an extreme example, basically revolve around cryptography, which can be used in a number of ways to protect digital intellectual property. Digital watermarking, a combination of cryptography and a technique for hiding data known as steganography,[37] ensures that copies, legal or illegal, can be traced back to their source; more advanced initiatives are supposed to lock the intellectual property, be it typeface, research report, or *Friends* video, inside a software box that can only be unlocked by the correct keys, supplied when the user pays.[38]

Fancier technology will impose even more limits. If Stefik's sort of scheme were to succeed, your printer might be one such system, able to mark printouts more or less undetectably with a time, date, and owner identifier while charging you for the job and sending out electronic payment over the network. All these technologies will make possible a new, fine-grained unbundling of rights that up until now have been taken for granted. It's easy to imagine, for example, that music files could be distributed using personal codes that match only a particular person's players.

Copyright holders love this kind of thing, but users hate it. In the early days of commercial software, when there really was no such thing as a cheap program, companies used copy protection schemes that hurt honest users more than dishonest ones, and few are in use any more outside of niche areas. Abandoned in response to public unhappiness, these schemes have crept back in the form of software that locks up if you haven't registered.[39] The Net-based version of copy-protection is likely to be forced registration, followed by required updates and additional payments—essentially meaning that consumers will no longer buy (or, rather, license) software but rent it, giving them even fewer ownership rights.

Users still hate copy protection, as the recent examples of DVD and Divx should have reminded everyone. The change from videotapes to DVD is a lot like the change from vinyl to CD: more stuff on the discs and clearer quality, but higher prices. DVD should represent big money to the studios, since they can both charge more for the disc *and* sell the same disc worldwide. But, like CDs, DVDs are perfect copies, lacking the gradual degradation of quality that occurs when you make successive generations of analog copies. Worse, movie and TV studios are used to being able to control when and how they launch their films in different countries around the world. British moviegoers are expected to be patient about waiting six months for American movies and TV shows to appear in their country. Digital distribution could change some of this because it will now cost no more to make an extra digital "print" of a movie to ship to the United Kingdom for distribution. However, film critic Roger Ebert has written a dissenting essay about digital distribution, pointing out that relatively inexpensive upgrades to current projection equipment will allow far superior quality using traditional film. Given the wonderful quality of light through celluloid and the importance for the exhibition industry of ensuring that theater-quality cinema stays ahead of home theaters, I hope he's right that this technology will win out.[40]

The movie studios pushed DVD player manufacturers into crippling the technology by adding cryptographic coding to prevent discs intended for one region from being played in another. The increasing leakage of videotapes from the United States, however, means that almost all new British VCRs can play American (NTSC) tapes on a British (PAL) set. So almost immediately a trade sprang up in Britain supplying hacked DVD players[41] that play American as well as European discs, and DVDs joined CDs and to a lesser extent videotapes in streaming eastwards from the United States to Europe in what must surely be one of the first effective ecommerce-enabled consumer rebellions. Although some people felt that supporting the British industry was important, a debate in the *dvd* conference on London's CIX conferencing system made it clear why American discs were so popular: not only were they cheaper, they typically had more features and came out sooner. Contrary to popular belief, the British *don't* like queuing up to wait for things.

Most Americans don't care that DVD is crippled. But they did rebel over Divx, an even more crippled form of DVD developed by Circuit City to replace rental videotapes. The idea was that you would buy the Divx disc for a relatively small sum of money—$5 or less—and then be free to watch the movie stored on it as many times as you liked in a two-day period. Thereafter, you could either throw the disc away or pay again to unlock it for a few more viewings or to open it permanently. Circuit City's thinking was that this would relieve consumers of the need to make that second trip to return tapes to the video store. The way those in the anti-Divx campaign[42] perceived it, however, they were buying a disc they then didn't own, a concept they found offensive. Despite Circuit City's efforts to push the technology—there was a flap over whether the company was behind what were billed as pro-Divx fan sites—the idea died.

My guess is that protection schemes involving micropayments will meet with the same kind of fate. People hate unpredictable payments and reviewing complex itemized bills. There's a reason why subscription cable channels are everywhere but pay-per-view is a minority interest, or why a $60-a-year subscription to eLibrary[43] is a better deal than buying articles one at a time from the *New York Times* or *Business Week* archives. Certainly, all the digital cash schemes so far tried have failed,[44] in part because most transactions are large enough to be handled by credit card. The most recent attempt, Beenz, is more like a glorified loyalty card system than a micropayments system.[45]

Software licensing is also getting tighter, as anyone who's ever troubled to read the license before clicking "I accept" knows. One has to assume that consumers have let the software companies get away with this at least partly because by the time the software license pops up, you've bought and installed the software and couldn't return it even if you wanted to. For most people the perception is that what you do in your own home with your own computer is private and those legal disclaimers don't really mean anything.

People should read more carefully, because software licenses are infecting other kinds of intellectual property. As James Gleick said in a column on the subject, inspired by the discovery that subscriptions to online magazines required users to accept software license–style agreements, the conditions users are being asked to accept are getting more sinister. Network Associates prohibits you from publishing a review of the product without prior consent, while Microsoft Agent's license says you may not use the animated characters it creates to disparage the company or its products. "Will the next version of Microsoft's operating system have a clause like that? I'll have to find a typewriter?"[46]

This is getting very close to the future I imagined for *Salon* for New Year's 1998, in which I surmised that by 2002 we would see copyright inspectors visiting schools to ensure that children playing with trademarked dolls and toys weren't bringing any of the fictional characters into disrepute.[47]

These licenses are the most common examples of the contractual way of managing copyright, and they display all of its problems. They are coercive: by the time you read the license, you have already bought the software. They are difficult to understand. Frequently, it is difficult to keep copies or to find the agreement from within the software if you want to read it again. They may, in the case of online services, be updated without your realizing it. When Yahoo! bought Geocities, it altered the user agreement to claim copyright in all user Web sites. Yahoo! backed down when warnings posted all over the Net led Geocities users to desert en masse. Worst, there is no negotiation: you can't call Microsoft and say you'll only buy Windows if they take out the bit about not being liable for any damage to your systems. If it were a building contractor putting in a new bathroom, would you sign?

Oddly, the validity of software licenses has always been questionable, because the contract terms aren't available to consumers until after the transaction has been completed. Some courts have argued that since the licenses are more or less an industry standard, consumers can be said to know what they're agreeing to even without reading them in the store. In any case, the software industry has set out to *make* them legal. The standard license terms were incorporated into changes proposed for the Uniform Commercial Code as a new section known as Article 2b. After that article failed to pass, it was reinvented as the Uniform Computer Information Transactions Act (UCITA). As of late 1999, the draft of the article is still being debated amid criticism from many quarters, including Samuelson and writers' organizations such as the National Writers Union.[48]

UCITA is intended to govern all transactions in software; it may even be allowed to govern sales of hardware that incorporate software, such as computers and personal digital assistants. The draft provisions represent the worst kind of bleed-through. Instead of applying the first-sale and fair-use doctrines to software, it takes software's licensing restrictions and applies them to every kind of intellectual property—books, music, films, photographs, the demented ravings of a drunken diarist at 4 A.M. Look at Gleick's online magazine subscriptions: no one applies such conditions to print publications.

Yes, the Net poses a challenge to the traditional control copyright owners have been able to exert over their work. But content providers themselves will be ill-served by a regime under which they have to pay for each piece of information used in the production of new work. Every creator of new ideas, however those ideas are expressed, is first and foremost a consumer of ideas. A regime in which we pay for every access to ideas in a fine-grained way will cost copyright holders more than they will lose by loosening their control. Time and time again in the history of intellectual property industries, we have seen that high prices mean a small market and low prices mean a bigger, much more profitable market.

It is time for copyright holders to stop fighting the Net and begin exploiting the new opportunities available to them. It is time for them to learn to behave in a way that doesn't make everyone from their own artists to consumers hate them for their greed and ruthlessness. If they really want people to buy instead of steal their products, their best strategy is to add value that people recognize is worth paying for. They could start by debugging their software.

Many of the restrictions in today's intellectual property fields are due to the limitations of older technology or existing rights arrangements. There is no technical reason why British TV viewers should have to wait six months after the original American showings to see new episodes of *Friends*. Given that they do, is it surprising that avid fans haunt Usenet for spoilers and download tiny, jerky offprints of home recordings so they can find out what happened?

As the Net develops, there will be more and more kinds of information whose ownership is contentious. Cybersquatting—another of the intellectual property–related areas legislated in 1999—first came to attention in 1994, when *Wired* magazine ran an article by Joshua Quittner, who, finding that many Fortune 500 companies hadn't registered their names yet, registered *mcdonalds.com* and tried calling the company to ask if it was interested in acquiring it from him.[49] Quittner noted that at least some of the registrants of the era demanded large sums of money for handing over recognizable domain names to the relevant companies, who viewed the practice as stealing their property and selling it back to them.

Cybersquatting has, if anything, become more common and more professional since then. In July 1999, the Senate passed the Anti-Cybersquatting Consumer Protection Act, which awards statutory damages to trademark holders whose names have been squatted. The bill was sponsored in the Senate by Patrick Leahy (D-Vermont) and Orrin Hatch (R-Utah),[50] who himself was the victim of a cybersquatter. Miami detective Joseph Culligan, who had registered 118 domains using familiar political names, offered Hatch *senatororrinhatch.com* for $45,000.[51]

There is, or will be, plenty of Internet-related fraud to go around, but there are few cases where domain name registration is outright fraud. Registering, say, *cocacola.com* is clearly different from claiming you are an official outlet for the Atlanta-based soft drinks giant and selling T-shirts, Coke bottles, and shares in the company. There are already adequate laws against that.

Amazon.com's August 1999 suit against a Greek imitator involved accusations of both cybersquatting and outright fraud. Amazon.com accused Greg Lloyd Smith and two of his companies of copyright infringement, trademark dilution, and violating the anti-racketeering RICO statutes, among others, via his "Greece's Biggest Bookstore" Amazon.com look-alike site at www.amazon.com.gr and www.amazon.gr. More cybersquatter-style, Amazon.com alleged that Smith had earlier offered to sell it a controlling interest in the holding company that owned the site for $1,632,000.[52] The case was settled in September 1999 with the Greek store agreeing to switch to greekbooksonline.com, though it retained the other two names.[53]

The cybersquatting bill also ignores the fact that a substantial percentage of domain name registrations in *.com* come from outside the United States. American politicians seem to have this problem of being unable to remember why we call the Internet "global" and that cybersquatters in, say, Brazil might feel free to ignore American laws.

This is a difficulty that RealNames and keyword systems like it can't solve entirely. These systems register single words to act as an easier-to-use navigation filling between users and the increasingly complex domain name system. But like domain names, keywords have to be unique. In its December 1998 report, WIPO made an example of the word "telecom," which under some keyword systems points at Symmetricom (telecom.com), completely ignoring the equal rights of Telecom UK Ltd (telecom.co.uk), TWX Telecommunications GmbH (telecom.de), Telecom s.r.l. (telecom.it), Telstra Communications (telecom.com.au), and Swisscom (telecom.ch).[54] With keyword systems integrated into some browsers (though not others), the report expressed concern that some companies would be given a marketing advantage. Technically, though, the problem is that keywords and the DNS share the same weakness.

WIPO's conclusion, when it was consulted by ICANN on the matter, was that people should not be allowed to register companies' trademarks.

University of Miami law professor Michael Froomkin, who served as a member of the Panel of Experts WIPO appointed as advisors, complained that this conclusion was biased in favor of trademark holders; failed to protect free speech; provided no privacy protection for registrants; created an expensive, loser-pays arbitration process that would intimidate legal registrants; tilted the legal playing field in favor of challengers; and was inconsistent in its approach to the use of existing law.[55] James Love and the Consumer Project on Technology challenged ICANN by requesting, on March 1, 2000, the creation of a number of new top-level domains to facilitate criticism and promote civil rights and movements (for example, the proposed *.union* domain). Registration in *.sucks*, anyone?[56]

Cybersquatting is only one example of the new forms of intellectual property being created almost constantly. Others include the compilations of messages that make up online communities, the collaborative database of user preferences built up by systems like Alexa (the technology that enables Amazon.com to recommend other sites to visit), and the system logs kept by ISPs, Web sites, and, soon, wireless network operators.

Most people never think about who owns the personal trails they leave behind in Web site logs, individual sites' transaction records, or archives of online discussions. Most probably think it's all too ephemeral to worry about. But take, for example, science fiction writer Douglas Adams's online project to create a collaborative *Hitchhiker's Guide to the Galaxy*, which requires contributors to relinquish all rights in any material they submit. Collaborative sites like this find it easier and simpler to demand all rights, just as publishers do, but there must be an alternative—after all, we have these things called computers that are rather good at managing just this sort of problem.

Conversely, companies may have good reasons for complaining when someone comes along and hacks their products to make them jump through different hoops. Take the case of the Diamond Rio, a palm-sized MP3 player. The Recording Industry Association of America (RIAA) attempted to block the product, but lost in court when Diamond argued successfully that it didn't contravene the 1992 Audio Home Recording Act because it was a playback device, not a recording device—unless it was attached to a computer. Thanks to a group of smart hackers, the Rio now can upload files to a computer, turning it into a recording device. Good for consumers, but potentially a legal minefield for Diamond. Like minidiscs, however, the focus on commercially recorded music obscures MP3 devices' usefulness for mass storage of the spoken word or for creating your own files. Underlying that, of course, is the arrogant presumption that anyone who's any good as a creator would have been snapped up under contract by the entertainment industries long ago.

Similarly, the coding (CSS) behind DVD was hacked in late 1999, leading to mass action on the part of the Motion Picture Association of America (MPAA) against anyone posting or linking to the source code. Making this type of hacking illegal will potentially criminalize many perfectly honorable activities (such as cryptography research, reverse engineering, and inspecting systems for safety), while failing to correct vulnerabilities in system design. It's also worth pointing out that for all the United States' self-righteousness over software piracy in China (for example), it was once notoriously unwilling to recognize foreign authors' copyrights. Most of Dickens's works were published in the United States in pirate editions, as was J.R.R. Tolkien's *Lord of the Rings*.

In a society where we trade information about ourselves every day for conveniences such as telephoning from home (creating a database of telephone records) or savings such as frequent flier miles (creating databases of our movements), it seems a small step to leave fragments of our thoughts trailing around cyberspace wherever we visit. But the consequence may be that one day we have to pay royalties to access our own thoughts or live in homes filled with objects we must pay to use.

9

The Future of Public Information

> Education is here placed among the articles of public care, not that
> it would be proposed to take its ordinary branches out of the hands
> of private enterprise, which manages so much better all the con-
> cerns to which it is equal; but a public institution can alone supply
> those sciences which, though rarely called for, are yet necessary to
> complete the circle, all the parts of which contribute to the im-
> provement of the country, and some of them to its preservation.
> —Thomas Jefferson, Sixth Annual Message, 1806

In 1993, *Wired* magazine considered the future of libraries.
At the time, it seemed as though electronic books might take over the
world, and writer John Browning mulled over the possibility that libraries might need to charge for access to them:

> If libraries do not charge for electronic books, not only can they not reap
> rewards commensurate with their own increasing importance, but li-
> braries can also put publishers out of business with free competition. If
> libraries do charge, that will disenfranchise people from information—a
> horrible thing. There is no obvious compromise.[1]

Then the Web happened. The issue is no longer whether or not libraries
should charge for access to electronic books but what libraries should
be doing in a world where it's actually faster for me to find the reference to an article in the *Columbia Journalism Review* on the Web than
it is for me to search my own paper archives.

If there were three categories of people that might logically have
thought their jobs would be safe in a world of exploding information,
they would be teachers, librarians, and government workers. And yet,
what we're seeing is a push to put college courses online, an extended
debate over what the future will be for libraries if all information
sources are digital and easily accessible on the Web, and plans on the

part of various governments to streamline their services and cut costs by switching to electronic delivery. The Net challenges all three.[2]

There are, of course, plenty of ways in which technology can improve public services. The availability of texts on the Internet, for example, means much faster access to material you waited weeks for in the past. Given the technology, small libraries in rural areas can provide access formerly available only in large urban areas. Similarly, technology enables students in remote areas to gain access to teachers and learning they could not have reached before, and with more interaction than in correspondence courses of the past. A class of teachers in training scattered all over a rural area like Wales, for example, can be brought together once a week online for group discussions where meeting in person is impossible.

Governments, meanwhile, look at electronic delivery of services in part as a way of cutting costs, but also as a way of cutting down the frustration most people experience in trying to get through the maze of government regulations and departments in order to accomplish simple things like changing an address or registering a death.

But there is a cost to electronifying these services and interactions that goes beyond the simple problem (discussed in chapter 8) of locking off access by demanding payment. Putting courses online may de-skill the teaching profession. Streamlining government departments means merging databases of information in ways that no one ever expected when those databases were first created, opening the way to the long-feared surveillance state. Assuming that the Internet will take over where libraries leave off ignores how much information is not on the Internet—telephone books from the 1920s are an obvious example. On the other hand, it is truly astonishing how much is out there now. I was going to use ancient Icelandic sagas or the works of British novelist George Gissing as examples of material not available online, but there they are in full text, wonderful stuff that just ten years ago was available only in collections (mostly in Scandinavia, in the case of the sagas) or expensive library-bound reprints. It's common to assume that given the variety of people in the world sooner or later everything will find its way online, but there's no guarantee.

The biggest trouble lies somewhere in the gap between past and present media. One of my favorite drawings by *New Yorker* cartoonist Saul Steinberg is of an analog clock that has "NOW" written twelve times on the clock face where the numbers would normally go. The cartoon pre-dates digital watches but captures them perfectly. On a digital clock, it is always NOW; on an analog clock, time is relative. My personal information manager database, by analogy, makes it very easy to update records with new information—but does not automatically store the replaced information in a form that would let me go back to look at it, the way my Rolodex, with its multiple scratchings and changes, does. In the digital world, history is invisible; it requires discipline to retain it. In the analog world, it required more discipline to throw things away than to keep them.

A perfect example of this was the novelist Nicholson Baker's 1994 article in the *New Yorker* lamenting the trashing of library card catalogues, rapidly being replaced by electronic indexes.[3] The article was received with fury by many librarians, who insisted that many of Baker's criticisms—that, for example, the knowledge built up in decades of notations in the careful, back-slanted writing known as "library hand" was being discarded instead of added to the electronic databases were wrong-headed. Baker saw the old card catalogues as painstakingly compiled repositories of human knowledge, much the way software engineer Ellen Ullman, writing in *Salon*, said she regarded computer systems before Windows rendered them impenetrable.[4] By comparison, the uniform electronic records supplied by the Online Computer Library Center in Ohio have the bland sameness of suburbs.

Baker later commented, "It's fine to have silicon conduits to get you the information, but it's important to hold onto the paper source as well, whatever it might be—book, card catalogue, run of an old newspaper—those things are being thrown out much too casually."[5]

In a 1998 online discussion of Baker's article among librarians,[6] most still agreed Baker was wrong. The card catalog as an artifact may have emotional value, but online catalogs, as immature as the technology is, offer too many advantages. While they agreed that a lot of information was being thrown out, they also said a lot of it was pretty irrelevant: the date the seventeenth copy of a particular book was withdrawn, for example, or the date, source, and cost of each book. Somewhere I can hear a historian from five centuries hence keening. The value of information changes over time, and details like that are briefly valuable when fresh, fade quickly, and then become fascinating again when enough time has passed to make them revealing of a culture that's gone.

For a researcher, the Web is both wonderful and dangerous: wonderful because so much is out there; dangerous because you never know how long it will be there or whether you'll be able to find the same page next time you look. According to Brewster Kahle, founder of the Internet archive project, the average lifetime of a document on the Web is only seventy-five days.[7] Not everything gets mirrored and preserved, and there's no guarantee that the pages that are free today will be free tomorrow, or that the site someone currently maintains with such passion will still exist two years from now when you suddenly need to check a quote or a fact. The only really safe solution is to keep your own archives. But Web browsers are not designed by people who understand research needs. Netscape can be set to automatically stamp printouts with the source URL, date, and time (though not the creation date). A page saved to disk, however, retains nothing to indicate its origins. Adobe Acrobat, frequently used for fancier files whose owners want them to look exactly like the original, has the same flaw. A browser designed by information specialists would surely log all that information automatically and unalterably, and perhaps even be able to track multiple versions of the same Web page. No one is working on this, however; they're too busy adding features to support ecommerce.

Keeping old or out-of-print material so that anyone may access it has traditionally been a function of libraries. So far, they have not adopted this as a habit for the digital age. Instead, if you lose a piece of information and it disappears from the Web, you must rely on the kindness of strangers who may have archived their own copies. It's axiomatic, for example, that by the time this book is printed, a noticeable percentage of the URLs in the footnotes will be broken, even though they will all be checked at the last possible moment. As one example, Peter de Jaeger, whose year2000.com Web site was a resource for everyone remediating computer systems to get rid of Y2K bugs, put the domain name up for auction on eBay on January 3, 2000. The site is gone.

It only adds to the difficulty that the Web is not seamless. Many of the major commercial content sites (who at least do mark their material with a date and time) do not allow their material to be indexed by the search engines and so are not really part of the larger Web. Instead, they huddle, requiring you to search their sites individually. While requiring you to load three or four pages for every search is nice for their advertising revenues, it requires a researcher to search tens if not hundreds of sites instead of one or two.[8] An additional consequence is that to be a really effective user of the Web you must learn much more about the kinds of sites that are out there and what all their specialties are. Despite the Web's apparent ease of use for amateurs, professional-quality researching is no easier than it ever was, though it is infinitely more convenient.

Worse, one of the larger known problems with digitized information is its instability. I have books in my personal library that I've had for forty years; they are as readable as the day I acquired them. But the disks from my TRS-80 Model III computer, last used in 1990, are unreadable on today's machines without a special emulator. Digital data requires much more upkeep to ensure continued accessibility—transferring it from medium to medium as machines and formats die, keeping and testing backups—than do old books. Music is even worse: the 78-rpm records from my childhood and the reel-to-reel tapes I collected in my twenties are practically extinct now. For public archives, this kind of overhead is a nightmare.

Besides the format problem, there's the difficulty of ensuring the integrity of documents. People tend to presume that digitized documents are faithful copies of the originals, but without comparing the digital versions with an official hard copy there's no way to be sure. *Columbia Journalism Review* reported on a study of just this question in 1998. Bruce William Oakley, editor of *Arkansas Online*, discovered that even official electronic periodical databases like the high-priced Lexis/Nexus were riddled with errors, often because the database versions were taken from the reporters' original copy rather than the final pre-print version that had been fact-checked, copy-edited, and cut to length.[9] Transcription and other spelling and typographical errors are no surprise to anyone familiar with these types of databases. But what shocked Oakley was the discovery that a legally actionable statement had persisted electronically even though it had been excised from the print edition. "My study uncovered problems at every step," Oakley wrote, "from the first capture of information to the last connection between a commercial database and a searcher."

In many cases, therefore, we have multiple versions of the truth of what was published. Researchers can certainly rectify this by checking the printed or microfilmed versions, but only by adopting traditional, time-consuming methods that don't fit today's high-speed deadlines. This is a good example of why older methods of archiving, using hard, fixed, unalterable copies, are still vital if you want to ensure absolute accuracy. Eventually, the expectation is that cryptographic systems will provide an authentication trail, but that won't solve the kinds of errors Oakley talked about. Encryption also poses other risks: a misplaced key or a bit of corruption could render whole tracts of material unreadable.

Archiving is also complicated by intellectual property rights. Unquestionably, the social life that takes place on the Net every day and the knowledge base composed of the world's millions of Web sites is the kind of cultural snapshot that historians would be thrilled to have from earlier eras. But archiving the whole Web—as the Internet archive project[10] is trying to do—involves storing data that may be copyrighted, corrected, or withdrawn if there's a libel suit. Some online periodicals, such as *Business Week*, give away articles for only a short time and charge fees for articles retrieved from back issues. Respecting the fence around that material, though, makes the archive incomplete and therefore less useful.

This is where the distinction between an archive and a library becomes important. As Julie E. Cohen, an intellectual property law specialist then at the University of Pittsburgh, said in a panel on archiving the Net at the Computers, Freedom, and Privacy 1999 (CFP99) conference, archivists are pack rats and keep everything, while librarians are selective. It would be a logical outgrowth of today's libraries to create careful indexes of the material they believe is most interesting to their patrons. At the moment, both library-style selection and archiving are being left to newcomers online who are interested. Yahoo! has made an S&P 500 business out of its consistent indexing and search functions, and founder Jerry Yang said in 1997 that one secret behind the quality of the company's indexing is that it has involved librarians in its design.[11]

In the same CFP99 panel discussion, Marybeth Peters, head of the U.S. Copyright Office, talked about the difficulty of deciding what constitutes publication in the electronic era, which is critical in some areas of copyright law and affects whether or not the Library of Congress has access to materials. The Library of Congress is actively working on digitizing the older items in its collection, but it is not collecting electronic material. This seems like a terrible misstep. Surely the national library should be collecting copies of computer software, online databases, and original CD-ROM publications. A national archive of this type is needed, particularly for computer software. It is impossible to make sense of software culture or design without understanding the steps along the way to its creation, and a national repository would help users when software goes out of development and leaves its data orphaned. These are important parts of our communal history. Just as everyone agreed that one of the elements that makes an online community work is a sense of its own history, preserved through archives of old discussion topics, so it is with offline communities.

The impact of digital media on the government sector is even messier. The easier availability of public information online is to everyone's benefit—it's wonderful to be able to search the Securities and Exchange Commission and Congressional archives or look up Food and Drug Administration pamphlets without having to go to great lengths to ferret out the correct address and wait weeks for copies to arrive in the mail.[12] Equally, it makes sense for governments to adopt the 24/7 operation and immediate response we've become accustomed to from businesses. But the instability of media is just as big a complicating factor for governments as for others,[13] while the cryptographic schemes that can be used to ensure the authenticity and integrity of those records can also render them inaccessible—or worse, falsely authenticated—if the cryptographic keys are mismanaged.

These were some of the issues that Britain's Foundation for Information Policy Research (FIPR) was set up in 1998 to research. The year before, one of FIPR's co-founders, British cryptographer Ross Anderson, concluded that the solution to both the problems for archivists and the potential for rampant copyright restrictions and censorship was a collaborative, anonymous archiving service.[14] Among the many situations in which the protection of records may be important, Anderson lists medical malpractice, pollution cases, immigration disputes, fraud, and computer security. "Preventing the powerful from rewriting history or simply suppressing embarrassing facts is just one of our goals," he says, going on to specify how such an archive could be constructed.

At the moment, the risk is more from the withdrawal of information than its alteration. Such a case occurred in 1999, when Congress debated whether to make available online a database of risk management plans and worst-case scenarios for the 66,000 industrial sites working with extremely hazardous substances. A 1990 decision required plants to submit the information, and as recently as 1997, when submissions were due, the government intended to make a searchable database of these risk management plans available over the Internet.

Even in 1997, however, some people were concerned that allowing full access to the data to anyone who wanted it, anywhere in the world, might make it easier for "amateur" terrorists to attack those facilities. In 1999 the Center for Democracy and Technology (CDT)[15] and other interested groups raised the alarm after hearing that proposals to limit access to this information were before the Commerce Committee. In a publicly released letter to the committee's chairman, Thomas Bliley, the CDT's executive director, Jerry Berman, argued forcefully that the Freedom of Information Act mandates that information must be supplied in the format requested as long as it's easily producible. On May 19, Bliley introduced H.R. 1790, the Chemical Safety Information and Site Security Act of 1999, which restricts how (mostly paper) and to whom (local government officials and the public under controlled conditions) the information may be given.[16]

Proponents of publication point out that the information is likely to be readily available whether or not the database appears on the Net. For example, local newspapers have made it their business to learn about hazards surrounding chemical plants, and many of these themselves are online. In addition, as John D. Dingell (D-Michigan) said in a statement in his capacity as the ranking Democrat on the Commerce Committee, the risks to the public at large are much greater from ordinary industrial accidents than they are from terrorist activity. A 1997 report by the Environmental Protection Agency (EPA) itself said that between 1980 and 1987 there were 11,058 accidental releases of toxic chemicals in the United States that killed 309 people and caused 11,341 injuries and the evacuation of nearly 500,000 people.[17] Having information about chemical plants, therefore, could help communities protect themselves better, as could knowing what kinds of accidents have happened around other, similar plants.

At CFP99, however, representatives of the EPA, the House Commerce Committee, the Chemical Manufacturers Association, and the National Security Council vehemently backed the idea of restrictions, arguing that the FBI opposed putting the information on the Internet, and that it's not uncommon for rules to specify how even public information may be released and used. The Office of Management and Budget's representative countered by saying, "If we put this information out, we will double terrorism. But a doubling of terrorism is still zero."

In the meantime, activists were compiling and posting information on the Net about chemical plants collected from a variety of public sources.[18] Among other things, the Community Right-to-Know site analyzes the areas around ten DuPont chemical plants. Claiming that up to seven million people in surrounding areas may be vulnerable to worst-case accidents, the site argues that the chemical industry should not be lobbying Congress to help keep its activities secret, but should be looking at ways to reduce the hazards it poses to the communities around its facilities.

While governments struggle with what to tell the people and how, educators are trying to figure out how to deal with copyright issues. Putting courses online that use copyrighted material and extending educational exemptions under the copyright laws to the electronic media could hurt publishers, but not extending those exemptions could deny people access to education.[19]

The last few years have seen a race by higher education institutions to get online. Everyone, from traditional universities such as UCLA and distance-learning specialists such as the University of Phoenix to start-ups such as the Western Governors' Virtual University project and the California Virtual University, is putting everything from individual courses to whole degree programs online. Management guru Peter F. Drucker has predicted the death of traditional residential higher education within thirty years.

But a report published in April 1999 questioned whether online learning can really solve our longstanding educational problems and inequalities.[20] The report, written by the Institute for Higher Education Policy (IHEP) on behalf of the American Federation of Teachers and the National Education Association, concludes that the proof is not there that the "learning outcome" is on a par with traditional classroom teaching (not that you'd expect a teachers' organization to conclude anything else). The report criticizes research efforts for, among other things: studying individual courses instead of overall programs; ignoring the drop-out rate in assessing the overall success rate of students; failing to control for extraneous variables so that cause and effect are not shown; not randomizing subjects; and failing to show the validity of the instruments used to measure learning outcomes. In addition, the report complains that the research does not look at differences between students, explain why drop-out rates are higher in distance learning, look at technologies used together, adequately assess the effectiveness of digital versus physical libraries, or consider how different learning styles relate to specific technologies. In other words, we're racing headlong into a new set of educational techniques we don't really understand. Given that an ever-increasing percentage of the U.S. economy depends on knowledge workers, and that those workers need to be highly educated and skilled, this could be a really stupid move.

On the other hand, opening up online access gives a large sector of the population a crack at higher education who otherwise wouldn't get one. Plenty of bright people lose out on education every day because of difficult family circumstances or lack of money. Not everyone can use online education to bridge the gap, but many can. In the thirty years Britain's Open University has been in existence, it's seen more than two hundred thousand people complete degrees using everything from televised lectures to Internet-based conferencing and short residential courses. It is pure snobbery to pretend that only classroom-based education is worth having.

Nonetheless, there are drawbacks to putting many courses online, a topic which few have considered critically. An exception is historian David F. Noble, now teaching at Toronto's York University, who in October 1997 began circulating the first installments of what has over time become a treatise called "Digital Diploma Mills."[21] Noble, who compares the drive online to the early twentieth century craze for correspondence courses, connects the soaring cost of a university education with what he calls the commercialization of academia since the mid-1970s, when industrial partnerships and other commercial exploitation of university-based discoveries and research became common. Noble believes that moving courses online is part of a larger drive to "commodify" university education: "In short, the new technology of education, like the automation of other industries, robs faculty of their knowledge and skills, their control over their working lives, the product of their labor, and, ultimately, their means of livelihood."

Even England's Oxford University intends to find a way to replicate its famed personal tutorial system online. As Noble says, universities struggling with overburdened staff may see the Internet as a way to make themselves more economical, but with computer vendors looking at higher education as a huge, new potential revenue source, what are the odds that many universities will buy courseware from the same five or six commercial vendors, reducing diversity and academic freedom? Meanwhile, the dream the top universities will be selling is that anyone can have access to the finest education available: would you sign up for Podunk's online course or Harvard's?

Replicating the student experience online is much harder than creating courseware, however, and although online communities represent a way of doing it, as we've seen they're not easy to create or maintain. Interaction between students is as important a part of a college education as interaction between students and faculty. A residential education is the special privilege it is because nowhere else can you rub shoulders with such a variety of people with so many different interests.

This is not to say that online learning has no place in the world, or that it shouldn't happen. But the issues keep surfacing. How do faculty members find time for their own lives and/or research in an environment where they're on call via email twenty-four hours a day? What about student services, extracurricular activities, and, as the IHEP report said many times, libraries?

There is a final intriguing consequence to the proliferation of information sources and online searching. Traditionally, knowing and being able to quote learnedly from a wide variety of authors was a sign of an educated person. When everything is online and finding a quote to bolster your argument is a simple matter of dropping the right few words into a search engine, what new language will evolve whereby scholars can recognize each other? Just how do you think I found the Jefferson quote that begins this chapter?

10

Falling into the Gap

For the first time in modern human history, there is an opportunity to abolish educational discrimination based on class-ism, age, race, or economics. Modern personal computers are dropping below the $700.00 range. Internet Service Providers (ISPs) allow discounts for college attendees (at least mine does). If the universities follow true Internet form and allow many classes for no-pay or lesser fees—the bell of Freedom in America will ring again and science can once again experience the likes of Benjamin Franklin, George Washington Carver and Alexander Graham Bell.
　　　　　　　　　　—A *Scientific American* reader rebutting criticism of
online education

Vinton Cerf, one of the authors of the TCP/IP protocols and now a vice-president at MCI Worldcom, has a stock speech that begins, "The Internet is for everyone. But it won't be if . . ."

The great dream of the Net in the early days—and, of course, in many quarters still—was that it could act as a leveler to promote democracy, equalize opportunity, and end divisions of rich and poor. Distance education, as discussed in the last chapter, is one way some have claimed the Internet will increase equality and democracy.

In a report published in early 1999, the College Board, purveyor of standardized college admission tests, cast doubt on the idea that new technology can cut costs in delivering education and that it will bring equality of access:

Most educational technology introduced over the past 50 years has supplemented and often enhanced—not supplanted—traditional classroom instruction, thus *adding* to its cost, not reducing it. Cutting-edge information technology tends to be expensive and have a short half-life, straining education budgets, not relieving them.

Nonetheless, the vision of packaging courses with name instructors and mass marketing them around the world through the Internet is a powerful lure to providers, especially those that already have substantial investment in the necessary infrastructure.[1]

The report quotes the head of the Open University, who says that the notion of distance learning in which teaching is presentation and learning is absorption—what you might call the broadcast model—will fail, or at least have massive drop-out problems, similar to those found in the teachers' report quoted in the last chapter. Even the Open University's programs typically require one- to two-week residencies.

Other problems cited by the College Board report: the technology favors those who are already advantaged. School access to the Internet is not a good indicator of student access. In some schools the only access is in the library or the principal's office. The report notes, "Virtual space is infinite, but it does not promise universality or equity." It goes on to say, "While education is the great equalizer, technology appears to be a new engine of inequality. Access to technology is not only about hardware and software. It is about effective use, teacher training, and careful integration of technology into the curriculum."[2]

You cannot expect to throw technology at education and solve long-standing problems of policy, as psychologist Sherry Turkle has pointed out. "I see a lot of positive educational benefits," she says, "but it's not a substitute for giving kids free lunches or putting a piano in their school." Wiring the schools in no way solves the serious problems in education or social services for kids. "It's a fantasy that's a displacement of our very real anxieties about kids and the state they're in." Most of the children she studies "don't need more information; they need to learn to use a little bit of information well, first."[3]

These critiques of online learning are only part of a series of studies that show that although the Internet could *potentially* help us to fulfill the same democratic dreams we have every time a new technology is invented, so far it is increasing existing disparities of income, race, and education.

The most important of these studies is the Department of Commerce's series *Falling through the Net: Defining the Digital Divide*.[4] The Department has carried out three of these studies since 1995, and the latest (released in mid 1999), shows that the gap is widening, not narrowing.

Among the report's key findings:

- Households with incomes of $75,000 and higher are more than *twenty times* more likely to have access to the Internet than those at the lowest income levels, and more than *nine times* as likely to have a computer at home.
- Whites are more likely to have access to the Internet from home than Blacks or Hispanics have from *any* location.
- Black and Hispanic households are approximately *one-third* as likely to have home Internet access as households of Asian/Pacific Islander descent, and roughly *two-fifths* as likely as White households.
- Regardless of income level, Americans living in rural areas are lagging behind in Internet access. Indeed, at the lowest income levels, those in urban areas are more than twice as likely to have Internet access than those earning the same income in rural areas.
- The gaps between White and Hispanic households, and between White and Black households, are now more than six percentage points larger than they were in 1994.
- The digital divides based on education and income level have also increased in the last year alone. Between 1997 and 1998, the divide between those at the highest and lowest education levels increased 25 percent, and the divide between those at the highest and lowest income levels grew 29 percent.

This pattern is being duplicated in other countries. The Virtual Society program studying issues of equity and access from 1997 to 2000, for example, has so far concluded that the power structures developing in cyberspace are the same as those we already have.[5] The program, managed at Britain's Brunel University, is coordinating work at twenty-five universities in Britain and two in Amsterdam and Copenhagen.[6]

Vanderbilt University professors Donna Hoffman and Tom Novak's widely reported 1999 study for the journal *Science* discussed race and its impact on Internet access.[7] They concluded, "Although African Americans are online in impressive numbers, significant disparities in access indicate the presence of a racial divide on the Internet." The gap, their research shows, is greatest among secondary and university students—exactly the group in whom you would least expect it.

Hoffman and Novak make several important policy points. "Ensure access and use will follow," they say, suggesting that it's particularly important to encourage multiple points of access, including home, work, school, and other locations. Noting that white students, whether or not they have a home computer, are more likely to use the Web than African Americans, they say, "This suggests the importance of not only creating access points for African Americans in libraries, community centers, and other non-traditional places where individuals may access the Internet, but also encouraging use at these locations."

In addition, as their survey showed that African Americans are currently more likely to want access to the Net than whites, they stress the importance of encouraging home computer ownership and the adoption of low-cost devices that enable Internet access, particularly over TV sets.

An important point Novak and Hoffman make is that when communities insist on installing filtering software in libraries, they are imposing censorship on those who have no other access to the Net.

The paper also cites a number of studies showing that although 70 percent of the schools in this country have at least one computer connected to the Internet, less than 15 percent of classrooms have Internet access, and that access is not distributed randomly but correlated strongly with income and education.

Similarly, a National Science Foundation–funded study carried out in Pittsburgh and reported at the Association for Computing Machinery's Policy '98 conference in Washington, D.C., found that without special care access tended to gravitate toward already advantaged schools and students. The privileged schools were better able to write the proposals necessary to get the equipment and access in the first place. Once a school was connected, the students who got to use the access tended to be the most academically gifted, either because using the Internet was seen as a reward for good work or because the teachers didn't know enough about the Internet to be able to introduce it to all students equally and relied on the already knowledgeable students to lead the way.

There are all kinds of reasons for wanting to ensure equality of access in education as well as in the rest of life, from the practical (we need the skilled work force) to the idealistic (it's only fair). It's also clear that if we are to have any diversity in the design of technology, we also need to have equality of access. And as our interactions are increasingly mediated by these technologies, diversity of approach to design becomes important, as we saw in chapter 2.[8]

When I wrote *net.wars* I was optimistic about the prospects for women in the networked world. The numbers of women online were growing, a lot of the early stupid media scare stories about how hostile the Net was to women had stopped appearing, and I thought the real answer—ensuring that women were equally represented in technical fields as well in online positions of control—was secure. That was before the news became public that the numbers of women in computer science have been steadily dropping.

After all the advances toward equality for women, you might assume that there are lots of women programmers. But according to statistics presented at the Policy '98 conference by Tracy Camp, an assistant professor at the University of Alabama, the number of undergraduate degrees in computer science awarded to women has been shrinking steadily, both in real numbers and as a percentage of degrees awarded, since it peaked in 1983–1984 at 37.1 percent (which then represented 32,172 BA/BS degrees). Other science and engineering disciplines, she notes, do not show the same pattern.[9]

However, *Business Week* reported in August 1999 that the number of women completing higher-level economics degrees has also dropped—only 20 percent of Ph.D. degrees awarded in economics in 1997 went to women, down from 26 percent in 1995 and 35 percent in 1993, compared to law (46 percent of first-year law students are women) and medicine (42 percent of medical graduates are women). *Business Week* went on to joke that perhaps the dismal forecasting record of economists in the last few years had something to do with it. A more important factor may be that both computer science and economics are math-oriented disciplines and girls are still not typically encouraged to think of themselves as good at math.

The 1995 book *Failing at Fairness* presents a clear picture of the way computers and math both wind up as boys' domains, at home, in school, and at computer camps.

> In a study of students who had not received computer instruction in school, more than 60 percent of boys but only 18 percent of girls had a computer at home. And when boys and girls play computer games, for education or recreation, they manipulate mainly male figures in adventures involving technology, sports, and war.
>
> These lessons learned outside school shape in-class performance. Boys are more aggressive when it comes to grabbing space at a classroom computer, and they often fail to share with girl classmates. They are the ones

who monopolize the spaces in the school's computer courses in high school and college. When boys study computers, they learn to program. When girls study computers, it is often for word processing.[10]

There has always been a shrinking pipeline effect for women in computer science. Girls make up 50 percent of high school computer science classes, but in 1993–1994 women accounted for only 5.7 percent of full professors in the field. But what Camp is talking about is a shrinkage in the number of women entering the profession in the first place. For example, the percentage of MS degrees peaked (logically) in 1985–1986, when women won 29.9 percent of the degrees awarded, and Ph.D. degrees peaked at 15.4 percent in 1988–1989. Those percentages decline further through the ranks of faculty members. Even though the absolute number of MS and Ph.D. degrees awarded has continued to increase, these numbers are likely to begin decreasing soon.

Why is this happening? To attempt to find out, Camp, who heads the Committee on Women in Computing for the Association for Computing Machinery (ACM), conducted a survey of ACM members.[11] This is, as she herself said when she presented the survey results at the Policy '98 conference, not the right sample: you need to ask the people who didn't join the profession.

But many of those surveyed agreed that male-oriented computer games tended to get boys more computer experience than girls in the 1980s, and that the long hours, gender discrimination, lack of role models within the profession, as well as the antisocial hacker image of professionals (Marimba's glamour CEO Kim Polese notwithstanding) have tended to lead women to choose other fields. Proposed solutions include making more visible the female role models that exist, improving mentoring, and encouraging equal access to computers for girls in grades K–12. One issue that was not on the survey but was brought up a lot (including by a large systems specialist I consulted) was sexual harassment.

Many of these disadvantages are common to other professions. Doctors also work very long hours. But the perception is that in computing you never gain control of your time (as you might in medicine), most of those hours are uncompensated, and you have relearn everything you know every three to five years. As women are typically more conscious of the difficulties that face them in juggling work and family, it's understandable why these might be deterrents.

This pattern is not unique to the United States. In Britain the decline is even more marked, with the percentage of women entering university degree programs in information technology courses declining from a third to about 5 percent. The reasons given by British observers such as Rachel Burnett, a council member for the Institute for the Management of Information Systems, are similar to those listed above, though minus the long hours.

This is a depressing phenomenon. Everyone agrees that the quality and variety of software could only benefit from having a less homogeneous group of people working to create it. Anita Borg, founder of the Systers mailing list for professional women in computer science, has pointed out that involving women in technology design makes a difference in its accessibility to women. Even stupid details like the belt clips on cases for handhelds and mobile phones make them unusable by the many women who don't usually wear belts.[12] If technology is going to change *everyone*'s lives, shouldn't everyone have some kind of input on the direction it's going to take? In the technology world, the only kind of input that's respected is producing a working prototype.

Borg, also founder of the new Institute for Women and Technology and a research scientist at Xerox PARC, told *Wired News*, "There's an incredible brilliance in people who know nothing about technology, but the culture of technology doesn't respect it. It's hard enough for them to respect the opinion of women and minorities who have credentials." She went on to cite a study of high school students conducted by the University of British Columbia, which found that most students did not believe that studying computer science and engineering would enable them to have a positive social impact—odd, given most technology folks' belief that their inventions can change the world. In fact, Microsoft uses exactly this hook to recruit top researchers for its labs.

Camp argues that this "shrinking pipeline" does matter, especially given that the industry claims that there is currently such a severe shortage of computer scientists in the United States that Congress needs to grant more visas to would-be immigrants.

In the context of the online world, you could say that it doesn't matter, since women are close to parity in numbers, certainly as a percentage of users of email and the Web. But because women are underrepresented in the technical fields that create the architectures of online spaces, they rarely control the spaces they use. In turn, this may have direct consequences for the kinds of discussions that are allowed and the treatment that's handed out to participating females, as well as the kinds of uses women make of the new tools. Most online moderators of all types (MUDs, IRC channels, discussion forums) are men, as are the CEOs of most electronic commerce companies and the designers of most online communities—a fact that may go some way toward explaining why ecommerce sites intended for women incorporate so many stereotypes you'd think would be dead by now. Women such as Hewlett-Packard CEO Carly Fiorina, Marimba CEO Kim Polese, online community founders Stacy Horn (Echo)[13] and Candice Carpenter and Nancy Evans (iVillage),[14] and the ubiquitous Esther Dyson (interim chair of the Internet Corporation for Assigned Names and Numbers) stand out in a sea of guys in khakis precisely because they are relatively rare. They shouldn't be.

What's become plain also is that on the Internet *everyone* knows you're a dog. It is, as Horn observed in her book *Cyberville*, not possible to jettison a lifetime of cultural conditioning unless you're determined to create a false persona. The same is true of race online. No one who has spent any time on Usenet can have missed the racism, sexism, and general intolerance that permeate even the most innocuous subjects (even *rec.sport.tennis*), and it's often easy to identify racial or gender identity. As Byron Burkhalter writes, there's no ambiguity about a thread entitled "All niggers must die."[15]

One class of people you would expect to be helped by the electronic era is the disabled. In the Web's first few years of widespread use, its graphical interface wasn't a problem—despite a few pictures, bandwidth and other technical limitations meant the Web was mostly text. It's relatively easy to equip a computer with a text translation program that will output the contents of a computer screen in Braille or synthesized speech. Now it requires constant vigilance to keep the Net in a universally accessible state, however, as sites add graphics, animations, and other bells and whizmos without regard to the difficulties they may impose on others—not just the disabled, but the bandwidth-impaired.

In 1997, the World Wide Web Consortium (W3C), the international group that oversees the development of the Web, officially launched the International Web Accessibility Initiative, a program to promote the Web's accessibility for people with disabilities.[16] The program was endorsed by President Clinton and has support from the National Science Foundation and the European Union as well as W3C members, including IBM, Lotus, and Microsoft.

For ordinary graphics, provisions were added to HTML for an "ALT" tag, which can be read by screen access software and displays a text caption in place of a graphic. It's simple to add, but not everyone bothers—which is dumb, since surveys show that at least 25 percent of Web users browse at least some of the time with graphics turned off. According to Geoff Ryman, a Web developer for Britain's Office of Central Information, a very high percentage of those accessing the government's servers do so text-only.

The current situation is a travesty because the Internet and computers for the first time made it possible for blind people to make independent choices about what they read. Peter Bosher, who is blind and gives training and installations for speech access to the Internet and works with Britain's Royal National Institute for the Blind, says that before the Internet, "You would read absolutely anything because so little was available in Braille." Even what was available tended to be limited by the agenda of the sponsoring organization. "The real revolution was when I realized that using a computer I had access to an unbelievable range of information," he says. "The big difference is that you are no longer dependent on someone choosing what should be available."[17]

In late 1999, the National Federation for the Blind (NFB) announced it was suing AOL because of the service's graphical design, which effectively prohibited blind people from using the service. In version 5.0 of AOL, some of the menus are keyboard accessible, and hover text pops up if you hold your mouse over some of the graphical buttons for a few seconds to tell you what they are. But the service's non-graphical access is patchy, and hover text only helps you if you know where to hold the mouse. According to the NFB filing, even the sign-up screens are impassable.

The NFB's case against AOL seeks to establish that the Americans with Disabilities Act extends to cyberspace, a principle that ought to be embedded in the architecture of the Net. When you think about it, it's ridiculous to design anything in cyberspace that locks people out. Yet an AOL staffer's first reaction to news of the NFB suit was to say it was impossible for AOL to recode its many millions of pages to make the service accessible. Why wasn't it obvious from the beginning that by not considering the needs of these users they were locking out potential customers? Why isn't it obvious to Web designers that as the population ages many more of us are going to have increasing difficulties with sight, sound, and mobility?

The advent of XML (for eXtended HTML) may help—or it may make things worse. XML, which supplies a way to code data about data ("metadata") via extensions to the Web's coding language, HTML, is intended to allow the Web to handle many more types of data than is possible today and to make Web pages machine-readable. XML will make possible functions such as real-time authentication and two-way linking between individual documents. It should also make the Web truly interactive. (Anyone who thinks pointing and clicking on links is interactive needs to have his TV remote taken away.)

If, for example, medical systems use a set of codes developed specifically to handle patient data, an individual practitioner should be able to fill out a form electronically as easily as dragging and dropping a patient record onto an application form. Tagging, which might identify elements such as name, address, allergies, and so on, would direct each piece of information to the correct slot in the form. With a standard set of tags across the medical profession, that form could be designed flexibly according to each organization's needs. Creating a system for handling metadata could take the Web a long way back towards Tim Berners-Lee's original vision of user control, lost when designers took over.

One of the first XML applications is the Platform for Privacy Preferences, which is intended to allow users greater control over what personal information sites may collect and how they may use it. There seems to be no reason why XML should not be used to create accessibility profiles, too.

One thing you can't hide on the Net is your level of literacy and command of language. The adoption of Unicode[18] ends the limitations imposed by the ASCII[19] character set, especially that of trying to represent non-English characters on screen Non-English-speaking people can finally post online without looking illiterate in their own language.

Oddly, it seems to come as a surprise to Americans that a substantial portion of the rest of the world fears that the increasing pervasiveness of the Net, perceived as largely American, might spell doom to local languages and cultures—a different kind of limitation on equality of access. Europe's economic unification during the 1990s in no way changes this: in 1994 the European Commission passed a directive requiring member states to protect minority languages.[20] It is obvious to Europeans that human culture is embedded in language, and that when a language dies it takes a whole culture with it. One of the great things about the Net is its ability to foster diversity by uniting widely scattered members of the same culture, however small a minority they may be. From that standpoint, it would have been more logical and more useful had the domain name system been designed to reflect native language rather than geographical location.

English is not as dominant as we believe it is, even though it's estimated that there are more English speakers in China than in the United States.[21] In many of the larger European countries—France, Italy, Spain—it's surprisingly rare to find business people, even younger business people, who speak any second language. When they do, it's often not English: Spanish speakers are more likely to learn French.

According to San Francisco–based market research company Global Reach, non-English-speakers accounted for 43 percent of all Internet users in 1999, and their numbers were expected to pass the 50 percent mark in 2000. After English, the most common languages on the Net are, in order, Japanese, Spanish, German, and, in a tie, French and Chinese.[22] With surveys indicating that the Internet is due to explode in China and Latin America,[23] expectations are that by 2003 more than half the Web's content will not be in English.

I remember asking someone circa 1994 what it would be like when other languages dominated Usenet, and his response was that English speakers would just ignore it, "like they do now." This will not be so easy on the Web, where clicking takes you along unexpected pathways. For monoglots, the Web may become an uncomfortable maze where more than half the doors are closed—an outcome that may at last convey to today's dominant group what it's like to be a minority. Machine translation and efforts like Google's multilingual searching will only help somewhat.

If whole sections of our society are being left out of the developing electronic world, this is quite rightly regarded as a policy issue by governments around the world. What's not clear is how a universal access policy like that applying to telephone service could be designed for the Internet, or what universal access would mean. Do we want Internet kiosks scattered everywhere like phone booths, subsidized with government or cross subsidies in areas where private companies refuse to go? Public points of access in all schools and libraries? Guaranteed access to the same information offline? Government-sponsored free access for people who can't afford connections? Even if we have these things, will Internet access mean anything if people can't take advantage of it because they lack the education and training to use it, or because the circumstances under which they use it limit what they do?

It seems to me that we need all of these things. More than that, we need the same things we've always needed: better resources for education, literacy programs, and libraries (who could add to their range of services assistance in finding information and resources online). Using the Internet won't automatically become simple for blind or illiterate people as soon as everything is voice-enabled. For one thing, as usability specialist Donald Norman has persuasively argued in his book *The Invisible Computer*, throwing voice at computer systems is not going to make them any easier to use than throwing graphics at them did.[24] For another, text is a greater leveler than any other format: it can be displayed on small, cheap machines, sent through the Net at a tiny cost compared to audio or video, and processed by specialized access devices.

The fact is that the Internet boom itself is economically favoring the advantaged. The inequity between rich and poor in the United States, as in other countries, increased in the final decade of the twentieth century, and it applies as much to high-tech jobs. In her Easter 2000 column, for example, Molly Ivins points out that seven out of ten jobs being created in Silicon Valley pay less than $10,000 a year.[25]

In *The Silicon Boys*, David Kaplan quotes Mike Moritz, the British venture capitalist who funded Yahoo! as a start-up, on this subject: "One of the dirty little secrets of the Valley is that all the job-creation we like to talk about is probably less than the Big Three automakers have laid off in the last decade. . . . Look at our companies. Maybe they've produced 100,000 jobs or 150,000. But what kind and for whom? Jobs that 250 million people in this country aren't qualified to apply for. Jobs for guys out of MIT and Stanford. Jobs that in many ways gut the older industries in the Midwest and on the East Coast."[26]

Access can't be divorced from the other topics examined in this book. Access is meaningless if all the content is locked away behind restrictive intellectual property regimes or requires expensive, proprietary technology to display it. On the other hand, these issues may become less relevant if the entire Internet is converted into a giant shopping mall.

11

Divide by Zero

> Suddenly somebody began to run. It may be that he had simply re-
> membered, all of a moment, an engagement to meet his wife, for
> which he was now frightfully late. . . . Somebody else began to
> run, perhaps a newsboy in high spirits. Another man, a portly gen-
> tleman of affairs, broke into a trot. Inside of ten minutes, every-
> body on High Street, from the Union Depot to the Courthouse
> was running. A loud mumble gradually crystallized into the dread
> word "dam." . . . Two thousand people were abruptly in full
> flight. . . . A visitor in an airplane, looking down on the straggling,
> agitated masses of people below, would have been hard put to it to
> divine a reason for the phenomenon.
> —James Thurber, "The Day the Dam Broke"

A lot of elements had to come together before Amazon.com
could set up its operation in Seattle and start selling books online, go
public, sign up 13.1 million customer accounts, hit $2.6 billion in an-
nual sales, reach a market capitalization (on January 4, 2000) of $27.9
billion (about half that of General Motors), and get founder Jim Bezos
named *Time*'s man of the year for 1999, all while losing $1 billion (by
March 31, 2000).[1] (By November 2000 its market cap had dropped to
$12.1 billion, in line with other dot-coms.) The technical underpin-
nings of the Internet had to be in place and solidly reliable; there had to
be a relatively simple way of displaying linked information; there had
to be a critical mass of potential customers; and there had to be tolera-
ble security available, including strong cryptography to ensure the safe
transmission of sensitive information such as credit card numbers and
personal details. Even more important, the infrastructure had to exist
for electronic (credit card) payments and, perhaps most vitally, as Malcolm Gladwell pointed out in the *New Yorker*, there had to be the in-

frastructure of roads, shipping companies, and warehousing techniques to enable all those remote orders to be fulfilled.[2] The stock market valuation required much less: a bubble market and some amplification from the media.

This is not to say that Amazon.com is not a great site. I love shopping there and am probably one of their most consistent customers. But it seems to me premature to talk about a business as a big success until it's actually proven some ability to make money.[3] Just being able to lose money at an ever-increasing clip is not in itself an indicator that a company is going to be one of the long-term giants of cyberspace. Just like the business folks say, the four great brands of the early years of ecommerce are AOL, Yahoo!, Amazon.com, and eBay. Maybe eTrade makes five. But even famous brands fail: as I write this Fruit of the Loom is filing for bankruptcy.

It's fashionable in ecommerce circles to talk about "first-mover" advantage. Yahoo! was the first directory service for the Web, eBay the first auction site, and Amazon.com the first (or close enough) online retailer. All three were founded by people who participated in the Net enough to understand it. The Yahoo! founders began making lists of favorite sites in the days when no one could find anything on the Web, and they quickly realized they were creating a tool that everyone needed. Amazon.com and eBay not only saw the commercial possibilities in the developing infrastructure of the Web, but also understood how to use databases and good search tools to create something online that actually functioned better than the existing physical-world alternatives. All three understood the workings of online community enough to harness it for their fledgling businesses.

These companies were not successful solely because they were first, but also because they were good at figuring out what the right next step was in a new and rapidly evolving medium, and because they started early enough that they didn't have much competition. Lack of competition bought them time in which to figure out what they should be doing, a luxury that does not exist for most of the companies entering the ecommerce market today. AOL's situation was slightly different. It was not the first online service, or even close to it, and it faced far greater competition in its early years. But it was the first to take advantage of Windows and figure out how to package the online world in a graphical interface acceptable to the mass market. It upended the command-line driven corporate online services CompuServe (owned at the time by H. and R. Block) and Prodigy (owned by Sears and IBM) in much the same way that Microsoft Word for Windows up-ended WordPerfect for DOS.

The growth of electronic commerce has been a boon primarily for the already affluent, both customers and retailers. Increasingly, we hear less about the "little guys"—the mom-and-pop shop in Singapore competing worldwide so beloved of Net pioneers' dreams—than about the large (or start-up turned large) companies dominating the Web. For every Tony Sleep whose one-man Web site of in-depth film scanner reviews[4] attracts a worldwide community of professional photographers there's a consultancy firm saying that the *average* ecommerce Web site costs $1 million and five months to build.[5] The killer, however, is the back-office stuff, which is no different online than it is in the physical world. If you're selling physical goods, you still need a packing warehouse full of objects and people to stuff them in boxes. Even if you're selling only computer files (audio, video, text, software), unless you're selling something so unusual or necessary that people will go to any lengths to get it, you have to be able to provide superb customer service, requiring money and staffing levels that many small businesses just don't have.[6] The media play their part too: the standard advice dished out by TV programs and mainstream news tells people to buy from "reputable" companies, that is, ones they've heard of, presumably through advertising, word of mouth, and media coverage.

The problem with the "little guy wins" idea of the Internet was always that in an unfamiliar environment filled with strangers, the familiar names have a huge advantage. Early successes like Amazon.com and CDNow only seem to contradict that rule. Amazon.com itself was not familiar when it started, but the goods it carried were solid and familiar from a thousand bookshop or music store visits. More, by offering superior search functions and fast access to a wider range of inventory than a physical-world store, those online businesses captured sales from people who knew what titles they wanted but not where to find them quickly. As soon as you move into more complex and less predictable items such as clothing, shoes, insurance policies, or consumer electronics, the big brand names are even more important, as they give customers the security and familiarity lacking in the retailer itself. A Sony Discman is a Sony Discman, whether you buy it from some Minnesota-based outfit you've never heard of found by searching on MySimon or from a physical-world chain retailer. All you need is a credit card company that insures the goods' arrival.

Branding was 1999's cyberspace buzzword, just as 1998's was community, 1997's was Java, and 1996's was portals (I'm oversimplifying here, but not by that much). In 1999, AOL spent an estimated $807 million (16.9 percent of revenues) on marketing its brand name; Yahoo! spent $206 million (35.9 percent of revenues), and Amazon.com $402 million (25.9 percent).[7] By then, brand pressure was such that new start-ups were spending heavily on TV and newspaper advertising at the expense of building good sites and good back ends. According to *The Economist*, in December 1999 as little as 5 to 20 percent of ecommerce start-ups' funding was going on merchandising, logistics, and fulfillment, and Swedish sports-fashion retailer Boo.com spent $100 million on public relations before finishing debugging its Web site. (This may help to explain why Boo went spectacularly bust in late 2000).[8] Meanwhile, sites like Pets.com were stumping up $2 million in cash up front for their thirty-second Super Bowl spots[9] so old media could be sure of getting their money. For the 2000 Super Bowl, "dot-com" companies accounted for 30 percent of ad revenues.[10]

Given the difficulties of providing good customer service and order fulfillment,[11] it's not surprising to learn that there are companies that specialize in handling all the horrid back office stuff on a contract basis. Even so, as *The Economist* pointed out, problems persist.[12]

Let's assume that all these logistical problems get solved. After all, only a couple of years ago the Web was widely dismissed as slow and filled with useless garbage. There's still a problem here, in that almost no one is making any money other than via the stock market. In that sense, nothing's changed since 1995, when the class of people trying to figure out how to make money out of the Net was primarily content providers, from Time-Warner, News International, and Disney to scores of local newspapers and Internet start-ups.

"The Internet is the single most important development in communications in this century. It not only combines radio, television, and telephone but dwarfs them and has begun the process of making them obsolete. The Internet is changing our lives, and we can look forward to it [*sic*]," Michael Wolff quotes himself as saying at an early 1995 Internet conference in his book *Burn Rate*. "Why did I say this other than the fact that I could get away with saying it? Not that it wasn't possibly true. But it was true like astrology."[13]

Wolff, founder of NetGuide, a failed early attempt at creating a *TV Guide* for the Net, goes on to say, "The people at *Time* especially—and Judson [Bruce Judson, general manager of Time Media] particularly—knew the economics of businesses that sold advertising. And they knew that for the foreseeable future, if ever, advertising as the sole source of revenue could not support online content. Simple."[14] In 1995, Wolff noted, *Time* had a burn rate of $20 million on Pathfinder, a content aggregator for a number of well-known publications, with projected revenues of only $4 million. Time-Warner finally gave up throwing money at Pathfinder in May 1999, just as it had dumped its Netly News online news service a year before.

Even so, the advertising dream dies hard. "Internet eCommerce sites that lose money hand-over-mouse in their core business offerings are quick to reassure Wall Street: 'But we make it up in banner ad sales!'"[15] advises Andersen Consulting's Web site, going on to recommend that ecommerce sites focus first on pleasing users—who will then be willing to pay for the value they receive and, in turn, become more valuable to potential advertisers.

Things haven't, therefore, changed all that much since 1995, of which time Wolff wrote, "Because no enterprise has found the formula to create a profitable business, this failure, oddly, inspires a host of others to try. The thinking (my own included) goes something like, Hell, if that's success, you can't fail." If Amazon.com is deemed a massive success with no profits, and a company like FreeServe, a free ISP subsidiary of the British mainstream retailer Dixons, can float successfully after only ten months in business, during which time the company operated at a loss on a business model that will be extinct by 2002, well, let's go, the mid-2000 drop in stock prices notwithstanding.

To me, one of the most significant figures mentioned in Amazon.com's earnings statement for the third quarter of 1999 was that 72 percent of its sales were to repeat customers, up from 70 percent the previous quarter. The company had piled on customer accounts; the 13.1 million cumulative accounts were 2.9 times the number of the year earlier.[16] On the other hand, sales were "only" 2.3 times as much—$356 million, up from $154 million. Amazon.com can justifiably claim that it's hanging onto its existing customers (note that "cumulative" probably means they've probably never deleted anyone since they opened in 1995), but average sales per customer went down over that year, from $34 to $27.17.

While it would take a more thorough survey of online retailers to see if this pattern is repeated across the board, these are not numbers that seem to me to bode well for the leading online retailer of 1999. They suggest there may be limits to electronic commerce.

The mail-order business, which went through massive growth at first and then leveled off at about 10 percent of the retail market, has stayed level for decades. Online shopping suits people who know a lot about what they're buying and cannot stand dealing with human customer service personnel. The limit for these people is not, as Esther Dyson has said, attention,[17] but *patience*. Compared to mail-order catalogues, ecommerce comes out about even: the pictures and browsability of catalogues are better, while the searching functions are better on the Web. The interactive features on the Web give virtual "trying-on" possibilities unavailable in a printed catalogue, but the catalogue can be carried around, marked up, and retained for reference. In late 1999, Land's End reported that about 10 percent of its sales were coming in via the Web.[18]

In a *New Yorker* article about the way ecommerce was changing its business, Land's End explained that the Web has not lessened the need for customer service, but it's changed the level and type of service being requested. Instead of asking if an item is available (as that's built into the Web site's ordering facilities), customers ask live service staff for advice about designs and styles.[19]

In addition, while the U.S. moratorium on taxation of Internet transactions is very nice for technology companies and those who like to shop online, it's not fair and can't last. Since Net-based commerce is largely the province of the relatively affluent, the tax moratorium favors the already advantaged, a trade-off that presumably we hope will pay off in increased jobs and an extra boost to the economy. It does, however, give the United States a chance to dominate ecommerce. The European Union's system of value-added taxation has not (yet) been harmonized, and the administrative burden it places on smaller businesses is horrendous. Recognizing this uneven playing field, the EU wants to require U.S. businesses to pay VAT.

I am in no way suggesting that Web-based commerce is a fad, the way it was fashionable in the slew of anti-Net books that were released in 1995 to say that the Internet would go the way of the hula-hoop. CB radio, the craze of the 1970s, continues to be useful as a tool to professional long-distance drivers who either don't have cellphones or can't get them to work in the long, empty distances in the midwestern United

States. People who a few years ago would have demanded to see and touch everything they bought are taking to the Web to buy the strangest things: cars, cellphones, gourmet foods, stocks and bonds. But not everyone, and not all the time.

The people Web shopping suits tend to be educated, comfortable with technology, and more patient with waiting for goods to arrive than they are with the people serving them in stores or on customer service lines. People for whom shopping is entertaining—and, mysteriously, there seem to be a lot of these—or who insist on seeing and feeling the goods they buy are not going to take to it. Products that are heavy and/or repetitively purchased (like bags of flour or printer refills) are obvious candidates.

I am exactly this kind of impatient person: I live in one of the world's best-supplied cities, but I loathe shopping, and physical-world stores have reinforced that by becoming increasingly uncomfortable: loud music, limited merchandise, store clerks who either don't look at you or can't hear you to answer questions, crowding. I buy everything from Christmas presents to groceries online and walk around the corner to a local shop to get perishables such as fresh vegetables, milk, and newspapers in between. Where I used to find books or new music serendipitously by browsing in bookstores, I now collect recommendations from online discussions and from friends.

The issue is what benefits consumers perceive from shopping online. With cars, the history of lying salesmen is so long and the expense so great that if a system offers—as the Web does—a way of both avoiding an untrustworthy middleman and getting a substantial discount, it's going to succeed. Buying a cellphone involves wading through hectares of fine print to understand the intricacies of the airtime contracts. Even though most people would like to see the screen clarity and feel the weight of the actual phone before buying, the benefit of having time to read all that stuff in peace may be worth it.

The phenomenon that took many people by surprise in 1999 was the rampant growth of online stock trading. The same people who wouldn't deposit a cent in a First Virtual account[20] or buy electronic cash were apparently perfectly happy to deposit $10,000 with newly established online brokers. In retrospect, stock trading online is ideal. The major currency of the financial industry is information—the more immediate, the more valuable—and securities, bonds, or policies, whose physical representations are pieces of paper. The heaviest thing anyone needs to send is a prospectus—and those can be made readily available online.

What the U.C. Davis study mentioned in chapter 2 didn't—maybe couldn't—address is how different trading online feels compared to going through a broker. There's a sense of secret sin about online trading that isn't there when you have to explain your choices to another human being before they're enacted. If you fail, no one has to know. More, the direct control gives you the sense of how the financial markets must feel to those involved in them. Because constantly changing stock prices and buy/sell spreads are so readily accessible, in the days or moments before you make a trade, the cash in your brokerage account seems a lump of dead numbers, and buying shares feels like setting it free to breathe. It's only natural, therefore, that even an experienced investor's performance might differ after moving to online trading. That will change over time as the new environment becomes more familiar.

Gavin Starks, who raised enough cash to start up an Internet multimedia company by trading online from the United Kingdom, says, "Clicking around stuff on the Net is what you do and, then to be plus or minus $10,000 is a completely different use and quite surreal. Over the last year I've probably quadrupled the amount I actually put in, and seeing the number on the screen is quite surreal because it doesn't relate to anything in the tangible world."

The flap over the Red Hat IPO shares showed just how little any of this is really democratizing finance. As C. Scott Ananian, one of the lucky Linux hackers who got shares, wrote in *Salon*, "We had no power in this world; no one cared to listen to what we had to say."[21] (Practically speaking, they shouldn't have worried so much. Another 1999 study showed that most high-flying IPO stocks sell below their first-day close within the following few weeks.[22] In fact, despite a huge price rise after the guilty verdict in the Microsoft anti-trust case, a year later Red Hat was selling at roughly a third of its first-day closing price.)

Even experienced brokers say they think that individual investors now have more impact on the market than they did, making prices less clearly predictable. More immediately, Starks says on his occasional forays into day-trading, you can see the United States wake up and come online, then a visible lull over lunchtime and a second peak mid-afternoon. The planned move to extended-hours trading and then, inevitably, electronic trading 24/7 will tip the balance for short-term (longer than a trading session, shorter than a year) trading back toward institutional investors, who have the staff to monitor the markets in continual shifts. An individual investor could not hold something volatile overnight that might crash while he was asleep.

The first business model for the Net was ad-supported content, supported by a mix of community areas to keep customers coming back and shopping (the Web magazine *Salon* sells branded coffee and hats, and even "I kiss you!!!!!!!!!" Mahir Cagri, the Turk whose amateurish Web site launched a craze, has a line of T-shirts). The second was sales of physical objects. The next will almost certainly be digitized versions of audio, video, and other data. Egghead Software, formerly a chain of physical-world stores, converted itself into an online-only store in 1998, and many software companies sell direct to consumers over the Net. But the distribution of audio and video has been held back by the ferocious protectionism of the recording and film industries.

At any given time, there are huge numbers of talented musicians who can't get a recording contract but can, given the chance, attract a devoted coterie of fans. For them, MP3 provides a way to make their music available directly to fans all over the world. For recording companies, MP3 and its successors, most notably the music-sharing service Napster, could completely rewrite the way the music industry does business. Sites like MusicMaker and MP3.com bet millions on digital distribution as the future of the music biz before launching IPOs. The former lets you make custom CDs; the latter indexes music from a large collection of independent artists.

Another Net trend could also prove instrumental in turning the music industry upside down: home radio stations. These are going to be more and more possible as people get flat-rate, permanent, high-bandwidth Internet connections over ADSL and ISDN and mobile phones that can play Net audio. The ImagineRadio Web site, for example, lets you design your own custom-made radio station. You pick the general type of music you like and fine-tune the selection the site plays by removing songs and artists you don't like. How does a site like that fit into the current scheme, whereby music industry publishing organizations ASCAP and BMI distribute fees to artists and songwriters based on calculations made from a selection of stations' standard playlists?

The fact is that the new digital world could be very good for artists and consumers, eliminating a number of middlemen and marketers and allowing direct contact with fans. It may even restore to artists some of the power they've typically had to sign away to get distribution. Recording companies, with their superior ability to afford high-quality recording and production and finance tours, also have a chance to find new ways to exploit the new medium, selling anything from handsomely boxed personalized love songs for Valentine's Day to customized greatest hits compilations (why should you take *their* choices?). The people whose livings are most at risk in this new world will be songwriters, who rely on royalties from recordings of their work.

Despite music industry claims to the contrary, digital distribution is much cheaper[23] and more flexible. Why, for example, shouldn't the industry be collaborating with Net-based radio stations so you can click a button to buy a copy of the song that's playing? Instead, dickering over the Secure Digital Music Initiative means that it will be at least 2001 before consumers see industry-distributed digital music. Most of 2000 was wasted in lawsuits; at the end of the year, Bertelsmann finally saw some sense and decided to collaborate with Napster.

At the same time, some companies are beginning to get the idea that they can manipulate the Net. There were, for example, accusations that the apparent grassroots support for the unexpected hit movie *The Blair Witch Project* was manufactured.[24] *Wired News* reported that the "fan" sites supporting Divx[25] seemed a little too slick and polished to be true fan sites. What's fascinating about this is that throughout the history of the Net we have been fed warning after warning of the dire consequences of hacking and fraud. The presumption has always been that the big danger was that rip-off artists might pass themselves off as famous names or that hackers would falsify a company's information. But here we have a case in which a corporation might be passing itself off as a group of disinterested fans. This is the logical continuation of the trend started by corporate PR agencies and lobbyists, who learned the value of creating what appears to be a grassroots campaigning organization, but which in fact merely represents corporate interests.[26] Creating a Web site is easy by comparison.

What I object to about all this is that it crosses the line from advertising to tampering with reality, like the story of the book publicist who hired two actors to sit on the London tube all day and talk about the book they were supposedly reading, just loud enough so the nearby passengers could hear them and get curious. We are, of course, all in the habit of assessing any given speaker's biases in determining how much weight we should give to what he says, and certainly the Net is no different in that respect. ("Oh, that guy's always a bozo, forget about it.") Even so, if I want my reality tampered with, I'd rather do it myself.

A lot has to change for ecommerce to fit the established norms of physical-world trading. For buying, say, a new VCR, today's ecommerce sites are inadequate, because models change frequently and sites generally make available only the sketchiest list of features and specifications. What I want is to be able to read the user manual online, as I do in stores, to see whether there are hidden annoyances and how the remote control is laid out. Similarly, in my experience online grocery shopping is severely limited by the lack of availability of the information that's printed on can labels and the size/price calculations commonly posted on supermarket shelves. All this means that today's version of ecommerce is crude and unsatisfying and is failing to extend the consumer protection mechanisms we have carefully constructed into cyberspace. As long as ecommerce is regarded as experimental and there are plenty of physical-world alternatives, this may not matter as much; but the precedent it sets is poor.

Many of ecommerce's most difficult problems remained to be solved at the end of 1999. Within the banking community, for example, you could find complaints that the Secure Electronic Transactions (SET) system designed by MasterCard and Visa in 1996 was expensive to implement and support and would not scale to the mass volumes required.[27] Also, the ecommerce model that assumed that consumers and companies would risk dealing with strangers and leave the burden to fall on the credit card companies would work only as long as credit card companies were willing to carry that burden.

In a presentation at a London seminar on ecommerce for the Association for Biometrics, Bill Perry, the senior manager for the emerging products group at Barclay's Bank, laid out a plan for an alternative business model that he claimed would eliminate fraud. Instead of today's situation, where customers must pass their information to sites whose security they can never test or be sure about and vice versa, all transactions are controlled by the issuing bank, which authenticates both the seller's and buyer's halves of the transaction, thereby improving security for both parties. The advantage, according to Perry, would be that the seller and buyer no longer have to trust each other; instead, they trust their own authenticators, who in turn trust each other (because there are very few authenticators, where there are millions of buyers and sellers). In many ways, a situation like this makes more sense than going through a third-party authenticator like Verisign, which issues certificates but otherwise is not a company you have an ongoing relationship with. The bank's control over transactions has other consequences, however, as Perry noted casually: besides eliminating fraud, it builds in an infrastructure for taxation.

Perry's proposal is a perfect example of the kind of far-reaching social and economic decision that Harvard lawyer Lawrence Lessig argues in his 1999 book *Code and Other Laws of Cyberspace* can be embedded in code apparently designed for a completely different purpose.[28] You can certainly argue that the ability to tax Internet transactions is desirable, that without it entire nations will collapse because tax evasion will reach such levels that they will not be able to provide their citizens with necessary services. But such an argument should be made explicitly and debated publicly, not be hidden in a structure no one knows is being developed that banks and governments agree on without involving citizens.

No one expects anything different from Barclay's Bank: it is an old, profit-making institution that naturally seeks to extend its power, influence, and profits into new markets as they develop. What's much harder to watch is the way some of the bigger Net start-up businesses have lost sight of their own roots. As 1999 drew to a close, for example, Amazon.com found itself settling a case with the Minneapolis-based Amazon Bookstore Cooperative, which had been using the Amazon name since the 1970s and got sick of being confused with a branch of Amazon.com. The start-up eToys, now public, was embroiled in a fight for market share with both Amazon.com (which by then had added toys, consumer electronics, auctions, CDs, videos, and shopping search services to its original bookselling activities) and Toys "R" Us's online extension, but it still found time to sue the Zurich-based artists' media group eToy over its similar domain name. The fact that eToy had registered and marketed the name for two years before eToys went into business apparently didn't matter, either to eToys or to the first judge to hear the case, who issued a preliminary injunction removing eToy.com temporarily from the Net—and during the Christmas season, too.

Other stupid cases abounded. Amazon.com (again) sued Barnes and Noble, claiming that the latter's "Express Lane" checkout violated a patent held by Amazon.com on its "One-Click" facility. The case was promptly settled. The movie industry sued seventy-two hackers and related sites (including Slashdot.org) for violating the law by cracking DVD's regional coding—or even just linking to the explanation of how to do it. The Recording Industry Association of America sued then small start-up Napster, still beta-testing its site, over alleged copyright violations: the site was designed to allow members to exchange copies of their MP3 collections.[29]

What's especially frustrating about this is that the old Net culture could help these companies. If, for example, retailers weren't so anxious to lock customers into their sites, they could link to manufacturers' own databases of product information, which would only have to be created once. Similarly, manufacturers that are not doing their own online sales could take a cue from aggregator search sites like MySimon and allow you to search among both physical and online retailers according to a variety of user-defined parameters—these might include price, but they also might include nearby suppliers with the item in stock, or delivery speed. However, as my friend Geoff Ryman, science fiction author and head of the new media department for Britain's Central Office of Information, said in 1998, "They will raze the old Net culture if it's good for business."

Lessig argues persuasively that this is already happening. He reminds us that cyberspace's open design is not a law of nature but the result of a lengthy series of human decisions whose effects can be undone if we make certain types of changes to the code, both legal and technical, that supports them. Lessig contends that we are in the process of allowing those types of changes to be made. Despite every belief of the old Net, Lessig argues that the Net certainly could be turned into the kind of regulable top-down medium early Netheads claimed it could never become. While some of the older technology that formed the early Net—such as Usenet, whose extensive numbers of news articles can be copied from machine to machine without traversing the Internet—can certainly provide a way around a heavily controlled Internet, the Web is much more controllable because it requires real-time connections between live machines.

The saying goes that during the Gold Rush, the people who made money were not the miners, but the people who sold them picks and shovels. Today's stock market analysts, therefore, by analogy figure that you should buy into the companies that sell the Internet equivalent: routers (Cisco), workstations and Java (Sun), back-end services (IBM, Akamai, and any number of start-ups), wireless (Nokia, Qualcomm, Ericsson), and telecommunications companies (MCI Worldcom, AT&T, the Baby Bells). Those companies have made money, true. But the picks and shovels equivalent of the Internet era is not any of these things: it's money. The people who are really making money are the venture capitalists and the Wall Street crowd who are taking these fragile companies public. And they're doing it largely at the expense of the investing public. John Doerr has famously called Silicon Valley's newfound riches "the largest legal creation of wealth in history." It would be more accurate to call it redistribution.

Not that this crazed market will last. There have been stock market bubbles before, as Edward Chancellor recounts in detail in his *Devil Take the Hindmost: a History of Financial Speculation*:

> "Stock prices have reached what looks like a permanently high plateau," declared the eminent Yale economist Irving Fisher in the Autumn of 1929. . . . Why did Professor Fisher get things so wrong? The answer is that he had fallen for the decade's most alluring idea, a thesis which underpinned the great bull market of the late 1920s: He believed that America had entered a *new* era of limitless prosperity.[30]

As Benjamin Graham, the Wall Street giant who defined value investing, asked in his last (1977) update to *The Intelligent Investor*, referring to a different stock and a different era, "Has anyone in Wall Street any responsibility at all for the regular recurrence of completely brainless, shockingly widespread and inevitable speculation in this kind of vehicle?"

12

The Haunted Goldfish Bowl

> The makers of our Constitution undertook to secure conditions favorable to the pursuit of happiness. They recognized the significance of man's spiritual nature, of his feelings and of his intellect. They knew that only a part of the pain, pleasure, and satisfaction of life are to be found in material things. They sought to protect Americans in their beliefs, their thoughts, their emotions and their sensations. They conferred, as against the government, the right to be let alone—the most comprehensive of rights and the right most valued by civilized men.
>
> —Supreme Court Justice Louis D. Brandeis,
> "The Right to Privacy"

In the end, all roads lead to privacy. Or rather, all of these debates lead to debates about privacy: how much people should have, who should enforce the limits beyond which outsiders may not intrude, whom we most need to be protected from. Deciding what we may read, whom we may interact with and how, and what access we will have to the many present and future databases all lead to tradeoffs regarding our individual and collective privacy. Any attempt to control information, whether it's to keep illegal or harmful material away from the wrong people or to enforce intellectual property rights, perforce requires some kind of policing mechanism. In the case of intellectual property rights, policing means restricting access to those who are authorized, making it necessary to track who those people are and what they access for billing purposes. Policing censorship regimes means investigating what individuals read and/or access. For this reason, a team planning an Anonymous Server, a system to give citizens of countries with institutionalized censorship access to banned material, talked at the 1999 Computers, Freedom, and Privacy (CFP99) conference about the facilities they'd need to include to ensure that no one could trace specific Web page requests to any particular user.

The proliferation first of computers and then of the Internet seemed to bring new forms of privacy invasion almost every day. Databases, junk mail, and easily searchable electronic records are commonplace by now. But most steps you take on the Internet create a trail of Reese's Pieces that lead back to you, and which a determined investigator can follow.

The first line of defense is encryption, which provides two vital functions. First, it protects the privacy of data by scrambling it so it can't be read by anyone who happens to intercept it, and second, it authenticates the data so that its integrity and source are assured. On the Net, encryption has many applications, from protecting your credit card information in transit to an ecommerce site to enabling certificates built into your Web browser that help prevent fraud by giving you the means to check that the site you're dealing with is legitimately the one it appears to be.[1] Encryption is also the technology that makes possible digital signatures. Slowly gathering legal recognition across the United States and Europe, a framework for giving digital signatures the same legal weight as handwritten ones is necessary as business turns electronic and needs a way of creating a binding contract.[2]

The battle over deregulating strong cryptography isn't over, but the uneasy alliance of businesses and privacy activists on this issue seems to be having an effect. Throughout the 1990s, the U.S. government led the push to keep cryptography restricted, first through export controls under the International Traffic in Arms Regulations and then through attempts to require key escrow.[3] Both efforts were generally loathed by the technical community, who fought back first by being clever technically (as when Colorado consultant Phil Zimmermann wrote the free cryptography software PGP and AT&T researcher Matt Blaze cracked the Clipper chip) and second through the courts (as in the cases brought by mathematics student, now professor, Daniel Bernstein and security specialist Philip Karn). But cryptography regulations are loathed by the business community, too. The software industry hates the expense and complexity of maintaining domestic and export versions of products, while no business (particularly non-U.S. companies) wants to hand copies of its private keys over to the U.S., or probably any other, government.

The late 1990s saw the American cryptography battle replayed in

Britain, where Department of Trade and Industry (DTI) proposals for an electronic commerce bill (eventually renamed the Electronic Communications Act) started out by falling more or less into lock-step with the United States. The first proposals, released in 1997, required any business selling cryptographic services to the U.K. public to get a license as a Trusted Third Party. Claiming that licensing was necessary to build the public trust, the proposals required the implementation of key escrow as a condition of getting such a license, on the grounds that widespread use of strong cryptography without retaining copies of keys posed too great a problem for law enforcement. As the proposals were updated and released, a series of public meetings called "Scrambling for Safety" were held to explain and debate the proposals. The first of these was organized by Simon Davies, the head of Privacy International. Later meetings were organized by the new think-tank the Foundation for Information Privacy Research (FIPR), created to consider the policy implications of new technologies.[4] FIPR commissioned a human rights audit of the third and last set of draft proposals, as well as the legislation actually introduced into Parliament. The audit showed that the design of the proposals, which created a situation in which someone who had been sent unsolicited email containing an encrypted file could be jailed for not being able to produce the key to descramble it, violated the European directive on human rights by upending the presumption of innocence. A more rebelliously activist outfit, Stand,[5] proved the point by sending Home Secretary Jack Straw just such a file.

By the final version of the bill, licensing was voluntary, the law enforcement provisions had been moved to a separate bill still to be announced (as everyone had been asking the DTI to do for two years), and key escrow was prohibited in one clause and allowed in the next (perhaps reflecting the government's general desire to please both business and law enforcement). Amusingly, one of the later proposals contained the note that until recently only a few civil libertarians opposed key escrow—it was clear that the wave of protest took the government by surprise. As late as 1997, DTI officials involved in drafting the proposals imagined that cryptography was an esoteric technology no one cared about.

Internationally, however, the United States and Britain were not typical, even though the United States claimed in late 1998 that it had achieved an international consensus requiring the regulation of strong cryptography under the Wassenaar Arrangement.[6] Within a few months of that announcement, it became clear that other countries felt themselves free to interpret the agreement in their own way, and that few wanted the tight regulatory regime the United States did, seeing in unfettered electronic commerce an economic opportunity for themselves.

A more interesting legislative approach was taken by Australia and the Isle of Man, both of which opted for very simple legislation that recognized electronic transactions and signatures without touching the morass of other possible complications. (It was generally held that the British licensing approach was going to be expensive, slow, and complicated to implement, with few benefits for electronic commerce, even though the government's claim was that it wanted to make Britain the most hospitable place for ecommerce by 2002.) Even Canada has many fewer regulations than the United States, to the point where the start-up Zero Knowledge was able to set up, legally, a service to sell cryptographic products that guaranteed online anonymity and protected profiles online.

Zero Knowledge's service was based in part on the idea that most people have multiple roles or identities in real life—the tennis club you belong to, for example, knows nothing about your banking transactions, your bank knows little or nothing about who your friends are, and your telephone company has no idea what foods you like to buy at the supermarket. The company's idea, therefore, was that there was no reason why encryption software couldn't create a similar situation online, so that you have different, unlinked identities in different online situations, such as online communities, shopping sites, and so on. None of these identities need necessarily be linked to your real-world identity.

Although the idea revived all the old debates about the value and/or toxicity of anonymity, it is an important one. As more and more of our transactions move online, there are many more risks to our personal privacy than simply the possibility that some hacker will steal credit card details en route to a shopping site. For one thing, growing databases of personal information are retained by these sites, not just the information we enter on registration forms, but shopping and browsing patterns, shipping addresses of friends and relatives, wish lists, and, most of all, the large amounts of information we divulge about our tastes, feelings, and experiences in online communities attached to those sites.

You may not think you're revealing much about yourself or the people you know in such places, but research carried out by Latanya Sweeney, an assistant professor at Carnegie-Mellon University, examined the identifiability of details contained in a couple of Usenet postings exchanged between two women. From the information in those postings, she sent out two email messages containing a few odds and ends of description of an unnamed guy one of them had met in Harvard Square. Five people eventually replied, all supplying the same, correct name.

Any scheme that prevents a site from knowing too much about you acts as an antidote to some of the more common types of security problems, such as design flaws in or poor implementation of the site's security systems. The hacking of the regional coding for DVD, for example, shows that encryption by itself is not impenetrable. As cryptographer Bruce Schneier observed afterwards in a posting to the RISKS Forum,[7] for a movie to be watchable on a screen it has to be decrypted by the device that's displaying it. The upshot is that all the necessary information is there to be hacked—a built-in security flaw that can't be changed by legislation such as the Digital Millennium Copyright Act.[8] Similarly, a Web site that is managed badly may display one customer's data to the next arrival, use inadequate protection such as easily guessable information, or silently collect data customers don't know about. All three of these scenarios have happened in the last few years.

The first version of the Social Security Administration's site, for example, set up in early 1998, authenticated people checking their Social Security records by requesting only their social security number and their mother's maiden name. As security specialist Simson Garfinkel pointed out, for company CEOs this information is public record. Some states even use social security numbers as the identifying numbers on drivers' licenses.

Silent data collection had been brewing as an issue for some time—the earliest uses of cookies, small files of gibberish that reside on your computer and track your visits to specific Web sites, and targeted ads based on browsing data raised this sort of fear—but it was brought to the forefront when a few Net users discovered that Deja News, a search and archiving service for Usenet, was tracking the email addresses users clicked on—for no apparent reason other than that could.[9] In a weirder case, free software made by Comet Systems that replaces the cursors in Web browsers with cartoon characters or other images when the users are browsing participating sites was assigning each user a global user ID (GUID), though the company said it was not connected to individuals' physical-world identities. After a spate of bad publicity over the issue, Comet said it would delete the serial numbers. Nonetheless, the company went on counting visits to sites, as the animated cursor is intended to enable more efficient advertising.[10] Only a few weeks earlier, Real Networks had come under the same kind of fire for collecting data via its RealJukebox software, again using a GUID. This, too, has been disabled.[11] Finally, a GUID secretly embedded in Microsoft Word files helped law enforcement trace the author of the Melissa virus.

The Comet Systems case offers a perfect example of what we're facing: no one would have thought that an animated cursor would provide the excuse for invading privacy, and the company didn't seem to feel it was necessary to explain its identifier scheme up front. You could say it's a fair trade for getting the cursor software for free, but if that's the case it needs to be made explicit when you download the software.

These worries can get exaggerated. Cookies, the little files of gibberish sites store on your hard drive to keep their place in your browsing sessions, for example, still spook people. Yet, they are necessary if you want to be able to store an item in a site's shopping cart long enough to put together an order and see it through to a purchase, because the connection you make to a Web server does not persist between page requests.

Under the European Union's privacy directive, collecting data without the user's consent and then handing it on to third parties—which was apparently not Comet Systems' plan—is certainly illegal. Not only does the United States not have such legislation, but resistance to it seems entrenched at the top. One of presidential aide Ira Magaziner's last acts before leaving the White House was to hand over to the Clinton administration a report on cyberspace issues that recommends greater consumer protection and privacy rights, but advises leaving these to industry self-regulation rather than government intervention. The report follows a series of similar recommendations, such as a two-year moratorium on Internet taxation and other policies designed to keep the Internet free of regulation while it grows and continues to develop. The U.S. government seems to be in a minority in thinking that privacy is best left to industry self-regulation. It's out of step both with other countries and with the American public, who in polls cite privacy concerns as a serious deterrent to the growth of electronic commerce. Things may be changing a little: when the defunct dot-com retailer Toysmart tried to sell its customer data as an asset in its bankruptcy proceedings, the FTC moved to block the sale.

We'd be free to sit around and debate this in our own time while our privacy eroded if it weren't for the fact that in October 1998 the European privacy directive came into force. This legally binding document requires all European member states to pass legislation meeting the minimum standards it establishes. The kicker in the directive and its supporting legislation as far as the United States is concerned is that, besides giving European consumers much greater privacy rights, it prohibits member states from transferring data to countries that do not have equivalent protection. Privacy activists have been warning the U.S. government for some time that without a change in its policy American companies may find themselves prohibited from transferring personal data for processing, either to business partners or to their own overseas subsidiaries. Nonetheless, the Clinton administration still clung to the idea that market pressures will force the industry to regulate itself.

A white paper by the Online Privacy Alliance, an association boasting members such as AOL, Bank of America, Bell Atlantic, IBM, EDS, Equifax, and the Direct Marketing Association, outlines how those in the industry think self-regulation can work. The paper argues for a "layered approach" of publicly announced corporate policies and industry codes of conduct, backed by the enforcement authority of the Federal Trade Commission (FTC) and state and local agencies, coupled with specific sector-by-sector laws to protect the privacy of specific types of information. This approach, the Alliance argues, will offer the same level of protection as the European directive and will provide a "safe harbor" for companies that follow the guidelines. Bear in mind that few of these companies are organizations privacy advocates love to trust. EDS is the contract holder for many government databases worldwide. Equifax is one of the two main credit agencies in both Britain and the United States, where it holds comprehensive data on tens of millions of households; the Direct Marketing Association brings you all that junk mail; and AOL keeps getting hauled into court for violating its members' privacy.[12]

As the Online Privacy Alliance's paper points out, the United States already has many privacy laws, starting with the Fourth Amendment and leading up to the 1998 Child Online Privacy Protection Act, which directs the FTC to promulgate regulations to control the collection, use, and disclosure of personal information obtained by commercial sites from anyone under the age of thirteen. No such law is proposed for adult online users, who arguably have as much or more to lose, though several schemes—including TRUSTe and BBBOnLine—try to give the Web some consistent privacy standards, and the W3 Consortium's proposed Platform for Privacy Preferences is intended to allow users to create a standard profile for their browser that will give them control over what information is sent out. The paper's unsurprising conclusion is that the United States doesn't need privacy regulation.

Simon Davies, director of Privacy International and a visiting fellow at the London School of Economics, disagrees. "When the U.S. government approaches this issue, they approach it as if it were a domestic affair," he says. "Safe harbor is condemned by everybody because it lacks all the primary requirements for effective protection."

Under the self-regulatory model, customers have to do all the legwork. They have to do the complaining and the investigating, and they have to muster the proof that their privacy has been invaded. Any arbitrator is hampered in such a regime, because companies are notoriously reluctant to give third parties access to internal records that may be commercially sensitive. Meanwhile, says Davies, companies are "pathologically unable to punish themselves," so a customer seeking redress is unlikely to find any without that third, external party. A lack of effective regulation means that even if companies successfully regulate themselves there are no curbs on *government* invasions of privacy. For many, government intrusion is the greater concern, especially because of projects under consideration, such as putting all medical data online, switching to electronic delivery for benefits payments, and the withdrawn "Know Your Customer" program that would have required banks to notify government officials if customers displayed a change in their banking habits.

The United States may be in for a shock if Europe, flexing its newly unified muscles in a globally networked world, refuses to budge and companies find themselves unable to trade because of data flows. Davies, for one, thinks this is an all too likely scenario. "They still think that because they're American they can cut a deal, even though they've been told by every privacy commissioner in Europe that safe harbor is inadequate," he says with exasperated amusement. "They fail to understand that what has happened in Europe is a legal, constitutional thing, and they can no more cut a deal with the Europeans than the Europeans can cut a deal with your First Amendment."[13]

Of course, it's not just weird, new, unexpected abuses that are illegal under European law; it's even common practices in American business. For example, European law bans companies from collecting data for one purpose and then using it for another without the individual's consent—opt-in, instead of opt-out. The opposite is true in the United States, where you know that every time you subscribe to a magazine you're going on a dozen more mailing lists. If one possible cause of a trade war in the early twenty-first century is intellectual property rights, the other is privacy.

Privacy advocates tend to argue that we sell our privacy very cheaply, trading it away for minor conveniences. You give up a piece of your privacy every time you pay for something with a credit card instead of with anonymous cash. The same goes for using loyalty cards and frequent flyer programs, or making telephone calls from your mobile phone instead of using a phone booth. Or, as an extreme example few think about, we trade our privacy for access to professional skills, such as when we have photographs developed professionally instead of owning our own darkroom.

Many of these giveaways are justified in the name of preventing fraud. We give our credit card billing addresses so the clerk accepting the card can ensure that we are genuinely the cardholder. We sign for packages so the delivery company can prove they delivered the package, these days using an electronic device that keeps our signatures permanently in easily copyable form. More pervasively, communities tolerate closed-circuit TV cameras in the belief that the cameras prevent— or at least assist in punishing—crime. In many parts of Europe now, these cameras are almost everywhere. They're posted by the sides of thoroughfares to catch speeders, in town centers to spot crime, and in private premises to detect trespassers. As these cameras become digital and the cost of storage goes down, it will be become possible to store the data they collect for longer and longer periods of time, making it possible to create a database of everyone's movements.

In New York, many people have adopted the EZ-Pass system, an electronic card that you attach to your window in a location where it can be read electronically by the tollbooths on any of New York's highways. A conspiracy theorist driving over the Henry Hudson Bridge would conclude that the city was pushing the system and that cash customers were deliberately limited to three backed-up lanes in order to create a dire comparison to the no-wait EZ-Pass lanes. From the privacy standpoint, however, the system poses a danger by creating a way of tracking people's movements in and around New York. Nonetheless, it's convenient not to have to stop every few miles on pay roads or worry about having enough cash.

How do we put a price on privacy? In at least some cases it should be fairly simple to come up with some rough figures. Say I buy $200 worth of groceries and get $10 off my next purchase because I racked up points on my loyalty card. Is it worth the $10 to avoid the junk mail and the "personalized" offers? Or say I spend half an hour setting up a $200 book order at Amazon.com. To buy the same books, I'd have to travel (one and a half hours round-trip) and probably visit three stores, fairly close together, spending an average of half an hour in each. Even if I manage to find all the books and they cost the same, that's two and a half hours. If you're self-employed, you can precisely value that time.

Most people do not make these specific calculations, though they could. An interesting experiment would be a Web site to calculate such differences given a dollar value on your time and some basic data on the effort it would cost you to buy the desired object in person with cash. It would make a great Java applet.

In his book *The Internet Edge*, Xerox PARC scientist Mark Stefik talks about the resistance to change that constitutes the "edge" of new technologies. One such resistance is the growing awareness of commonplace intrusions of privacy. It doesn't take many follow-up junk email messages about how "We've improved our site!" before consumers start lying routinely on Web site registration forms or setting up one-time free email addresses to get the registration password. Sometimes, the exchange of value for personal information is fair enough: when you want to buy a site's services or products, you have to give billing and shipping addresses to complete the transaction. Other times, it's way out of line, both in terms of the time and effort it takes to fill out the forms and in terms of the balance between benefits to the company versus benefits to the customer. No one should have to fill out an extensive, detailed form just to do a quick search to determine if any of a site's content is what they want. The physical-world equivalent would be stationing someone at store entrances demanding your business card before letting you in.

A fancier version of this is the tracking that advertising services like DoubleClick do so they can serve up ads to Web pages that reflect the interests of the person visiting a site. Again, people seem more irritated by the length of time it takes those banner ads to load than they do by the implicit loss of privacy in the form of the profiles the service is building up. The services insist that they do not sell identifiable data to the companies they supply with ads.

This was the other shocking piece of research Latanya Sweeney presented at CFP99. Sweeney has developed techniques for what she calls "triangulating data"—restoring identification to supposedly anonymous data, thereby disproving the common claim that reselling the data is all right because individuals won't be identifiable. In one example, data collected by a Massachusetts insurance commission, to assist in negotiating for health insurance policies on behalf of state employees and their families, had its explicit identifiers removed and was sold to researchers for pharmaceutical companies and a couple of universities. For $20, Sweeney bought two floppy disks containing the voter register for Cambridge, Massachusetts, and linked those to the supposedly anonymized medical information. The birth date alone was unique for 12 percent of the population. Birth date and gender uniquely identified 29 percent. With only four elements she was able to identify 97 percent of the data.

"People have misconceptions about what is identifiable data," she said. In addition, she noted, "Every time you look, data collected for one purpose is used for another." Sweeney concluded that the problem doesn't just involve rare cases like "the billionaire in Washington. There is incredible detail about each one of us."

This is one reason privacy advocates were right to be concerned when, for example, DoubleClick wanted to buy Abacus Direct Corp. and its purchasing data on 88 million households.[14] Information may want to be free, as Stewart Brand famously said (though he less famously went on to add that information also wants to be expensive), but data wants to merge. Worse, databases seem to infect something in human nature. As software engineer and essayist Ellen Ullman says in her book *Close to the Machine*, systems alter as they grow: the existence of a capability makes the system's owner want to exploit it. It is a *Labour* government in Britain that is pushing to keep and reuse electronically stored fingerprints and DNA samples and that wants to link its databases together to allow cross-checking between benefit claims and tax returns, and even to delve into individuals' bank account records. In the United States, it's a *Democratic* government that wants to do the same kinds of things.

Ullman calls this "the fever of the system." First the systems are benevolent (in her example, let's help the office manager we've had for twenty-six years do her work more efficiently), and then they infect their owners with an inexorable Orwellian logic (let's keep a record of her keystrokes and find out what she does all day). If the existence of computer databases tends to make their owners want to do things because they can, the safest answer is not to create those databases. It isn't enough to say, as one police spokesman did in explaining the police's desire for increased powers to collect and store fingerprints, "It's not a threat to civil liberties because it's to protect the public."

That phrase goes right up there with "raising public trust in ecommerce" as a sample of the justifications we are given for invasions of our privacy. We must be protected from crime, so we must have closed-circuit TV cameras everywhere. We must be able to have confidence in the businesses that want to sell us products over the Internet, so encryption should be kept in chains to prevent terrorism. Just as in the fuss over the online chemical databases in chapter 9, what's at work here is people's fear and poor assessment of risks. Crime seems real and specific, while the loss of privacy seems distant and diffuse. The terrorists, drug dealers, pedophiles, and organized crime unfailingly invoked as fearsome specters whose activities can be cloaked by the use of strong encryption seem more frightening and dangerous than the everyday menace of credit card theft. A perfect example of this kind of skewed thinking popped up during the worries about the Y2K computer bug: a man in the Philippines withdrew his life's savings from the bank, fearing the bank's systems would crash; about ten days later his house was robbed and all the money stolen. The fear of the new, high-tech risk blinded him to the bigger risk banks were created to protect against.[15]

Outside the United States, the answer to the creation of these many databases of consumer profiles is data protection legislation. For example, "That would be illegal in the UK," was the response of British data protection registrar Elizabeth France to the kind of data matching Sweeney discussed, since such cross-matching would constitute the kind of change of use specifically prohibited by law. Few would realize, though, that this type of re-identification would be possible, just as a lot of people are surprised to find that Amazon.com and Amazon.co.uk operate a single, shared database stored on U.S. servers. The credit card information and addresses you enter on the U.K. site pop up on the U.S. site when you enter your user name and password. (The British data protection registrar frowns on this, too.)

Things are only set to get worse with always-on wireless, something that's on the way, particularly in Europe, which is ahead of the rest of the world in this area. Americans often don't realize just how bad their cellphone service is compared to Europe's. By 1997 you could buy a mobile phone anywhere in Europe and have it work everywhere in Europe. Wireless is also growing fast in the developing world, where it typically costs less and takes less time to get a new mobile phone connection than a land line.

As Web-enabled cellphones roll out worldwide starting in 2000, there is a new threat. The Wireless Application Protocol (WAP) standard is specifically designed to allow operators to gather extensive detail of every transaction for billing purposes—what Web sites a user visits, what content is downloaded (both volume and time), and so on—since no one knows yet exactly what kinds of services will be chargeable.. While this sort of exhaustive detail is appealing to those who want to provide paid services via wireless, which according to some studies may make up half the world's Internet use by 2003,[16] it also ought to raise alarms for privacy advocates. As the Internet becomes the source of everything from reading matter to personal communications to theater tickets, data that was once widely dispersed will be brought together into individual logs. This goes beyond the logs currently kept by most ISPs, since these providers were not designed with the idea in mind that every "event" would be paid for. ISPs measure access by the hour, not by the transaction, and the logs are generally discarded within a day or two.

WAP, on the other hand, was designed at least in part by people who think that "the Internet is ultimately about ecommerce,"[17] comparing the Net to a shopping mall, which, although built for the purpose of retail trade, also plays host to a variety of human interactions. This is, of course, a very one-sided view: probably none of the Net's original founders thought of themselves as building a giant shopping mall, and at least some would have found it depressing if they had. Money may make the world go round, but turning everything on the Net into a billable service is the kind of danger people worried about in 1994 when

AOL opened its gateway to the Net. It may seem less unacceptable when wireless phone companies do it, because we're still accustomed to thinking of their services as exotic and expensive.

These plans may not work, of course: customers have generally been resistant to per-byte or per-transaction pricing (just as they hate copy-protection schemes), even though everyone in the business world wants it. Micropayments, the idea whose time keeps receding over the horizon, too, will create a detailed trail of everything we access. Depending on how micropayments are implemented, they will eventually have to link in some way to real-world payments. The early scheme DigiCash aimed to create anonymous digital cash so that those links couldn't be traced by others, but the company that pioneered the idea of using encryption to create electronic cash filed for bankruptcy in 1998, and most other such schemes do not seem to care about privacy in the same way. Current schemes are more like loyalty schemes, awarding points you can spend, than like anonymous cash. But the Net is young, and who knows what experiment is next?

Broadband connections such as ADSL and cable modems represent an emerging security risk. Early broadband users discovered that one of the consequences of being continuously attached to the Net is that, unless you secure your machine (and Microsoft should take the blame for creating consumer operating systems that are inherently insecure), you are much more vulnerable to outside attacks of all kinds, from remote monitoring software to implanted viruses. Early cable modems, for example, linked a local group of users into a virtual private network. The upshot was that anyone in the group could use the "Network Neighborhood" button on his Windows 95 desktop to browse the contents of his neighbors' computers. If those neighbors had a Webcam or a microphone attached, you could even reach into their computer and turn it on surreptitiously. Full-featured bugging, just like professional spies, right on your home PC!

It won't stay this way, of course. The designs of cable modems changed, and consumer-level firewalls are coming onto the market, and either those or the security software (such as Zone Alarm) available on the Net will help individuals secure their systems. Even so, the risk extends beyond the user's own computer. Subscribers with secure access to their companies' corporate networks may place those corporate networks at risk, too, if their systems are hacked. In addition, if a cracker installs software that monitors keystrokes, all the person's user names and passwords for secured systems, including Web-based shopping sites, could be compromised.

What users have to fear isn't just having their systems cracked so some teenager halfway across the world can read the details of their checking account balances or their email. This is another of those risks that people don't assess correctly. Having someone read your personal data is much less devastating than having someone send out email purporting to be from you. With access to your computer, your personal hacker can run your machine with its stored cookie files containing user names and passwords that unlock your personal profiles on sites from booksellers to bank accounts, online trading accounts, and telephone bills. How could you possibly prove that you did not originate transactions that came from your computer and are logged as such?[18] Electronic identity theft is likely to be the first major new crime of the twenty-first century.

This kind of issue was raised in the RISKS Forum, a heavily moderated list focusing on security issues, shortly after David L. Smith's guilty plea to charges of writing and releasing the Melissa email virus that infected more than 100,000 computers worldwide. Smith was caught because of the previously unknown GUID in Microsoft Word. As poster Russ Cooper pointed out, the presence of a particular GUID on an illegal document is at best circumstantial evidence that needs to be backed up by a trail definitively linking the user to it—any evidence that's electronic can be easily copied, pasted, or altered.[19] So few people understand how their computers really work that it's easy to give such identification systems more credibility than they deserve.

This is especially going to be a problem as encryption becomes widespread and digital signatures become legally binding. The draft British electronic commerce legislation talked a lot about non-repudiable signatures. But most of today's digital signature schemes rely on encryption keys stored on a user's hard drive and protected by a passphrase. Presuming that these keys are definitively tied to a particular individuals seems to me extremely dangerous. A greater audit trail is needed, especially now that the average Internet-faring individual is having to manage a large number of user IDs and passwords. Assign the same password and user ID to all sites, and any time someone cracks one, they've got them all. Assign different ones, and how do you remember them?

The answer the industry is pushing is biometrics, one of those technologies that until recently seemed too chilling—see the movie *Gattaca* for examples of why—in its implications to be acceptable.

Users identify themselves to access control systems in one of three ways: something they know (passwords), something they have (a key card or smart card), or something they are (a fingerprint or iris scan). More commonly, a good system will use some combination of the three, such as cash card and PIN, required in combination to get cash out of a bank's machine. But users lose cards and forget passwords, like the story that surfaced online recently: a customer who had never been able to remember his PIN complained to his bank manager about a spate of redecorating—he'd written the PIN in pencil on the bank wall next to the ATM, and it had now been painted over. Theoretically, biometrics should solve problems like these, since you can't lose your eye or your fingerprints, at least not easily.

There have, of course, been many criticisms of the idea of using biometrics. First of all, there's the physical discomfort of having the biometrics collected. Fingerprinting using ink pads has unpleasant criminal associations, and most people don't like the idea of being stared intensely in the eye by a laser. Iris scans, retinal scans, facial recognition, and voice prints all either make people uncomfortable or have a high failure rate. Worse are the privacy implications of creating a system that stores personal identifiers such as DNA samples or iris prints. What if the system gets cracked? A person can't get a new eyeball or set of fingers as easily as a new password or PIN.

Second, with all technological solutions there's a tendency to throw more technology at a problem than it needs. It's entirely predictable that biometrics will be misused in many ways, creating databases full of perfect identifiers that then can't easily be erased. For example, even though privacy has already been identified as a major issue with biometrics, and even though it's known that an important factor in deciding when and how to use them is determining how important it is to tie a given transaction to a specific person's identity, Clive Musgrave, vice-president of IriScan, still proposed at a London conference that iris scanning could help make many of the world's underground systems profitable because it would reduce the costs of handling money. But this is like using a ten-ton truck to run over a squirrel: the New York subway does not need to know who you are when you travel, it just needs to know that you have paid for your trip. Few schemes think in terms of limiting the amount of information collected to no more than what's actually needed, the way DigiCash did.

The push into electronic commerce is focusing attention on security. Electronic commerce is growing at a rate that leaves at least some large organizations convinced that today's models of trust and security won't scale to the volumes required, and that better authentication is going to be needed. Visa International, for example, says a November 1998 survey of twelve banks in fifteen European countries found that although only 1 percent of transactions were Internet-based, 47 percent of disputed transactions came from the Internet. Of those problems, slightly less than half (or 22 percent of all problems), come from fraud; 25 percent are customer service issues.

Although the idea of biometrics makes a lot of people uncomfortable, they are likely to form the basis of many new security systems. The industry is now attempting to come up with answers to some of the many criticisms directed at these new technologies and to make biometrics sound friendly rather than menacing. Fingerprint scanning seems on the verge of becoming a mainstream function; it is being incorporated into both desktop and laptop computers and many other standard devices. To access a machine, users insert a smart card into a reader and then place a finger on a fingerprint scanner. Similar functions may, over time, become part of building access control systems so that a worker carries one card and can validate his or her identity against that card at any point where authentication is needed. A by-product of such a system is that staff can't accidentally leave their PCs open, as they need to keep the card with them.

One of the key points about a system like this is supposed to be that there is no central database storing everyone's fingerprints. Instead, the individual's print is stored in encoded form on the smart card, and the computer merely compares the user's actual print against the one stored on the card. This design is intended to answer civil liberties arguments, by placing users in control of their data, and to prevent problems with data protection laws.

Facial recognition is also likely to become readily available soon as part of standard devices. The U.K. company Cambridge Neurodynamics is working on a system to capture 3D images, rather than the more commonly seen flat ones. Viewed as thumbnail images on a laptop, the 3D images look like ragged-edged smooth clay sculptures, similar to the intermediate rendered stage in creating computer-generated animation. The advantage of using 3D is that the system can recognize scanned faces at a much wider variety of angles. Even the company itself says, however, that facial recognition is not as accurate as fingerprinting, and probably never will be. Even though to a human a face carries infinitely more information than a fingerprint, to a computer the situation is reversed. A human sees color and emotion as well as shape. A computer doesn't appreciate any of that, but can calculate fine differences in the whorls and patterns of a fingerprint that a human can't, at least not easily.

One trend in devising biometric systems is using partial biometrics rather than an entire scan. A partial scan requires less storage space and allows for a replacement. Some systems additionally look for a pulse to insure against some of the more gruesome scenarios (like cutting off a finger or gouging out an eyeball to use for authentication).

Privacy advocates have always been unhappy about the idea of biometrics, believing that they ultimately create what Ian Brown, a spokesman on technology policy for Privacy International, called "a one-stop link between the individual and the machinery of the state." Even though newer systems avoid creating centralized databases, the problem, as Brown points out, is that under most legal systems authentication and identification are inextricably tangled together. Even the possibility of hooking the same fingerprint scanning that authorizes a user to a particular PC or network to cover building access control systems leads you inexorably back to building a database. If there's a burglary, the insurance company and the police are going to want a complete list, with names and addresses, of everyone who went in and out of the building for some hours on either side. If you're dealing with government benefits systems—exactly the kind of system where biometrics are likely to be pushed enthusiastically on the grounds that they will eliminate fraud—without a backup database, reissuing a lost card will be a lengthy and difficult process, during which the claimant will be essentially out of luck.

And yet, even some privacy advocates are being swayed by the anti-fraud argument and the claim that biometrics can be made both benevolent and harmless. At the 1998 Computers, Freedom, and Privacy conference, for example, Ontario Privacy Commissioner Ann Cavoukian claimed that by creating technical and procedural safeguards (such as encrypting the fingerprint scan), we could turn biometrics into "a friend to privacy." The controversial system for fingerprinting welfare claimants she championed then, however, was abandoned a year later.

What is notable as we move into the twenty-first century is that we are less at risk from huge monolithic systems than we are from what the TV show *Yes, Minister* called "salami tactics" (that is, the process of removing a thin slice at a time, eventually adding up to the whole salami). In 1948, when George Orwell wrote *1984*, and in the 1950s when Isaac Asimov and Robert Heinlein were writing their speculative fiction, the common theme was the fear of single global governments and computers. Orwell's Big Brother controlled every aspect of his proles' world. In Asimov's "The Last Question," the Galactic AC (for analog computer!) stored and processed all of human knowledge until all of human consciousness melded with it and turned it, after centuries of processing, into God.[20] None of the stories of that period imagined a world with computers everywhere (though everyone had their own robots).

Now, what we are seeing is splintered, distributed systems that mirror the ongoing fragmentation of everything else in our society. In this world, the threat to privacy is not the single, monolithic government system but the millions of tiny mosaic pieces. We give up our privacy bit by bit because each piece seems too small to be important, and we find out too late how easy it is for someone else to link all those disparate pieces of data together. Mining all that data is very much on the forefront of ecommerce companies' minds,[21] and while someone trying to sell you something is hardly the worst thing that could happen to you, you're looking at a whole new level of risk if casually browsing pages of AIDS information suddenly gets you a rate hike from your medical insurer or fired from your job.

Privacy is difficult to streamline into a single cause. Computer geeks tend to focus on cryptography and traffic analysis (prying outsiders may learn more from analyzing whom your communications go to and come from than they would from the contents of those communications). Data protection folks tend to think in terms of databases and suffer from the feeling that what they do sounds unbelievably boring. Still others focus on law enforcement and other government surveillance; their stories sometimes sound too paranoid to be true but sometimes are anyway (that sparrow flying around inside the CFP99 conference hall for the first two days: bird, or National Security Agency spy satellite?).

The result is that everyone has a different answer to what the biggest near-term threat to consumer privacy is. At CFP99, I went around asking people what they'd pick. "Data sharing and merging databases as organizations take a wider and wider brief," was Elizabeth France's choice, adding that her office's then most recent major source of trouble was utility companies in the newly deregulated British market. All industries are changing, whether because of new (de-)regulatory regimes, international mergers, or the advent of electronic commerce. In the United States, the repeal of parts of the Glass-Steagall Act means banks will start selling insurance and open brokerage services. In Britain, supermarkets are opening banking services, and the government is planning a major reorganization.

"Enfopol" was Simon Davies's pick, referring to the joint European Union and Federal Bureau of Investigation plan to design and implement a global surveillance network, which was proposed in the European Parliament in the fall of 1998. Twenty countries—the European Union's fifteen, plus the United States, Australia, Canada, Norway, and New Zealand—would participate in creating a network that would make it possible for law enforcement to access and transcribe all conversations. According to Lisa Dean from the Free Congress Foundation,[22] a conservative Washington, D.C.–based think-tank campaigning for freedom of speech and privacy rights, the battle over deregulating strong encryption and the use of key escrow is an important part of the context in which Enfopol is being proposed. Without ready access to decryption keys, such an international transparent network would achieve only part of its goal. Stephen Wright, who wrote the report on Enfopol for the European Parliament's Scientific and Technical Options Assessment Panel,[23] describes the existence of such a network as "preemptive policing." More commonly, you hear, "If you have nothing to hide, you have nothing to fear." In other words, guilty unless proven innocent.

On the other hand, FIPR's Caspar Bowden told science journalists in 1999 that traffic analysis is the greatest threat. Even though your messages can be made unreadable, encryption doesn't hide who your contacts are, and security services and other law enforcement can still track the flow of email and construct circles of contacts through which they can create pictures of interrelationships, progressively eating into the freedom of association we take for granted. Bowden's colleague in setting up the Foundation for Information Policy Research, Ross Anderson, notes as a follow-up to his paper on the subject that law enforcement relies much more heavily on this type of traffic analysis than on being able to access the contents of specific communications.[24]

The privacy dangers we face today are a mix of the old big-government intrusion fears—projects such as Echelon,[25] a global spy network for scanning all international data flows[26]—and the newer worries about the intrusive power of multinational corporations that didn't exist when the American Constitution was being written. The piecemeal erosions of privacy don't yet have an Orwell to fix the danger in people's minds; they've progressed slowly and almost imperceptibly.[27]

I believe that the biggest dangers are from our habits of mind, which give undue credibility to electronic data and apply extra technology to situations where it isn't needed in the name of public trust and safety. Data protection laws are a valiant effort to protect privacy, but they are probably doomed to eventual failure. For one thing, it does impede customer service if the person who's helping you can only access a small portion of your records. In all countries, citizens really do want easier, more streamlined, and more efficient access to their government records, not more splintered access that requires contacting many offices to make a simple change. People in the northeast want easier passage on toll roads. Traders want access to their brokerage and bank accounts online, even if that means the occasional security risk. For another thing, as the world is increasingly networked, the most likely scenario is that data is going to go where we don't want it to go. The best option, therefore, if you want your privacy guarded from merged databases that fall into the wrong hands is: do not create those databases.

What is important, then, is ensuring that people have enough physical-world *and* online choices to allow them realistic control, to shop and browse anonymously and opt into data collection only if they want to, rather than to be able to opt out only if they can find the right locked filing cabinet in the disused lavatory with a sign on it saying "Beware of the leopard."[28] This requires concerted effort and public policy decisions. It can't be created by companies who want to lock customers in, even if they are subtle about it by granting freedom in online communities.

The science fiction writer David Brin, in his book *The Transparent Society*, claims that as galling as it is to see companies making money off our personal information, the solution to privacy problems is not data protection legislation, which he has often described (at CFP95, for example) as legislation that protects the rich and powerful at the expense of the rest of us, to the benefit of no one but lawyers.[29] Brin proposes instead that we should embrace the loss of privacy. He argues that having cameras everywhere will end crime, and that complete openness will benefit us because it will subject the police and government, not just individuals, to surveillance. Both these outcomes seem remarkably unlikely, although the idea of reciprocity is interesting and can be valuable.

An experiment at the Olivetti Research Lab in Cambridge, England, for example, embraced reciprocity. A system of sensors and "active badges" used infrared to track the movements of staff members, log them on to nearby PCs (so any user could get his or her own desktop and applications on any machine), and so on. Staff could easily defeat the badge by taking it off and putting it in a drawer, but as long as they were wearing it anyone could use the network utility Finger to check on their whereabouts or availability. As guests were also given badges on arrival, a quick command to a computer could tell whether the staff member was in a meeting or on the phone. The key element, however, was that all those Finger requests were recorded, so that people could not be surveilled without their knowledge. A system that notified you every time your data was sold to another mailing list or was accessed for credit-checking would go a long way toward restoring some sense of control.

In one sense, technology changes nothing. Stores have always gotten to know their customers, and electoral rolls have always been public data. Today's databases of telephone calling patterns and credit card transactions aren't unprecedented in kind. Forty years ago they were the knowledge in the head of a town's nosy switchboard operator, like the one in the 1968 movie *The Russians Are Coming, The Russians Are Coming*, or local shopkeepers. Small-town residents from the Scottish Highlands to the rural American South don't have secrets even as small as whether they liked the fish they had for lunch; in the tiny County Wicklow town in Ireland where I lived in 1984, the local postmistress/newsagent/grocer/confectioner/coalmonger/dairy/butcher grilled you mercilessly about your every move.

But technology also changes everything. My Irish postmistress wasn't part of a permanently connected network of postmistresses; the knowledge she gained about me didn't follow me to the next post office to be stored and expanded, and my mail did not pass through her office written on the backs of postcards. Today's technology is enabling far greater surveillance and storage for less labor than ever before, when if you wanted privacy and anonymity you could move out of your small town into a large city. Few would agree with Brin that embracing surveillance is the answer.

The San Francisco computer security expert Russell Brand asked in conversation at CFP95 whether, if you could be sure that no one would use the information to damage you, it would be necessary to have secrets. It's an interesting question, because although most of us have secrets, recovery programs from AA's twelve steps to the confessions of the Catholic church include opening our inner dark areas up to another person and/or to whatever higher power one may or may not believe in, as a way of delivering oneself from crippling shame and guilt. Having the choice over which parts of ourselves are secret and which are public is our currency in human relationships. We show people their importance to us by telling them things about ourselves that no one else knows.

13

Twenty-first Century Snow

> It's here! It's here! The 21st century is here! You'd think this snow
> would be a little more high-tech.   —*Foxtrot*, January 2, 2000

The two great dangers for the Net have always seemed to me to be, first, that it would become dominated by a very few large players and therefore turn into a closed, proprietary system, and second, that the Net and its freedom would be strangled by government regulation. The Communications Decency Act, the Child Online Protection Act, and the International Traffic in Arms Regulations (ITAR) are all examples of exactly the wrong kind of government intervention, in that while the motives are reasonable enough the implementation is screwy. More children are harmed by poverty and abuse every day than have ever been harmed by the Net, and the ITAR's restrictions on the deployment of strong cryptography have harmed honest citizens, who need security and privacy far more than anyone else. Meanwhile, citizens have had to cope with other privacy threats such as the now dropped requirement that states put Social Security numbers on drivers' licenses and the plans to put medical data online.

People laughed at the oligopoly scenario only a few years ago. That was before the astonishing rise of MCI Worldcom, which didn't even exist as recently as 1984, when AT&T was broken up, but now owns an unnervingly large percentage of the world's Internet backbones. The company got its start when two guys scrawled a plan for a discount long-distance telephone service on a napkin at their favorite diner, and like many others since has grown huge through stock swaps, along the way acquiring MFS and its subsidiary UUnet and the networking divisions of both AOL and CompuServe. Meanwhile, Earthlink and Mindspring, now merging, are swallowing smaller ISPs like former leader Netcom whole. There are only two mainstream Web browsers and they are owned by AOL (20 million subscribers) and Microsoft, which also has a lock on millions of consumer desktops and, through its Web development product Front Page, which requires special extensions to run on the hosting servers, is making a play for the Web standard. Most of the world's routers are made by a single company, Cisco, and the local bulletin board systems and FreeNets of the past are vanishing. In the shakeout of ecommerce sites everyone expects in 2000, it would be surprising if more than one or two Web-only companies survived in each mass-market goods category, while the ones who have the best chance to survive without that first-mover advantage are the companies who are already successful in the physical world and can combine online and offline effectively—the "clicks and mortar" approach.

Ownership of the Net poses as great a danger as government regulation, not just because commercial companies are allowed greater latitude in setting rules, but also because so many technical decisions have social and cultural regulation embedded in them. Those who argue that technology is neutral may do so because the consequences of their decisions are too uncomfortable to think about; or perhaps the technology only seems neutral because the ideas embedded in it are theirs.

"Clicks and mortar," probably doomed to be the buzzword for most of 2000, seems to me as good a metaphor as any for what is going to happen next. Increasingly, the Net is not going to be a separate thing people do instead of watch TV. Rather, it will be entangled in everything we do. It shouldn't be a surprise if the cyber/physical blends are the successful ecommerce companies, since that repeats the pattern that's well established in online communities.

Always-on connections, both wired and wireless, will dramatically change the culture around Net access. You think very differently about online when you no longer need to collect a list of Web sites to check out next time you're online because you can visit them as soon as you hear about them, as easy as thought. The same is true of email when it's "here" any time you feel like looking at it instead of "out there" from where it has to be retrieved. This is the life academics have had since the mid 1980s, and it will be the first time mass consumers experience the Net as it was for its original users, just an ordinary extension of everything they do.

In his 1999 book *The Invisible Computer*, Donald Norman talks about the early days of electric motors, when you would buy one large, expensive motor and attach things to it for specific jobs; now electric motors are cheap and come embedded in all kinds of whizmos.[1] He predicted something similar would happen to the computer, but in a sense, it already has, since even people who boast that they do not own a computer probably have hundreds of computers—chips with embedded software, designed to do one particular job—in their cars, VCRs, breadmakers, TVs, and even credit cards like American Express Blue. The same thing is going to happen with Internet access. In an always-on world, why shouldn't an ordinary CD player be able to recognize the CD you put in it by accessing the online CD database? Why shouldn't a standard TV be able to retrieve the cast list and production background of the movie you're watching? It's my guess that within ten years, maybe within five years, there will be more machines on the Internet than there are people, and that increasingly Internet access will be invisible in the same sense Norman wants the computer to be. As I write this, Panasonic has announced a phone that will be able to make calls both through the ordinary telephone network and over the Internet, and we will see many more such hybrid devices in the 2000s.

A big danger as we move into this type of world (aside from the question of whether we'll be able to read the machines' newsgroups) is in imagining that technology and the market will solve everything. The gap between those who try to improve the world through technology and those who try to improve it through personal and governmental intervention in the form of diplomacy was nowhere made clearer to me than at the Virtual Diplomacy conference in Washington in 1998. It was bridging that gulf that Bob Schmitt, the conference's organizer, had in mind, when he began trying, three years earlier, to bring the two communities together. At the first meeting, he says, they found that computer industry leaders and diplomats had this in common: nothing.

"The culture of the computer companies is ruthless," he said on the first day of the 1998 conference, "but you just get another job. The stakes are different in diplomacy, where you have the weight of the world on your shoulders. People will die, there will be blood on the ground, and you can't wash it away."

That evening, John Gage, director of Sun Microsystems' science office, surveyed the people gathered over drinks, bounced like an eager terrier, and asked, "How can we make inroads into this community?" With Schmitt's story of Sun's 1995 refusal to donate old workstation hardware to Bosnia still fresh in the notebook, only one answer seemed possible: "I think they're asking the same thing about you."

Here, on the diplomatic floor, were the diametrical opposite of tech-nolibertarians: people who fight internecine turf wars over providing aid, but who believe, as World Bank vice-president Ismail Serageldin argued passionately, that there are moral obligations if you are a member of the 20 percent of the world's population who get 83 percent of the income when three billion people live on less than $2 a day.

The conference opened with this statement: "The information revolution will not only destroy the sovereignty of states. What we are witnessing changes the very nature of power." The speaker was Jean-Marie Guéhenno, the international director of the French Cour des Comptes.

The idea that governments are losing control, popular among tech-nolibertarians, probably originated with this group. Speakers like Guéhenno, public policy specialist Francis Fukiyama, and Walter Wriston (probably the only banker ever to be featured on the cover of *Wired*) have been writing books about the threat to nation-states for years, and the rise of non-governmental organizations (NGOs) all around them probably told them the story before anyone else.

Guéhenno, who said he felt obliged to be stereotypically European and pessimistic, finds the origins of today's nation-states in a different invention: the printing press. "Gutenberg shifted power from the few, the literati, to the hands of the people," he said. "The state replaced the sovereignty of the Pope, religions, and kings. Today, we are seeing the exact opposite. The distinction between domestic issues and international issues is less relevant every day."

The falling costs of communications and transport mean increasingly decentralized management; the growth of the global economy means that individual nations no longer have sole control over their fiscal policies, not even their ability to impose taxes—Guéhenno argued that even the European Union is simply old hierarchical power in a bigger box. Smaller, more flexible institutions will be the way of the future, and a key difficulty will be managing the interface between today's hierarchical national structures and tomorrow's diffuse sites of power. This is not a consequence of the Internet, but among those at the conference it was clear that the Internet is accelerating a pre-existing trend, though its impact pales beside that of CNN and the unique pressure it imposes on national leaders with its instant, worldwide pictures.

If anything, the assembled collection of NGOs and official representatives had grasped the essentials about the Internet—that it's a fast, relatively inexpensive, pervasive communications medium—more comprehensively than computer people have grasped the essentials about diplomacy. Jack Dangermond, a geographic information systems specialist, for example, began his talk by saying, "I don't know your field, but . . ." and went on to explain that maps are an essential tool for understanding any kind of conflict; all true, though disappointing to his audience because he neglected to say what made his systems different from what was already available.

A similar problem surfaced when systems consultant Paul Strassman's videoconferencing system demonstrated a built-in flow chart to help negotiators understand who's saying what and how often. "It costs under $3,000 to put this on each desk," he said enthusiastically. "Less than the cost of a transatlantic ticket these days." (Someone needs to get this man a travel agent.)

"I may sound like an expert who doesn't want to become obsolete," said Joan Dudik-Gayoso, a participation manager at the World Bank, surveying the system, "but I don't know what to do in a negotiation when people are talking about politics when the issue is economics, or vice-versa. I don't know what to do when a negotiation depends on reaching some kind of understanding of the problem before you can reach a solution. The diagram of the types of issues is very important, but I think the idea that we can sit in the Capitol and do negotiations has its limits."

Then there are the real problems for which the Internet is no help at all. Hans Zimmermann, a senior office in the United Nations Department of Humanitarian Affairs named one of the biggest barriers to networking and information sharing: the lack of an international agreement on the use and export of telecommunications equipment in a humanitarian crisis. You're a relief worker in an earthquake, and the choices are to give up the vital tool of communicating with your fellow relief workers, or to take that walkie-talkie out of your backpack and risk getting arrested. Negotiating this single, simple principle—which has been universally approved—into international law is taking eight years. By contrast, as Xerox PARC's Marc Weiser said, "The whole world has agreed in the last five years on how computers are going to talk to one another."

Speed may be the major unbridgeable gap between the two worlds. Time and time again, said Dudik-Gayoso, what surprises new recruits is the many layers of clearances messages must go through. Yes, it's slow, but it's designed to be slow: in the diplomatic world you do not want the two-second response to half-read messages common in the email world. You want people to think: what does this word mean in Nigeria? Let's not flatten hierarchies if the hierarchies have a useful purpose. Sometimes the side conversations between underlings unearth the key to what's going on: a country's delegation is mad because their national football team lost last night. How do you find that out in a virtual negotiation where no one meets over the ice bucket?

The Internet seems to feel less new to the diplomatic community than it does to the rest of us. As Tom Standage recounts in his book *The Victorian Internet*, the telegraph reduced the time it took for dispatches to reach India from thirty-three days to four minutes, leading India's British governor to complain about his loss of autonomy.[2] In the Crimean War, telegraphed foreign dispatches, printed in the *Times*, provided information for Russian spies to telegraph home; today much of this sort of information retrieval is moving to the Internet, where the availability of foreign papers and economic data save weeks of research. The telegraph, too, it was believed, would usher in an era of world peace by allowing leaders to communicate directly. It is just what Standage calls chronocentricity that makes us believe *our* revolution must be the biggest.

Jobs are certainly changing in the diplomatic world, but just as Land's End told the *New Yorker* that the biggest change in its business was not the Internet but bar codes, former ambassador John Negroponte, now the special coordinator for post-1999 presence in Panama (who doubles in real life as the more famously digital Nicholas's older brother), said the single biggest success for computers in the State Department was installing machine-readable visas.

It is, I suppose, an example of the way things never work out quite the way you think they're going to. Here's another: a report from Cyber Dialogue in November 1999 revealed that, even though roughly half of Americans are expected to be online by 2003, the Internet boom is slowing down.[3] The report blamed the digital divide for some of the slow-down, but it also noted an interesting statistic: 27.7 million Americans, three times as many as in 1997, had given up using the Internet. Only about a third of those expected to get back online in the near future. The report's conclusion was that ecommerce companies would have to try harder to get and keep customers. This pattern is not yet being repeated in other countries, where Internet access is still booming—expectations are that the Net will explode in China and Latin America in the early 2000s—but it seems logical to expect that eventually it will be.

What isn't clear is whether the limitation is in the Internet itself or in the way people access it. As mass-market as it seems to be compared to its earliest incarnation, the Internet is still intimidating. The computers people must use to access it are complex and difficult (yes, even Macs), and the Internet itself is a mass of bewildering new concepts, even if the action of pointing and clicking seems simple.

The news of a slow-down comes at a time when the Net seems to be on the verge of reinventing itself yet again, as broadband begins to change consumer Net access to always-on connections, and as wireless and mobile devices with built-in Internet access become available. A Palm VII user can stand on a city street, look up the nearest location of a Barnes and Noble store, and search its database of books. Mobile phones with built-in microbrowsers can display streamlined content—at the moment, mostly sports scores, stock prices, and news headlines from services like My Yahoo!, but major European content providers are already designing WAP (for Wireless Application Protocol, the emerging standard for wireless access) versions of their sites.

Early reviews say microbrowser-equipped mobile phones aren't ready for prime time, but my guess is that this is at least partly because they're trying to emulate the existing computer world. It's a logical first step, but wireless access to the Web will probably morph quickly into something different. Sending instant short text messages over mobile phones is already the latest teen craze in Europe—sort of ICQ without the heavy machinery. One intriguing possibility is mobile phone access to Net-based radio: it's easy to imagine selecting from a series of menus using the number pad and then storing favorites in the phone's memory. Even battery life isn't that much of a problem—phones consume power seriously only when transmitting.

In a typical geek argument on London's electronic conferencing system CIX, people complained about the new Web-enabled phones because some network operators had blocked off access to anything other than the Web services they wanted to provide (and bill for). The received opinion was that these services would learn better, just as telephone companies rolling out ADSL (such as British Telecom) have had to learn that their users do not want video-on-demand from telephone company servers, but rather the freedom to roam far and wide on the Net. In this case, I think the geeks are at least partly wrong, at least for large parts of the mass market. Constraining choices of course means a loss of freedom; but simplicity must have its virtues, or else no one would buy cars with automatic transmissions.

The trouble is that this kind of simplicity also takes you in the direction of control, and this is why it seems to me that none of these topics can be considered in isolation. Most books about the Net and its development pick a single topic and focus on it—privacy, say, or civil liberties, or the history of the Net's design. It is not possible to disentangle these issues. You can't talk about freedom of speech without considering online communities and what holds them together, and you can't talk about that without considering where the technical structure came from to support them. Business issues lead inexorably to questions of standards and of Internet governance, which you can't talk about without looking at the challenge of free software, which leads in turn to the future of intellectual property and public information, which in turn raise issues of public access and the impact of electronic commerce. All those roads eventually lead to the problem of guarding individual privacy in the electronic era. Given the nature of the Net, you can't talk about any of these things without examining Net culture and the way social groupings cohere, because it is possible for even a small group to change the entire debate sometimes, just by inventing a new bit of technology or defying someone's authority. Understanding how all these issues intermesh is vital in determining policy to guide the decisions we make about the Net and its further development.

As Paulina Borsook persuasively argues in her book *Cyberselfish*, technolibertarianism is becoming pervasive, especially as more and more technology CEOs find themselves managing billion-dollar companies.[4] The thinking basically goes that whatever the problem is the market will sort it out. Even the idealists who have become millionaires through the dot-com boom and want to give their money away believe their judgment is better than the government's. And yet, it is not ecommerce companies, presumably eager to gain every possible customer they can, who are leading the way to ensure equality of access or who are even leading the way in thinking about the problems of equity. It's those big, bad, old demons, governments. Before we throw out the school system, for example, as *Wired* co-founder Louis Rossetto told *ReWired* we should ("Schools are obsolete. We should be doing all we can to liberate children from the slavery of the classroom, not wiring their jail cells."[5]), we should think very hard about the alternatives we are proposing to put in their place. One of Borsook's points is that technolibertarians are failing to connect the decimation of education in California over the last couple of decades to the shortage of high-tech workers that is leading companies to demand an increase in the amount of immigrant work visas.

This is one area in which the development of the Net is likely to be significantly different outside the United States. It is axiomatic in Europe that social justice matters and that being fortunate enough to enjoy the economic and other benefits of a good education carries with it some kind of obligation, through taxes, to help support those who are not similarly blessed. The United States is the only developed country I'm aware of where public television has to routinely beg its viewers for money, and it is the only Western country without some form of medical safety net for its citizens. Great inequalities exist in all countries, and Europe's social justice platform brings with it other problems, but the insistence that all regulation should be left to market forces seems to be peculiarly American.

David Hudson, editor of the *ReWired* site, wrote in his book of the same name,

> From 1985 to 1994, I lived in Munich. That's nine years away from "the old country." When I came back to what is still my favorite city in the world, San Francisco, I was appalled. I understand the shock Koch [a German reporter who visited *Wired*] and so many other foreign observers go through when they set foot in America and see the stats translated into 3D, tangible human suffering. The administrations friendliest to *laissez faire* economics wreaked havoc on the US and its people, tearing them apart into two classes, and rewarding the minority while punishing the majority.[6]

It is my guess that as the Net develops these battles will play out differently in different countries: the "global" Net will support vastly different cultural norms while still sharing some common characteristics. The best analogy I can come up with is the American melting pot, which manages to foster cultures reflecting their origins in Boston

(Irish), Louisiana (French), and Texas (Mexico) while still infusing all of them with something that is distinctively American.

It is already clear that the same technologies mean different things in different places. At Virtual Diplomacy, for example, John Gage, in listing developments to be concerned about, commented that twenty countries will have sub-metre satellite imagery by the year 2002. That means the ability to resolve individual humans and track what they are doing: a serious invasion of privacy to everyone. But, as a different panel showed, in Africa's Great Lakes region, the same technology helps track and reunite refugees, chart crop movements, and give early warning of disasters.

If I had to unify all these battles with a single theme it would be openness: of software, of culture, of infrastructure, of ideas. It was common to criticize the Net in the early days because of the amount of garbage that was out there. But the Net's openness to all comers also fostered pockets of insane brilliance—and we need those more than we need overall bland mediocrity and the conservative choices that are made when the majority rules. Our world is, after all, governed by Sturgeon's Law: "90 percent of everything is crap."[7] It is those pockets of brilliance, amplified by the Net, that have the power to change the world in accordance with all our old democratic dreams of equality. Ultimately, the power of the Net is in the ideas of the people who use it.

Acknowledgments

This book thing started when an editor for NYU Press posted a message to the Usenet newsgroup *rec.sport.tennis* in early 1995 to the effect that he'd been reading everyone's thoughts on tennis for four years but had no idea what anybody did outside of watch or play tennis. So, who was everybody? He'd start: he was a book publisher. My first thought was, "Yeah, right." I figured, you know, a vanity press or one of those shady fleece-the-wannabe outfits. Then I looked again at the email address—*nyu.edu*—and realized he was probably on the level. So I posted and emailed something on the order of: hungry freelance, wants to write books, psst, little editor, wanna buy a book? A couple of months later, we met in person and he commissioned *net.wars*. That was Tim Bartlett, and he never got enough credit for what he did for that book in requesting rewrites and giving the kind of personal editorial attention that is generally supposed to have died out with the passenger pigeon.

Tim has moved on from NYU Press now (which is why I can tell the story of how we met), and the editor of this book, Stephen Magro, has been a worthy successor.

Lots of other thanks are due. To my agent, Diana Finch, who puts enormous effort into small things. To Rachel Carthy, Jack McDonald, Bill Steele, Simon Eccles, and Lucy Kewney Sherriff, for various types of assistance (and de-ssistance) with sorting papers, finding quotes, and boring typing. It was one of Lucy's friends, also, who came up with the phrase "haunted goldfish bowl." Paulina Borsook and David Kline kindly gave me a pre-publication glimpse of their works, and Alex MacKenzie gave me more leads and information about the early days of international networking than I was able to pursue properly.

Much of the material that went into *From Anarchy to Power* came out of research for articles for a variety of publications in the United States and Britain. Editors and other staff who deserve special mention are Ben Rooney, Tom Standage, Georgia Cameron-Clarke, and Mark Ward at the *Daily Telegraph*, Charles Arthur at the *Independent*, Philip Yam at *Scientific American*, Bob Kolasky at *IntellectualCapital.com*, and Dylan Armbrust at *ComputerActive*.

Each year at the Computers, Freedom, and Privacy conference I meet people who seek to peer into the future of this technological revolution and understand its consequences. Many of them either have contributed largely to the way I think about these matters or have patiently let me bug them for help at various times, in no particular order (and no particular conference year): Michael Froomkin, Mike Godwin, Caspar Bowden, Beth Weise, Whitfield Diffie, Bruce Koball, Simon Davies, Bruce Sterling, John Perry Barlow, Russell Brand, Donna Hoffman, and Frank Carey. Dan O'Brien has never been to CFP, but his and his buddy Dave Green's filled-with-smarts-and-attitude *Need to Know (Now)* weekly eletter is my role model (you can find it at http://www.ntk.net). Dave Farber doesn't maintain his Interesting People list for my personal benefit, but I'm grateful nonetheless, as it provides the best and most concentrated set of leads to important Net stories I might otherwise have missed.

Thanks also to London's CIX Internet Services for, as always, bearing the brunt of my online habits, and to the WELL for providing the best place in the world to procrastinate. Especially, thanks to the *byline* conference (and Fawn Fitter and Mary Beth Williams for hosting it) and to various cranky people who shall remain nameless but unbitten.

Notes

NOTES TO CHAPTER 1

1. "Syphilis Outbreak Traced to Internet Chat Room," *Nando*, August 23, 1999. Was at http://www.nandotimes.com/technology/story/0,1634,85261-134655-938407-0,00.html. "Syphilis Traced to Chat Room," Reuters wire story on ABC News, August 25, 1999. Available at http://abcnews.go.com/sections/living/DailyNews/syphilis_internet_990823.html.

2. *Need to Know (Now)*, May 14, 1999. Available at http://www.ntk.net/index.cgi?back=archive99/now0514.txt&line=37#1.

3. See, for example, Dan Colarusso, "Over the Edge: Amateur Traders Stressed Beyond Capacity to Cope?" ABC News/The Street.com, July 29, 1999. Available at http://abcnews.go.com/sections/business/TheStreet/daytraders_990729.html.

4. Brad Barber and Terrance Odean, "Online Investors: Do the Slow Die First?" At http://www.gsm.ucdavis.edu/~odean/papers/Online/Online.html.

5. "Report of the Day Trading Project Group, Findings and Recommendations," August 9, 1999. Available at http://www.nasaa.org/nasaa/scripts/fu_display_list.asp?ptid=16

6. See Margo Hittleman, "CU study: Average Investors Lose Out Consistently to the Professionals." Available at http://www.news.cornell.edu/releases/May98/bloomfieldstudy.mh.html.

7. Testimony of Thomas M. Gardner before the Permanent Subcommittee on Investigations of the United States Senate Committee on Government Affairs. Available at http://www.fool.com/specials/1999/sp990322tomstestimony.htm.

8. The project that produced the study, HomeNet, is at http://homenet.andrew.cmu.edu/progress/.

9. R. Kraut, M. Patterson, V. Lundmark, S. Kiesler, T. Mukophadhyay, and W. Scherlis, "Internet Paradox: A Social Technology That Reduces Social Involvement and Psychological Well-Being?" *American Psychologist* 53, no. 9 (1998). Available at http://www.apa.org/journals/amp/amp5391017.html.

10. At http://www.drudgereport.com.

11. *Need to Know (Now)*, October 29, 1999. At http://www.ntk.net.

12. For example, see "Bombs on the Internet: New Fears about Free Speech

vs. Public Safety," CNN, May 29, 1998. Available at http://www.cnn.com/ TECH/science/9805/29/t_t/bombs.on.internet/.

13. Ken Silverstein, "The Radioactive Boy Scout," *Harper's Magazine*, November 1998.

14. Mitnick went on to become famous as the hacker who was tracked across the country and arrested in North Carolina in 1995, a story recounted in no less than three books, one of which, *Takedown*, is being made into a film due to hit theaters sometime in 2001.

15. Schifreen is himself a former hacker; with technology journalist Steve Gold, he hacked into a mailbox belonging to Prince Philip on the early British online service Prestel (the mailbox was not being used). Their acquittal on technical grounds was the direct inspiration for the writing and passage of Britain's Computer Misuse Act in 1984.

16. Sherry Turkle, *Life on the Screen: Identity in the Age of the Internet* (New York: Simon and Schuster, 1995), 196–206.

17. Janelle Brown, "BS Detector: 'Internet Addiction' Meme Gets Media High," *Wired News*, December 5, 1996. Available at http://wired.lycos.com/ news/culture/0,1284,844,00.html. See also Howard Rheingold, "The Addiction Addiction," *Atlantic Monthly*, Web Citations, September 9, 1999. Available at http://www.theatlantic.com/unbound/citation/wc990909.htm.

18. Available at http://www.psycom.net.

19. Storm A. King, "Is the Internet Addictive, or Are Addicts Using the Internet?" December 1996. Available at http://www.concentric.net/~Astorm/ iad.html.

20. For an analysis of this phenomenon, see Wendy Kaminer, *I'm Dysfunctional, You're Dysfunctional: The Recovery Movement and Other Self-Help Fashions* (Reading, MA: Addison-Wesley, 1992).

21. John Suler, "Computer and Cyberspace Addiction." Available at http:// www.rider.edu/users/suler/psycyber/cybaddict.html.

22. *Wired* and *HotWired* were split apart in early 1998, after two failed attempts to take the original company public. Wired Digital, including *HotWired* (now mostly just *Wired News*), was bought by Lycos, a portal/search engine company; *Wired* was bought by Conde Nast.

23. At http://www.beatrice.com.

24. Howard Kurtz, "Cyber-Libel and the Web Gossip-Monger," *Washington Post*, August 15, 1997, page G01. Available at http://www.freerepublic .com/forum/a716.html.

25. Frazier Moore, "Matt Drudge, Fox News Channel Call It Quits," Associated Press, November 19, 1999. Was at http://www.foxnews.com/ js_index.sml?content=/news/wires2/1119/n_ap_1119_92.sml.

26. Frank Rich, "The Strange Legacy of Matt Drudge," *New York Times*,

December 4, 1999. Available at http://www.nytimes.com/library/opinion/rich/120499rich.html (requires registration).

27. See, e.g., the discussion of the Martin Rimm study in Mike Godwin's *Cyber Rights and Cyber Law* (New York: Random House, 1998).

NOTES TO CHAPTER 2

1. Russell Frank, "You've Got Quotes!" *Quill*, October 1999.

2. John Seabrook, "Email from Bill," *New Yorker*, January 10, 1994. Reprinted in *The New Science Journalists*, ed. Ted Anton and Rick McCourt (New York: Ballantine, 1995).

3. Mike Godwin, "Nine Principles for Making Virtual Communities Work," *Wired* 2.06. Available at http://www.wired.com/archive/2.06/vc.principles.html.

4. The review was originally posted in February or March 1999; it disappeared but was replaced when people made a fuss. It was gone again from the Amazon site in November 1999, but a copy is archived at http://slashdot.org/books/99/01/31/1246212.shtml.

5. Avatars are representations that stand in for users in online interactions. In today's graphical world, these are typically cartoon-like figures, but the word can refer to anything from a text-based description to . . . well, whatever they dream up next.

6. At http://www.slashdot.org.

7. Dan Shafer, "Amy Jo Kim: Common Purpose, Uncommon Woman." Dan Shafer. Available at http://www.onlinecommunityreport.com/features/kim/.

8. Posting to the *media* conference, November 29, 1999.

9. Personal interview.

10. Howard Rheingold, *The Virtual Community* (London: Secker and Warburg, 1994).

11. A killer application is one that is so compelling that it sells the underlying technology to users. For example, Lotus's original 1-2-3 spreadsheet was a compelling reason for users to buy PCs.

12. MUD stands for multi-user dungeon; MOO stands for MUD object-oriented. Both are text-based games that allow players surprising latitude in creating descriptions for themselves and building additions to the "world" where the game takes place. Essentially an outgrowth of the type of game first popularized in *Dungeons and Dragons*, MUDs have been described as very nearly addictive by both players and observers.

13. Formerly belonging to Fujitsu, Worlds Away was sold to Avaterra.com in the spring of 1999. Available at http://www.worldsaway.com.

14. At http://www.thepalace.com.

15. On Worlds Away and The Palace (as well as other similar services such

as Active Worlds), users interact with cartoon-like representations of each other known as avatars. Avatars have different capabilities on different services; they may be able to carry or wear items ("props" on The Palace), build structures, or move around. There are also different constraints on the kind of avatar you can design; on The Palace, you can paste in any graphic you like; on Worlds Away you're limited to the range of bodies and, especially, heads available on the system.

16. One of the older blogs is programmer Dave Winer's Scripting site, at http://www.scripting.com. I had been reading it on and off for a couple of years—it always has interesting links to carefully selected articles covering new technology issues—before I even found out it was part of a whole class of these things.

17. Katz sold the WELL to the Web magazine *Salon* in 1998.

18. News International dropped out in 1999 to set up Currant Bun, a service aimed primarily at readers of its tabloid, *The Sun*. It's notable that although News International and its owner, Rupert Murdoch, began trying to enter the online world as early as 1994 when the company purchased Delphi, at the time the only national U.S. service with full Internet access, it has yet to make any real impact online. A joint effort to develop a new consumer-oriented platform for Delphi with MCI never came to fruition.

19. John Hagel III and Arthur G. Armstrong, *Net Gain* (Boston: Harvard Business School Press, 1997).

20. Thomas Mandel and Gerard van der Leun, *Rules of the Net: Online Operating Instructions for Human Beings* (New York: Hyperion, 1996).

21. Robert Seidman's *Online Insider* site, at http://www.onlineinsider.com. The site was active in 1998, but largely abandoned by 1999.

22. CompuServe Forums are an endangered species as I write this, two years after the service's acquisition by AOL. But for most of the period from 1978 to 1997, CompuServe was the leading purveyor of online community through asynchronous messaging; its forum software and moderator structure was eminently well designed to support the needs of online community, and at one point it numbered as many as 2,000 subject-specific forums with audience sizes from a few hundred to a few tens of thousands. As of late 1999, the service was planning to consolidate its roughly 950 forums into fewer than 500. The final remnant of CompuServe's earlier plain-text (ASCII) culture died in July 1999, when the last ASCII forum was turned off after an all-night vigil by old-timers, who reminisced about long-dead character-string commands and tricks.

23. Bumgardner's own home page is at http://www.thepalace.com/jbum.

24. John Suler, "The Psychology of Avatars and Graphical Space in Multimedia Chat Communities, or How I Learned to Stop Worrying and Love My Palace Props" (Rider University, May 1996 to July 1997). Available at http://www.rider.edu/users/suler/psycyber/psyav.html.

25. As quoted in John Suler, "On Being a God: An Interview with Jim Bumgardner" (Rider University, June 1996). Available at http://www.rider.edu/users/suler/psycyber/jbum.html.

26. "Habitat Anecdotes and Other Boastings," by F. Randall Farmer, Electric Communities, Fall 1988. Available at http://www.communities.com/company/papers/anecdotes.html.

27. A similar incident, the so-called rape on LambdaMOO, was written up by Julian Dibbell for the *Village Voice* and reprinted as part of his 1998 book *My Tiny Life* (London: Fourth Estate).

28. Personal email, October 1997.

29. Amy S. Bruckman and Mitchell Resnick, "The MediaMOO Project: Constructionism and Professional Community," by *Convergence* 1:1 (spring 1995). Available at http://asb.www.media.mit.edu/people/asb/convergence.html.

30. See ibid.

31. Judith S. Donath, "Identity and Deception in the Virtual Community," in *Communities in Cyberspace*, ed. Peter Kollock and Marc A. Smith (London: Routledge, 1998).

32. Janelle Brown, "Avatars: Punching into Life Online," *Wired News*, October 24, 1997. Available at http://www.wired.com/news/culture/0,1284,7951,00.html.

33. Chip Morningstar and F. Randall Farmer, "The Lessons of Lucasfilm's Habitat," paper presented at the First Annual International Conference on Cyberspace, 1990. Published in *Cyberspace: First Steps*, ed. Michael Benedikt (Cambridge, MA: MIT Press, 1990).

34. See Andrew Leonard, *'Bots: the Origin of a New Species* (New York: Wired Books, 1997).

35. Peter Kollock, "Design Principles for Online Communities," on the CD-ROM *The Internet and Society: Harvard Conference Proceedings*. (Cambridge, MA: O'Reilly and Associates, 1997). Available at http://www.sscnet.ucla.edu/faculty/soc/kollock/papers/design.htm.

36. For an explanation of how moderation works on Slashdot, see http://slashdot.org/moderation.shtml.

37. Because ASCII interfaces ran on simple text commands, the services they ran on could be accessed by any standard communications package that would let you type in commands. While that limited the kinds of material the service could display—no graphics, audio, or video—it did have the advantage of being operable from almost any machine. AOL, by contrast, runs on a proprietary graphical client that is available only for Windows and Macs, locking out anyone using anything else. While it's a reasonable economic decision for AOL to target the largest, most profitable markets, the consequences in terms of diversity of hardware and software are undesirable. CompuServe's current Web view forums do use standard software in the sense that they are accessible via any Web

browser—but to post to them members have to have CompuServe's special "Virtual Key" software, which only runs on Macs and Windows.

38. The WELL was sold to *Salon* magazine in 1999, shortly before *Salon*'s IPO.

39. Personal email.

40. Lawrence Lessig, *Code and Other Laws of Cyberspace* (New York: Basic Books, 1999).

41. Available at http://www.ascusc.org/jcmc/vol2/issue1/lambda.html.

42. Dibbell, *My Tiny Life*, 304.

43. Columnist Jon Katz talks more about the size issue in "Here Come the Weblogs," *Slashdot.org*, May 24, 1999. At http://slashdot.org/features/99/05/13/1832251.shtml.

44. Rebecca Spainhower, "Virtually Inevitable: Real Problems in Virtual Communities" (Northeastern University, 1994–1996). Available at http://world.std.com/~rs/inevitable.html.

45. Personal email.

46. Rheingold, *The Virtual Community*.

NOTES TO CHAPTER 3

1. Full archive of the service is at http://www.usc.edu/webcast/events/postel/.

2. Barry M. Leiner, Vinton G. Cerf et al., "A Brief History of the Internet." Available at http://www2.una.edu/tsingleton/ISOC-History-of-the-Internet.html.

3. The RFCs that define the way the Internet works are stored in many archives around the Net, including http://www.faqs.org/rfcs.

4. See, for example, "Jon Postel: God van Internet Is Niet Meer," in the Dutch magazine *Computable*. At http://www.computable.nl/artikels/archief8/d44rs8sc.htm.

5. Letter read at the funeral by Joseph D. Bannister, head of ISI.

6. RFC2555, "30 Years of RFCs." Available at http://www.isi.edu/in-notes/rfc2555.txt.

7. See, for example, Carol Shapiro and Hal R. Varian, *Information Rules: A Strategic Guide to the Network Economy* (Cambridge, MA: Harvard Business School Press, 1999).

8. An account of some of the early funding struggles for the British part of the network is at http:// www.cs.ucl.ac.uk/research/darpa/internet-history.html.

9. Janet Abbate, "A Tale of Two Networks: Early Data Communications Experiments in England and America," paper given at the History of Computing and Information Processing Conference commemorating the Moore School Lectures 50th Anniversary, University of Pennsylvania, May 17, 1996. Available at http://www.rci.rutgers.edu/~jea/papers/2Nets.html.

10. Vinton Cerf, as told to Bernard Aboba, "How the Internet Came to Be," in *The Online User's Encyclopedia* by Bernard Aboba (Reading, MA: Addison-Wesley, 1993). Available at http://www.bell-labs.com/user/zhwang/vcerf.html.

11. Janet Abbate, *Inventing the Internet* (Cambridge, MA: MIT Press, 1999), 171.

12. Actually, it became clear during the Millennium celebrations that Britain certainly *believes* it owns time.

13. Made available in 1999–2000 to consumers, ADSL offers an affordable flat-rate connection to the Net. "Asymmetric" refers to the fact that the bandwidth coming into the consumer's home is much higher than the bandwidth going out. There are some concerns about that, since the underlying assumption is that private homes will be primarily consumers of data—video and audio coming in, for example, to supply homes with access to new movies and/or music—rather than publishers or producers. This negates some of what's best about the Net and its ability to empower individuals. On the other hand, ADSL is still a lot better and cheaper than anything consumers have had access to before.

14. Personal interview.

15. New Zealand Ministry of Commerce, "Summary of Leased Line International Price Comparison," June 1997. Available at http://www.moc.govt.nz/pbt/infotech/summary.html.

16. Information Market Observatory (IMO) ADMEDIA project report "The Future of Media and Advertising," Executive Summary, November 1995, http://158.169.50.95:10080/imo/en/final_ex.html. The project was sponsored by the European Commission—DG XIII/E. The project team was asked to investigate the future of advertising and the new media.

17. Kenneth Cukier, "Bandwidth Colonialism? The Implications of Internet Infrastructure on International E-Commerce." Available at http://www.isoc.org/inet99/proceedings/1e/1e_2.htm.

18. Tracy Cohen, "Access and Equity and the Global Internet: The South African Experience," talk given at the 1999 Computers, Freedom, and Privacy conference, Washington, DC, April 6–8. Available at http://www.cfp99.org/program/papers/cohen.htm. Cohen is a research associate at the LINK Center, School of Public and Development Management, and a part-time lecturer in the School of Law, University of the Witwatersrand Johannesburg, South Africa.

19. See Paulina Borsook, *Cyberselfish: How the Digital Elite Is Undermining Our Society, Culture, and Values* (New York: Bantam, 2000).

20. Abbate, *Inventing the Internet*, 179.

NOTES TO CHAPTER 4

1. On Usenet, for example, a name like *rec.sport.tennis* allows computers to sort newsgroups more and more finely as they proceed to the right. So you

can tell a system in a computer science library to skip all hierarchies but *comp* (for computer science), or to accept *rec* (for recreation) groups as well, but only those in the *sport* sub-hierarchy and not those in *rec.tv*.

2. Actually, the United Kingdom is an anomaly: the ISO country code for Britain is GB. However, the analogous domain name is *.uk*, presumably because by being the first country code set up Britain got a certain amount of latitude, and local politics dictate that UK, which stands for "United Kingdom of Great Britain and Northern Ireland," is more inclusive.

3. The funny thing is that time was when *.com* was something to be sniffed at. In the early days of the Net, you really weren't anybody unless you were *.edu*. You especially wanted to be from the right sort of *.edu*, which meant a school that had made a significant contribution to the development of the Net, such as *mit.edu*, *caltech.edu*, *cornell.edu*, or *ic.ac.uk* (Britain's Imperial College, *.ac.uk* being the British equivalent of *.edu*). If you weren't a *.edu*, you could still claim class if you were, perhaps, *well.sf.ca.us*, whose geographical domain structure identified the apparently local electronic conferencing system the WELL, where many of the early cyberspace pioneers, as well as a number of mainstream writers, hung out. (In the early 1990s, the WELL opened itself up to the outside Internet and took the name *well.com*; not quite the same cachet, but still, for $15 a month you can sound like an old-timer. My home page used to be hosted on the WELL, and even in London people look at the address and call it "cool" and presume that anyone equipped with a WELL address must be knowledgeable.)

4. Statistics from NetNames, at http://www.netnames.com.

5. The DNS places limitations on names: they must be between two and twenty-two characters long, and the only allowable characters are letters, numbers, and hyphens. The rules are slightly different for some of the country code TLDs; for example, under *.uk* domain names must be a minimum of three characters long unless the name is a letter and a number. Spaces are not allowed (because a computer can't interpret them).

6. Figures from Michael Roberts, interim president and CEO of the Internet Corporation for Assigned Names and Numbers (ICANN), set up in 1998 to take over the naming and numbering functions, at a press briefing in London in November 1999.

7. Dan Goodin, "NSI Antitrust Woes Not Over Yet," *ClNet*, February 24, 1999. Available at http://news.cnet.com/news/0-1005-200-339149.html?tag= [November 16, 1999].

8. Was at http://www.edns.net.

9. See, for example, Karl Denninger, "Top Level Domain Delegation Draft, Rev 0.1." Available at http://www.iia.org/lists/newdom/1996q/0013.html.

10. Was at http://www.edns.net [November 16, 1999].

11. Available at http://www.internic.net. Or it was: the InterNIC dates back to before NSI's involvement in domain name registrations; until 1993 it was run under government contract by SRI. Hence the general outrage when, in mid 1999, NSI suddenly pulled the site, claiming the database of registrations was its intellectual property. Although the search functions were restored shortly afterwards, they were limited compared to the original version. Try Betterwhois at http://www.betterwhois.com.

12. By late 2000, however, it became plain that third party organizations were interested in managing domains such as *.union.*

13. Janet Kornblum, "AlterNIC Founder Sorry, Won't Give Up," August 4, 1997. Available at http://www.news.com/news/0-1005-200-321099.html.

14. Chris Oakes, "Making Net Names Safer," *Wired News*, August 25, 1998. Available at http://www.wired.com/news/print_version/technology/story/14638.html?wnpg=a.

15. Oscar S. Cisneros, "Network Solutions Cracked," *Wired News*, July 2, 1999. Available at http://www.wired.com/news/print_version/technology/story/20567.html?wnpg=a.

16. The court filings are available at http://www.namespace.org.

17. In 1999, the co-founder of AlterNIC revamped the site in an attempt to continue the efforts without the controversy. Available at http://www.alternic.org or http://www.alternic.com.

18. "Establishment of a Memorandum of Understanding on the Generic Top Level Domain Name Space of the Internet Domain Name System (gTLD-MoU)," February 28, 1997. Available at http://www.gtld-mou.org/gTLD-MoU.html.

19. "Internet Domain Name System: Myths and Facts," printed copy taken from http://www.netsol.com/announcements/MYTHS4.htm on July 12, 1997. The page has since been taken down.

20. Declan McCullagh, "Domain Name List Is Dwindling," *Wired News*, April 14, 1999. Available at http://www.wired.com/news/news/technology/story/19116.html.

21. See http://www.interactivehq.com.

22. "Stop the Internet Coup," press release issued June 11, 1997, by the Open Internet Congress (founded by the Association of Interactive Media). Available at http://www.apnic.net/mailing-lists/apple/9706/msg00060.html.

23. Personal interview.

24. Archives of Farber's list are at http://www.interesting-people.org/.

25. Personal interview.

26. The full range of Department of Commerce documents on the DNS controversy is available at http://www.ntia.doc.gov/ntiahome/domainname/.

27. Testimony of Jon Postel, Director, Networks Division, Information

Sciences Institute, University of Southern California, before the Subcommittee on Basic Research and the Subcommittee on Technology of the Committee on Sciences, United States House of Representatives, October 7, 1998. Available at http://www.house.gov/science/postel_10-07.html.

28. At http://www.icannwatch.org.

29. David Post, "Where Is James Madison When We Need Him?" *ICANN Watch*, June 6, 1999. Available at http://www.icannwatch.org/archives/essays/930604982.shtml.

30. "Internet Domain Name Unit Seeking $2 Mln in Loans," Reuters, http://quote.fool.com/news/news.asp/?sid=7376866.

31. The complete archive of reporter Jeri Clausing's coverage of ICANN's formation and early struggles is on the *New York Times* site at http://www.nytimes.com. Because the site requires registration, it's not possible to give specific URLs, though the site's internal search engine will find the collection if you search on "domain name." (This limitation is one of the real problems with registration-protected Web sites.)

32. Paulina Borsook, *Cyberselfish: How the Digital Elite is Undermining Our Society, Culture, and Values* (New York: Bantam, 2000).

33. Andrew Brown, "You Say Toma.to," *New Statesman*, January 15, 1999. Available at http://www.consider.net/library.php3?Action=Record&searchStart=1&searchRange=10&searchWriter=&searchContent=domain+name&searchSection=&searchDayFrom=&searchMonthFrom=&searchYearFrom=&searchDayTo=&searchMonthTo=&searchYearTo=&URN=199901150037.

34. Businesses with their own networks tend to have permanent IP numbers assigned to them by their ISPs; domestic consumers typically are assigned one out of the pool of IP numbers that are available when they log in.

35. "At War for the Future of the Internet," *The Cook Report on Internet*, at http://cookreport.com/icannregulate.shtml.

36. A copy of the report and comments are at http://personal.law.miami.edu/~amf/.

37. Available at http://sunsite.auc.dk/RFC/rfc/rfc1591.html, among others.

38. Available at http://www.faqs.org/faqs/usenet/cabal-conspiracy-FAQ/.

39. An attempt at designing such a system is underway. See http://www.superroot.org.

NOTES TO CHAPTER 5

1. Contrary to what many people think, Usenet is neither part of the Internet nor wholly owned by Deja News. Instead, it's a collection of bulletin boards that are carried over the Internet, but that are also propagated by other routes, some as simple as having two computers phone each other and

exchange news. It was invented in part as a "poor man's ARPANet" in the days when only military, government, and academic research staff had access to the Net.

2. Personal interview.

3. See, for example, http://www.webreview.com/pub/97/04/25/imho/. By all accounts, Metcalfe tried to get out of it, first by saying the ink was toxic, and then by eating a piece of a large cake with his column recreated on it in icing. Finally, he put his column in a blender filled with liquid, poured the mess out into a bowl, and ate it as if it were porridge.

4. Michael Stutz, "InterNIC Who?" *Wired News*, July 16, 1997. Available at http://www.wired.com/news/news/technology/story/5232.html.

5. Edward W. Felten, Dirk Balfanz, Drew Dean, and Dan S. Wallach, "Web Spoofing: An Internet Con Game," Technical Report 540-96, Department of Computer Science, Princeton University, revised February 1997. Available at http://www.cs.princeton.edu/sip/pub/spoofing.php3.

6. Available at http://www.anonymizer.com.

7. "Fallout over Unsanctioned Domain Name Test," *Wired News*, February 5, 1998. Available at http://www.wired.com/news/politics/0,1283,10090,00.html.

8. Simson L. Garfinkel, "Fifty Ways to Crash the Net," *Wired News*, August 19, 1997. Available at http://www.wired.com/news/technology/0,1282,6184,00.html.

9. The Good Times "viruses" (a.k.a. PenPal Greetings, Join the Crew, etc.) all follow the same pattern. The name of the virus appears in the subject header; the text message explains that a major company such as IBM, Microsoft, or AOL has issued a warning about a new and deadly virus that arrives by email with the header Good Times (or whatever), and that you must immediately delete the message without opening it, as if opening the message will launch a powerful and malicious virus that will trash your hard disk and delete all your data. When the news of the virus first started circulating in about 1995, the threat was entirely mythical, as attached files had not yet been automated to be easy enough for most people to use. Now, sadly, what the hoax virus claims is possible, though the viruses that are genuinely dangerous do not announce themselves this way. Moral: before forwarding any mass-circulated warning, check it out on the constantly updated Hoax Virus Warning Page, at http://ciac.llnl.gov/ciac/CIACHoaxes.html.

10. One of Microsoft's more important business software packages is known as Back Office; it automates various typical administrative tasks. Naturally, the software to crack into it and corrupt data had to be called Back Orifice. Created by the Cult of the Dead Cow, it's readily available on the Net at http://www.bo2k.com.

11. See http://www.annoyances.org for instructions.

NOTES TO CHAPTER 6

1. The full set of legal documents pertaining to the Department of Justice action against Microsoft is at http://www.usdoj.gov/atr/cases/ms_index.htm.

2. For a timeline of the DoJ's antitrust actions against Microsoft, see http://www.wired.com/news/news/politics/antitrust/story/12385.html.

3. "Bill Gates's Statement on the Findings of Fact," November 5, 1999. Available at http://www.microsoft.com/presspass/trial/nov99/11-05billg.asp.

4. Michael Neubarth, "Microsoft Declares War," *Internet World*, March 1996.

5. Joshua Cooper Ramo, "Winner Take All," *Time*, September 16, 1996.

6. One of the specifically terminated practices was charging PC vendors as if all the computers they shipped had Windows loaded, whether or not this was actually true. The Finding of Fact made an interesting point about this per-processor licensing requirement, which has usually been seen as a way of keeping out other operating systems; Judge Jackson saw it as a way of preventing software piracy. Without the requirement to pay per machine shipped, manufacturers might find it tempting to pre-install some extra copies without paying for them.

7. Historical stock data is at http://www.historicaldata.com.

8. Figures from "The Netcraft Web Server Survey," correlating responses from 7,370,929 sites. Available at http://www.netcraft.com/survey.

9. Steve Hamm and Peter Burrows, "So What's in the Cards?" *Business Week*, November 22, 1999.

10. Jim Clark with Edward Owens, *Netscape Time: The Making of the Billion-Dollar Start-Up That Took on Microsoft* (New York: St. Martin's Press, 1999), 256.

11. Charles H. Ferguson, *High St@kes, No Prisoners: A Winner's Tale of Greed and Glory in the Internet Wars* (New York: Times Business, 1999).

12. See http://www.aolwatch.org.

13. Clark and Edwards, *Netscape Time*, 255.

14. Steve Hamm, "Microsoft's Future," *Business Week*, January 19, 1998.

15. Po Bronson, *The Nudist on the Late Shift* (New York: Random House, 1999).

16. "Analysis—'Browser War' Seen Brewing in Mobiles," Reuters, December 9, 1999. http://www.planetit.com/techcenters/docs/networks-advanced_ip_services/news/PIT19991213S0030/1.

17. The Bill Gates Personal Wealth Clock, at http://www.webho.com/WealthClock. As of January 6, 2000, each U.S. citizen's personal contribution was calculated at $453.79. The maintainer does not deduct charitable donations of Microsoft shares, on the grounds that the resulting PR helps maintain the company's market value.

18. A partial example is AOL's Windows client software. You can run it on NT and use it via Telnet, but it won't be able to dial the service directly, as NT and 95/98 have completely different dial-up networking modules.

19. Links to rulings in the *Sun vs. Microsoft* case are available from http://www.microsoft.com/java/issues/sunsuit.htm.

20. Michael Lewis, *The New New Thing* (New York: Norton, 1999), 194.

21. Clark and Edwards, *Netscape Time*, 49.

22. Available at http://www.operasoft.com.

23. Daniel Lyons, "Slay Your Rival," *Forbes*, December 14, 1998. Available at http://www.forbes.com/forbes/98/1214/6213055a.htm.

24. *United States of America v. Microsoft Corporation* and *State of New York, ex rel., Attorney General Eliot Spitzer, et al. versus Microsoft Corporation*, Court's Findings of Fact. Available at http://www.usdoj.gov/atr/cases/f3800.htm.

25. Amy Cortese, "The Software Revolution," *Business Week*, December 4, 1995.

26. Like the robots in Douglas Adams's *The Hitchhiker's Guide to the Galaxy*.

27. Press conference transcript, Claridges Hotel, London, October 14, 1999.

28. Just as a word processor is an application that runs on a single computer, the Web (and other Internet functions such as FTP) is an application that runs across the Internet using a technique known as client/server. Your Web browser is the client; the Web site you log onto runs the complementary server program. With open standards, such as those the Internet was built upon, the two pieces of software do not have to come from the same vendor in order to interoperate. In a system controlled by a single vendor, that vendor may seek to lock customers in by ensuring that client and server only work with each other. This is, for example, the situation with AOL, which can only be accessed via its own client software.

29. For a version of this argument, see Eric S. Raymond, "An Open Letter to AOL," November 25, 1998. Available at http://www.opensource.org/press_releases/aol-letter.html.

30. Ralph Nader and James Love, "What to Do about Microsoft?" *Le Monde Diplomatique*, November 1997, English edition. Available in French at http://www.monde-diplomatique.fr/1997/11/NADER/9458.html.

31. Eric S. Raymond, "The Cathedral and the Bazaar." Available at http://www.tuxedo.org/~esr/writings/cathedral-bazaar/ or in Raymond's book, *The Cathedral and the Bazaar* (Cambridge, MA: O'Reilly and Associates, 2000).

32. Ken Auletta, "The Trials of Microsoft," *New Yorker*, August 16, 1999.

33. Andy Reinhardt, "How Intel Played It Right," *Business Week*, November 22, 1999.

34. Andrew Leonard, "Is Linux the Real Remedy?" *Salon Magazine*, November 6, 1999. Available at http://www.salon.com/tech/feature/1999/11/06/open_source/index.html.

35. For some thoughts on breaking up the company, see James Gleick, "What to Do about Microsoft" (1999). Available at http://www.around.com/triplets.html.

36. Halloween memoranda at http://www.opensource.org/halloween/.

NOTES TO CHAPTER 7

1. Software programs are written in one of a variety of programming languages as a series of instructions to a computer. To make it easier for humans to program computers, the most popular languages are composed of English-like statements. Computers can't understand these directly, so another piece of software called a compiler translates those English-like statements into the gobbledegook—at its lowest level, just 0s and 1s that turn switches on and off—that computers do understand. The software you buy has been compiled; a programmer who wants to work on the software needs access to the original program before translation, known as the source code.

2. See the Hack Furby site at http://www.homestead.com/hackfurby/.

3. Since the mid 1980s, "hacking" has increasingly come to mean breaking into other people's computers. Old-style hackers resent this enormously as a betrayal of their ethic, which included the idea of sharing open systems, but not the idea of damaging or endangering them in any way. For the story of the original hackers, see Steven Levy's 1984 book *Hackers: Heroes of the Computer Revolution* (New York: Dell). An explanation of hacking in the sense the open-source/free software community/ies use the word is in "How to Become a Hacker," by Eric S. Raymond, available at http://www.tuxedo.org/~esr/faqs/hacker-howto.html.

4. Quoted in William C. Taylor, "Inspired by Work," *Fast Company*, Issue 29. Available at http://www.fastcompany.com/online/29/inspired.html.

5. See Phil Zimmermann, *The Official PGP Users Guide* (Cambridge, MA: MIT Press, 1995). Although free versions are still available, PGP is now a commercial product. In 1996, after the Department of Justice dropped its investigation into whether Zimmermann had contravened the ITAR by releasing PGP onto the Internet, he set up a company to exploit PGP commercially. The company, PGP Inc., was bought by Network Associates in 1998.

6. At http://www.opensource.org.

7. "The Open Source Definition," version 1.7. Available at http://www.opensource.org/osd.html.

8. Contrary to what some journalists believe after contact with Microsoft's

PR, Bill Gates did not invent BASIC. BASIC stands for Beginner's All-purpose Symbolic Instruction Code, and it was developed by John Kemeney and Thomas Kurtz in the mid 1960s at Dartmouth College. It is one of the first and simplest high-level programming languages.

9. William Henry Gates III, "An Open Letter to Hobbyists," February 3, 1976. Available at http://www.blinkenlights.com/classiccmp/gateswhine.html (and many other locations).

10. In *Hackers*, Levy says one of the first copies of BASIC was taken from the room where the program was being demonstrated Multiple copies were made and distributed freely at computer hobbyists' meetings on condition that anyone taking one would bring back two copies and donate them to the pool (pp. 228–29). Nonetheless, Gates's characterization angered many.

11. Personal interview, October 1999.

12. For a timeline of UNIX development, see http://www.datametrics.com/tech/unix/uxhistry/hst-hand.htm.

13. Apple bought NeXT at the beginning of 1997, about six months before fired CEO Gil Amelio and brought Jobs back in as an interim replacement.

14. Personal interview.

15. FreeBSD, like Linux, is a UNIX-like free operating system. FreeBSD is older than GNU, and suits by AT&T against its developers in the early days inspired the development of GNU/Linux, in part to ensure the availability of an entire suite of software programs that used none of the original UNIX code and so could not be the focus of legal challenges.

16. Andrew Leonard, in "The Saint of Free Software," *Salon.com*, August 31, 1998, makes reference to Stallman's revered status as the author of GNU Emacs, a text editor in common usage all over the world. Available at http://www.salon.com/21st/feature/1998/08/cov_31feature.html.

17. The "copyleft" GNU General Public License is at http://www.gnu.org/copyleft/gpl.html.

18. A note on pronunciation. There is a significant split in the open-source world between the people who pronounce it Linn-ux and those who pronounce it Line-ux. In fact, if you go to http://www.linux.org/info/index.html, you will be able to hear Torvalds' own pronunciation: he pronounces it Lee-nux.

19. A history written by Torvalds of the Linux kernel is at http://www.linuxworld.com/linuxworld/lw-1999-03/lw-03-pronunciation.

20. See http://www.gnu.org for Stallman's account of the development of GNU/Linux.

21. Figures cited in William C. Taylor, "Inspired by Work," *Fast Company*, November 1999. Available at http://www.fastcompany.com/online/29/inspired.html.

22. Ibid.

23. As an example of this argument, see François-René Rideau, "About Eric S. Raymond's Articles." Available at http://www.tunes.org/~fare/articles/about_esr.html.

24. Personal interview. See also Leonard, "The Saint of Free Software."

25. The complete collection of Andrew Leonard's (and other *Salon* writers') articles on the open-source movement is indexed at http://www.salon.com/tech/special/opensource/index.html.

26. Eric S. Raymond, "Shut Up and Show Them the Code." Available at http://www.tuxedo.org/~esr/writings/shut-up-and-show-them.html.

27. Stallman does not use the Web himself as a sort of penance ever since GNU project staff insisted on securing the project's Web server because they couldn't afford the time to reload the site every time it got hacked under the old system of total openness.

28. Richard Stallman, "Why 'Free Software' Is Better Than 'Open Source.'" by Richard Stallman. Available at http://www.gnu.org/philosophy/free-software-for-freedom.html.

29. Personal interview, October 1999.

30. Of course, there are people skills and people skills. Andrew Leonard tells in one of his *Salon* pieces the story of his contacting Raymond with a question, only to be "flamed hairless" when Raymond considered it too stupid to answer. See Andrew Leonard, "Let My Software Go," *Salon*, April 14, 1998. Available at http://www.salon.com/21st/feature/1998/04/cov_14feature.html.

31. Raymond, "How to Become a Hacker."

32. Tracy Kidder, *The Soul of a New Machine* (New York: Avon, 1990).

33. This essay, along with several follow-up essays on related topics, was published in book form under the title *The Cathedral and the Bazaar* (Cambridge, MA: O'Reilly and Associates, 2000).

34. This argument is laid out in more detail in Jonathan Eunice, "Beyond the Cathedral, Beyond the Bazaar," May 11, 1998. Available at http://www.illuminata.com/public/content/cathedral/.

35. Raymond, "How to Become a Hacker."

36. For a listing, see http://www.freshmeat.net.

37. The latest version of Mozilla is available at http://www.mozilla.org.

38. In the wake of the Microsoft Finding of Fact, all Linux-related stocks popped way up; by the April 2000 NASDAQ slide Red Hat was back down around its IPO price.

39. Andrew Leonard, "Who Controls Free Software?" *Salon*, November 18, 1999. Available at http://www.salon.com/tech/feature/1999/11/18/red_hat/index.html.

40. Clay Shirky, "The Interest Horizons and the Limits of Software Love." Available at http://www.shirky.com/Articles/interest.html.

41. See Douglas Coupland, *Microserfs* (New York: HarperCollins, 1996).

42. Clay Shirky, "View Source . . . Lessons from the Web's Massively Parallel Development." Available at http://www.shirky.com/OpenSource/view_source .html.

43. See Wendy M. Grossman, "All You Never Knew about the Net," *The Independent*, July 15, 1996.

44. Donald A. Norman, *The Psychology of Everyday Things* (New York: Basic Books, 1988). The book's title was changed for subsequent editions to *The Design of Everyday Things*.

45. Raymond, "The Cathedral and the Bazaar."

NOTES TO CHAPTER 8

1. Kristin Philipkoski, "Iceland's Genetic Jackpot," *Wired News*, December 10, 1999. Available at http://www.wired.com/news/technology/0,1282,32904,00 .html.

2. "Monsanto Receives B.t. Gene Patent; Initiates Enforcement Litigation," press release, March 20, 1996. Was at http://www.monsanto.com/ag/articles/ 96-03-20BtGene.htm.

3. Jennifer Kahn, "The Green Machine: Is Monsanto Sowing the Seeds of Change or Destruction?" *Harper's*, April 1999. A cut-down version is available at http://www.gn.apc.org/resurgence/issues/kahn195.htm.

4. See Wendy M. Grossman, *net.wars* (New York: New York University Press, 1997), chaps. 4 and 5.

5. Personal interview.

6. Martin Hellman, "The Mathematics of Public-Key Cryptography," *Scientific American*, August 1979.

7. Simson Garfinkel, "Patently Absurd," *Wired* 2.07, July 1994. Available at http://www.wired.com/wired/archive/2.07/patents.html.

8. Edmund B. Burke, "For Once, Law Anticipates Technology: The E-Data Saga," *Educom Review* 32, no. 2 (March/April 1997). Available at http://www .educause.edu/pub/er/review/reviewArticles/32206.html.

9. Seth Shulman, *Owning the Future* (Boston: Houghton Mifflin, 1999), 59–82.

10. According to author David Kline, trash patents have frequently followed the growth of new technology, eventually getting thrown out as Patent Office knowledge catches up. See David Kline and Kevin G. Rivette, *Rembrandts in the Attic* (Boston: Harvard Business School Press, 1999).

11. A copy of the judgment in *Sony Corp. v. Universal City Studios*, 464 U.S. 417, 104 S. Ct. 774, 78 L. Ed. 2d 574 (1984), decided January 17, 1984, is available at http://www.virtualrecordings.com/betamax.htm.

12. At http://www.dfc.org/.

13. Pamela Samuelson, "On Authors' Rights in Cyberspace," *First Monday* 1, no. 4 (1996). Available at http://www.firstmonday.dk/issues/issue4/samuelson.

14. This initiative was known as H.R. 3531; it failed and has been replaced by other legislation.

15. By British Telecom and the Post Office, respectively.

16. Starting in the early 1990s, British Telecom operated a dial-in character-based service called PhoneBase, which gave callers direct access to its database. Because it was originally designed for the telephone operators to use, the interface was difficult; also, the modem speed didn't increase from 2400 baud until late 1999. A private company, PhoneLink, sold a graphical software package that accessed both PhoneBase and other databases such as the Automobile Association's database of travel information much more efficiently, but with surcharges similar to those of the older online services prior to flat-rate pricing. A German CD compiled from public sources (in defiance of British Telecom) that allowed reverse searching (enter phone number, get owner), which is banned by British Telecom for privacy reasons, was inexpensive but full of errors and disappeared soon after its U.K. launch.

17. Available at http://www.phonenetuk.bt.com:8080/.

18. Full text of the No Electronic Theft Act is available at http://www.cs .hmc.edu/~smikes/property/net/.

19. Quoted in Wendy M. Grossman, "Downloading as a Crime," *Scientific American*, May 1998.

20. The list archives are at http://www.interesting-people.org.

21. The LaMacchia case is documented in the legal archives at http://www .eff.org.

22. A summary of the bill, plus documentation on other legislation, is available at the U.S. Copyright Office's site, http://lcweb.loc.gov/copyright/.

23. For a timeline, see http://www.dfc.org/Active_Issues/graphic/graphic.html.

24. Reverse engineering is a common practice in the technology industry. Essentially, you take something apart to identify its functionality, and then build something original that's functionally identical.

25. Barbara Simons, "Outlawing Technology" September 2, 1998. Available at http://www.acm.org/serving/cacm/outlaw.html.

26. Mark Stefik, "Letting Loose the Light," in *Internet Dreams: Archetypes, Myths, and Metaphors*, ed. Mark Stefik (Cambridge, MA: MIT Press, 1996).

27. Jesse Freund, "MP3 Continues to Play Big Music's Death Chimes," *Wired* 7.05, May 1999.

28. Steve Silberman, "The Dead Grateful for MP3," *Wired News*, February 8, 1999. Available at http://www.wired.com/news/news/culture/story/17796.html.

29. John Perry Barlow, "Selling Wine without Bottles: The Economy of

Mind on the Global Net." Available at http://www.eff.org/pub/Publications/John_Perry_Barlow/HTML/idea_economy_article.html.

30. Esther Dyson, *Release 2.0* (New York: Broadway Books, 1997).

31. At http://www.urbanlegends.com. Everything you could possibly want to know about the exploding whale is at http://www.perp.com/whale/, including a clip of the original TV news coverage of the event. It's a measure of how much the Net has changed that in 1994, when I first found the TV clip, it was 12Mb and took more than two hours to download from an FTP site. In 1999, you can watch it in real time.

32. In Article I, Section 8, Clause 8. See http://fairuse.stanford.edu/primary/ for the text, plus links to a number of other relevant laws and legal decisions.

33. Frames are a technique for creating Web pages that allows a site owner to design a page so that part of the page—say, a navigation bar, ad, or logo at the top and a menu to one side—remain constant while the internal content changes. They pose problems for certain types of browsers, such as the older text-based ones, which display the material in the frame as a list preceding or following the content itself. They also pose problems for researchers or people wanting to bookmark specific pages, as the URL in the window often remains constant rather than reflecting the actual location of the displayed material (you can get around this by opening the frame in a new window, an option available in most browsers). In this case, the content inside the frame was actually pulled in from another site—but minus the frame the site itself had put in place.

34. The case is documented in detail at http://www.nwu.org/tvt/tvthome.htm.

35. Answer: four. In 1994 he bought Delphi and tried to expand it into Europe, eventually selling back the American side to its original owners and shutting down the European section. A failed joint venture with MCI intended to create a Windows-based online platform. In 1996, in conjunction with the Mirror Group and British Telecom, News Corporation founded the British service Line One, pulling out in 1999 to set up a free ISP with the *Sun* newspaper, called Currant Bun (it rhymes). By 2000, he was starting over, pinning his hopes on yet another new venture.

36. This subject has been frequently discussed on the Web-based forum I co-manage for British media, at http://www.fleetstreet.org.uk.

37. Steganography is the art of hiding data within other data, anything from creating an apparently innocent message in which the first letters of the words spell out a different message to hiding text in the least important bits that go to make up a picture file on a computer. The hidden data is undetectable unless you know how to find it.

38. A simplistic version of something like this has been used for years by Adobe, which cut distribution costs by putting hundreds of fonts on the same CD; users phone in or send in payment, and in return are given a code to unlock the fonts they've just bought.

39. For example, Intuit's Quicken.

40. Roger Ebert, "Start the Revolution without Digital," *Chicago Sun-Times*, December 12, 1999. Available at http://tvplex.go.com/BuenaVista/SiskelAndEbert/.

41. See Link Online, at http://www.linkonline.co.uk.

42. The Anti-Divx page is at http://www.dvdresource.com/divx/.

43. At http://www.elibrary.com.

44. DigiCash, the first of these, filed for bankruptcy in 1998, and its technology was bought up by a new company, Seattle-based e-Cash Technologies; Cybercash is now a specialist in secure electronic commerce payment solutions.

45. See http://www.beenz.com.

46. James Gleick, "Click OK to Agree," *New York Times Magazine*, May 10, 1998. Available at http://www.around.com/agree.html.

47. "Top Ten New Jobs for 2002," *Salon*, January 5, 1998. At http://www.salonmagazine.com/21st/feature/1998/01/05feature.html.

48. See http://www.nwu.org/pic/ucita2.htm.

49. Joshua Quittner, "Billions Registered," *Wired* 2.10, October 1994. Available at http://www.wired.com/wired/archive/2.10/mcdonalds_pr.html.

50. James Glave, "Hey, Orrin, Dot Com This," *Wired News*, August 5, 1999. Available at http://www.wired.com/news/news/politics/story/21122.html.

51. The pages at http://www.senatororrinhatch.com in early January 2000 were designed to look like campaign pages for New York City Mayor Rudy Giuliani's Senate run but were obvious fakes.

52. "Amazon.com Takes Legal Action against Cybersquatter," *PR Newswire*, August 18, 1999. Available at http://www.prnewswire.com/cgi-bin/stories.pl?ACCT=105&STORY=/www/story/08-18-1999/0001005413.

53. Troy Wolverton, "Copycat Amazon Site Changes Name," *ClNet*, September 2, 1999. Available at http://news.cnet.com/news/0-1007-200-346743.html?tag=st.cn.1.

54. "The Management of Internet Names and Addresses: Intellectual Property Issues, Interim Report of the WIPO Internet Domain Name Process," December 23, 1998. All the interim materials were removed from WIPO's site in mid-2000. The final report is at http://wipo2.wipo.int/process1/report/index.htm.

55. A. Michael Froomkin, "A Critique of WIPO's RFC 3." Available at A. Michael Froomkin, http://www.law.miami.edu/~amf.

56. The Consumer Project on Technology is at http://www.cptech.org.

NOTES TO CHAPTER 9

1. John Browning, "Libraries without Walls for Books without Pages," *Wired* 1.01, January 1993. Available at http://www.wired.com/wired/archive/1.01/libraries_pr.html. Excerpted as "What Is the Role of Libraries in the Infor-

mation Economy," in *Internet Dreams: Archetypes, Myths, and Metaphors*, ed. Mark Stefik (Cambridge, MA: MIT Press, 1996).

2. Bear in mind that the Net community, despite appearances, has a great deal of respect for librarians, who have led many fights against censorship and for freedom of speech and privacy. In recognition of librarians' importance, "librarians everywhere" were the recipients of a Pioneer Award from the Electronic Frontier Foundation at CFP2000.

3. Nicholson Baker, "Discards," *New Yorker*, April 4, 1994. Reprinted in *The Size of Thoughts: Essays and Other Lumber* (New York: Random House, 1996,) 152–81.

4. Ellen Ullman, "The Dumbing-Down of Programming," *Salon*, May 12–13, 1998. Available at http://www.salon.com/21st/feature/1998/05/cov_12feature .html.

5. Eric Lorberer, "Nicholson Baker, without Blushing," *atrandom*, July 1998. Available at http://www.randomhouse.com/atrandom/nicholsonbaker/. Reprinted from *Rain Taxi* 3, no. 2 (summer 1998).

6. At http://www.si.umich.edu/cristaled/postings/V78.html.

7. Brewster Kahle, "Archiving the Internet," *Scientific American*, March 1997. Available at http://www.archive.org/sciam_article.html.

8. Some commercial sites, however, such as Amazon.com, have made all their listings searchable, so that when you look up a particular topic some of the books on that subject also appear on the list of hits, with links straight to the book title for purchase.

9. Bruce William Oakley, "How Accurate Are Your Archives," *Columbia Journalism Review*, March/April 1998. Available at http://www.cjr.org/year/ 98/2/archive.asp.

10. At http://www.archive.org.

11. Personal interview.

12. Bear in mind that while Americans expect government information to be free in any format that's available, elsewhere citizens often must pay for such material. Counterintuitively, at least to the British government, the Central Office of Information found that putting the material online for free actually increased sales.

13. The Commission on Preservation and Access in Washington, D.C., was set up to consider these issues. Available at http://www.rlg.org/ArchTF/. The European equivalent is the European Commission on Preservation and Access, at http://www.knaw.nl/ecpa/.

14. Ross Anderson, "The Eternity Service," June 17, 1997. Available at http://www.cl.cam.ac.uk/users/rja14/eternity/eternity.html.

15. At http://www.cdt.org.

16. The text of H.R. 1790 is at http://rs9.loc.gov/cgibin/query/D?c106:43:./ temp/~c106ykRFij::

17. The EPA report is available at http://www.house.gov/waxman/caa/airover.htm.

18. Community Right-to-Know is at http://www.rtk.net/wcs.

19. See "Reply Comments of Educause to the US Copyright Office Concerning Promotion of Distance Education Through Digital Technologies," March 3, 1999. Available at http://www.educause.edu/issues/digitaltech.html.

20. "What's the Difference? A Review of Contemporary Research on the Effectiveness of Distance Learning in Higher Education," by Ronald Phipps and Jamie Meriotis, Institute for Higher Education Policy, April 1999. At http://www.ihep.com/PUB.htm.

21. David F. Noble, "Digital Diploma Mills." Available at http://communication.ucsd.edu/dl. The series attracted quite a bit of controversy; for a dissenting view see Frank White, "Digital Diploma Mills: A Dissenting Voice." Available at http://www.firstmonday.dk/issues/issue4_7/white/.

NOTES TO CHAPTER 10

1. Lawrence E. Gladieux and Watson Scott Swail, "The Virtual University and Educational Opportunity: Issues of Equity and Access for the Next Generation" (College Board, Washington, D.C., April 1999). Available at http://www.collegeboard.org.

2. Ibid.

3. Personal interview, January 1996.

4. Available at http://www.ntia.doc.gov/ntiahome/digitaldivide/.

5. Dan Jellinek, "There's Virtually No Equality Here," *The Guardian*, September 9, 1999.

6. See http://www.brunel.ac.uk/research/virtsoc/.

7. D. L. Hoffman and T. P. Novak, "The Evolution of the Digital Divide: Examining the Relationship of Race to Internet Access and Usage over Time." Available at http://ecommerce.vanderbilt.edu/papers.html.

8. This is particularly true if you accept the arguments of Harvard lawyer Lawrence Lessig in his book *Code and Other Laws of Cyberspace* (New York: Basic Books, 1999), in which he argues that technology is not neutral, and we embed in its design our ideas about how the world should work.

9. Camp's original paper is at http://www.mines.edu/fs_home/tcamp/cacm/paper.html.

10. Myra Sadker and David Sadker, *Failing at Fairness* (New York: Touchstone, 1995).

11. The survey results are at http://talus.Mines.EDU/fs_home/tcamp/results/paper.html.

12. Theta Pavis, "ISO More Women in Tech," *Wired News*, November 15, 1999. Available at http://www.wired.com/news/print/0,1294,32533,00.html.

As an aside, if someone really wants to do something to help women in business, they could start by designing pockets into women's clothing.

13. The story of Stacy Horn's system, Echo, is recounted in her book *Cyberville* (New York: Warner Books, 1998).

14. For an account of iVillage's successful IPO, see Erik Larson, "Free Money," *New Yorker*, October 11, 1999.

15. Byron Burkhalter, "Reading Race Online," in *Communities in Cyberspace*, ed. Peter Kollock and Marc A. Smith (London and New York: Routledge, 1999).

16. Information about the program is at http://www.w3.org/WAI/.

17. Personal interview.

18. At http://www.unicode.org.

19. American Standard Codes for Information Interchange: a character set that includes the English alphabet (upper- and lowercase), Arabic numbers, and standard punctuation. The set is also sometimes known as 7-bit as there are 128 codes.

20. Available at http://www.riga.lv/minelres/eu/re940209.htm.

21. See http://www.edusainc.com/ezine/sum99/king.html.

22. Statistics from http://www.glreach.com/globstats/index.html/

23. At, for example, http://www.nua.ie.

24. Donald A. Norman, *The Invisible Computer: Why Good Products Can Fail, the Personal Computer Is So Complex, and Information Appliances Are the Solution* (Cambridge, MA: MIT Press, 1998).

25. Molly Ivins, "Taking the Gospel to Silicon Valley and Beyond," *Fort-Worth Star-Telegram*, April 22, 2000.

26. David A. Kaplan, *The Silicon Boys and Their Valley of Dreams* (New York: William Morrow, 1999).

NOTES TO CHAPTER 11

1. Market capitalization figure from http://www.quicken.com, January 4, 2000. Loss data from Amazon's 10-Q SEC filing for the period ending September 30, 1999, at http://www.sec.gov/Archives/edgar/data/1018724/0000891020-99-001938.txt.

2. Malcolm Gladwell, "Clicks and Mortar," *New Yorker*, December 6, 1999.

3. You'd think. But for an account of Amazon's success, see Robert Spector, *Amazon.com: Get Big Fast* (New York: Random House Business Books, 2000).

4. At http://www.halftone.co.uk.

5. Survey by Gartner Group, May 1999. Press release at http://www.gartnergroup.com/public/static/aboutgg/pressrel/052799site_costs.html.

6. Sadly, online technical support may be more widely accessible now, but it is not nearly as good as it was in the days when every hardware or software

company of any aspirations maintained a Forum or section of one on CompuServe. The design of CompuServe's software made it easy to get efficient responses to user questions. The Forums, however, were paid for in part by the royalty system then in existence, something that is not available on the Web. In addition, companies may have breathed a sigh of relief at no longer having to deal with the downside of creating a community of your customers: listening to them agree on their complaints.

7. Paul C. Judge and Heather Green, "The Name's the Thing," *Business Week*, November 15, 1999.

8. "Wish Fulfilment," *The Economist*, December 18, 1999.

9. CBS Marketwatch, December 30, 1999.

10. CNBC, January 6, 2000.

11. A piece on *All Things Considered*, National Public Radio, December 29, 1999, highlighted the problem of returns for online startups. Available at http://search.npr.org/cf/cmn/cmnpd01fm.cfm?PrgDate=12%2F29%2F1999&PrgID=2.

12. "Wish Fulfilment," *The Economist*, December 18, 1999.

13. See http://www.skeptic.org.uk.

14. Michael Wolff, *Burn Rate* (London: Weidenfeld and Nicolson, 1998). Wolff got a lot of flak for his book, both because of disputes over its accuracy and because of the attitudes it demonstrated toward the people who worked for him.

15. Paul F. Nunes, Andersen Consulting, "We Make It Up in Advertising." Available at http://www.ac.com/ideas/Outlook/pov/pov_makeit.html.

16. "Amazon Announces Financial Results for Third Quarter 1999," press release, October 27, 1999. Available at http://www.amazon.com/exec/obidos/subst/misc/investor-relations/1999-third-quarter-press-release.html/002-8590550-8766669.

17. In Esther Dyson, *Release 2.0* (New York: Broadway Books, 1997).

18. Gladwell, "Clicks and Mortar."

19. Ibid.

20. First Virtual was set up in 1994 to safely process credit card transactions. Essentially, it allowed you to avoid the risks of sending your credit card number over the Net by setting up an account with a PIN code used to reference it when purchasing online; the merchant would contact First Virtual with your PIN and First Virtual would email you to confirm or deny the transaction. While the system had some advantages—buyers were protected from fraud and were allowed to conduct anonymous transactions, and neither buyer nor merchant had to install special software—it required merchants to accept all the risk and imposed a long waiting period for settlement. The company went public in 1996, but by 1999 it was gone.

21. C. Scott Ananian, "Inside the Red Hat IPO," *Salon*, August 13, 1999. Available at http://www.salon.com/tech/feature/1999/08/13/redhat_shares/index

.html. See also Ananian, "A Linux Lament," *Salon*, July 30, 1999. Available at http://www.salon.com/tech/feature/1999/07/30/redhat_shares/index.html.

22. See for example, "first-day close" on the IPO Fund's glossary, at http://www.ipo-fund.com/glossary.asp.

23. John Gartner, "Digital Music Will Cost You," *Wired News*, December 8, 1999. Available at http://www.wired.com/news/technology/0,1282,32674,00.html.

24. Patrizia diLucchio, "Did the *Blair Witch Project* Fake Its Online Fan Base?" *Salon*, July 16, 1999. Available at http://www.salon.com/tech/feature/1999/07/16/blair_marketing/index.html.

25. Was at http://www.prodivx.com.

26. See John Stauber and Sheldon Rampton, *Toxic Sludge Is GOOD for You* (Monroe, ME: Common Courage Press, 1995).

27. For the specification and other background on SET, see http://www.setco.org.

28. See Lawrence Lessig, *Code and Other Laws of Cyberspace* (New York: Basic Books, 1999).

29. Jack McCarthy, "Studios Sue MP3 Startup Napster," CNN, September 9, 1999. Available at http://www.cnn.com/1999/TECH/computing/12/09/napster.suit.idg/index.html.

30. Edward Chancellor, *Devil Take the Hindmost: A History of Financial Speculation* (New York: Farrar, Straus and Giroux, 1999), 191.

NOTES TO CHAPTER 12

1. The security options built into browsers allow you to compare information sent back by the site with certificates authenticated by third parties such as Verisign (http://www.verisign.com).

2. Encryption is not the only option for this, but it's the one most commonly talked about. An interesting project in Britain, for example, is a product called PenOp, which uses a touch-sensitive handheld device, such as a Palm Pilot, to capture a handwritten signature electronically and append it to a document. What's interesting about the system is that physically signing something gives a human a sense of ritual and closure, while the software built around the signature allows specific conditions, plus a date and time stamp, to be appended to the document itself, along with a function to allow the document's integrity to be checked afterwards.

3. Key escrow, now more often (and incorrectly) called key recovery, is the practice of requiring users to store copies of their private keys with a third party, typically one or more government agencies. In Britain, implementing key escrow was intended to be a requirement for anyone seeking a license to sell cryptographic services to the public in Britain. From 1997 to 1999, the proposals

changed so that licensing went from being mandatory to voluntary, and key escrow was dropped as a requirement. The final legislation, the Electronic Communications Act, both prohibits and allows key escrow, perhaps reflecting the schizophrenic desires of the government to please everyone.

4. At http://www.fipr.org.

5. Ibid.

6. At http://www.wassenaar.org.

7. Bruce Schneier, "More on DVD Encryption Cracked," *Risks Digest*, 20.64. Available at http://catless.ncl.ac.uk/Risks/20.66.html#subj14.1.

8. In *Risks Digest* 20.66. Available at http://catless.ncl.ac.uk/Risks/20.66.html.

9. Reported in *Risks Digest* 20.34. Available at http://catless.ncl.ac.uk/Risks/20.34.html.

10. Deborah Ashrand, "Privacy Story Moves Like a Comet," *Industry Standard*, December 6, 1999. Available at http://www.thestandard.com/article/display/0,1151,8100,00.html.

11. See http://www.realnetworks.com/company/privacy/jukebox/privacyupdate.html?src=000103realhome.

12. In 1999, for example, an eighteen-year Navy veteran, coincidentally named Timothy McVeigh, was threatened with discharge from the military under it's "don't ask, don't tell" policy when AOL revealed the identity of the person behind a screen name. McVeigh had listed himself as gay in his online profile. Also in 1999, users began complaining that a year after they'd turned off the service's advertising in their "marketing preferences" profiles, the ads began reappearing; it turned out that you had to renew your decision not to receive ads every year or your opt-out expired.

13. Personal interview.

14. Heather Green, "Eureka! The Information Gold Mine," *Business Week* (E.Biz), July 26, 1999.

15. *Risks Digest*, 20.69, December 16, 1999. Available at http://catless.ncl.ac.uk/Risks/20.69.html.

16. For example, Gartner Group, quoted in Denis Murphy, "The Mobile Economy Becomes a Reality," *Telecommunications International*, November 1999. Murphy is operations manager for Phone.com.

17. Ibid.

18. Carla Sinclair's novel *Signal to Noise* (San Francisco: HarperCollins, 1997) explored just such a plot, when a staffer for a magazine that sounds suspiciously like *Wired* leaves his computer at home open during a drunken party and several guests gamble away six figures of his own money in an online casino, failing to realize the casino was genuine and they were betting real funds. The staffer spends the rest of the novel on the lam from the casino owners in search of their settlement, trying vainly to convince a variety of people he didn't do it, honest.

19. *Risks Digest,* 20.70, December 19, 1999. Available at http://catless.ncl.ac.uk/Risks/20.70.html

20. "The Last Question" appears in several Asimov anthologies.

21. See, for example, Green, "The Information Gold Mine."

22. At http://www.freecongress.org.

23. "Development of Surveillance Technology and Risk of Abuse of Economic Information," at http://www.xs4all.nl/~tomh/echelon/.

24. See http://www.cl.cam.ac.uk/users/rja14/.

25. For one example, see Nicky Hager, "Exposing the Global Surveillance System." Available at http://www.caq.com/caq59/CAQ59GlobalSnoop.html. The article is about Echelon, one of the big privacy scares of 1999. The book from which the article is an excerpt, *Secret Power,* seems to be published only in New Zealand.

26. "BBC: Echelon Exists," *Wired News,* November 3, 1999. Available at http://www.wired.com/news/politics/0,1283,32296,00.html.

27. At CFP2000, the science fiction author Neal Stephenson did a greatly admired speech enlarging on this theme and the importance of having the right threat model. A recording is available at http://www.cfp2000.org.

28. See Douglas Adams's *Hitchhiker's Guide to the Galaxy.*

29. David Brin, *The Transparent Society* (Reading, MA: Addison-Wesley, 1998), 91.

NOTES TO CHAPTER 13

1. Donald A. Norman, *The Invisible Computer: Why Good Products Can Fail, the Personal Computer Is So Complex, and Information Appliances Are the Solution* (Cambridge, MA: MIT Press, 1998).

2. Tom Standage, *The Victorian Internet* (London: Weidenfeld and Nicolson, 1998).

3. At http://www.cyberdialogue.com/news/releases/1999/11-29-ic-slowdown.html.

4. Paulina Borsook, *Cyberselfish: How the Digital Elite Is Undermining Our Society, Culture, and Values* (New York: Bantam, 2000).

5. Quoted in David Hudson, *ReWired* (New York: Macmillan Technical Publishing, 1997). Also available at http://www.rewired.com.

6. Ibid.

7. Named for science fiction writer Theodore Sturgeon, who said: "Ninety percent of science fiction is crap. But then, 90 percent of everything is crap."

Selected Bibliography

Alderman, Ellen, and Caroline Kennedy. *The Right to Privacy*. New York: Knopf, 1995.

Baden, John A., and Douglas S. Noonan. *Managing the Commons*, 2d ed. Bloomington and Indianapolis: Indiana University Press, 1998.

Berners-Lee, Tim, with Mark Fischetti. *Weaving the Web: The Original Design and Ultimate Destiny of the World Wide Web by Its Inventor*. San Francisco: Harper San Francisco, 1999.

Brockman, John. *Digerati*. London: Orion Business Books, 1997.

Burstein, Daniel, and David Kline. *Road Warriors: Dreams and Nightmares along the Information Highway*. New York: Dutton, 1995.

Cairncross, Frances. *The Death of Distance*. London: Orion Business Books, 1997.

Davies, Simon. *Big Brother: Britain's Web of Surveillance and the New Technological Order*. London: Pan, 1996.

Diffie, Whitfield, and Susan Landau. *Privacy on the Line*. Cambridge, MA: MIT Press, 1998.

Foner, Eric. *The Story of American Freedom*. New York: W. W. Norton, 1998.

Furger, Roberta. *Does Jane Compute?* New York: Warner Books, 1998.

Godwin, Mike. *Cyber Rights and Cyber Law*. New York: Random House, 1998.

Goldman Rohm, Wendy. *The Microsoft File*. New York: Random House, 1998.

Grossman, Lawrence K. *The Electronic Republic*. London: Penguin Books, 1996.

Grove, Andrew S. *Only the Paranoid Survive*. New York: Doubleday, 1996.

Hafner, Katie, and Matthew Lyon. *Where Wizards Stay Up Late*. New York: Simon and Schuster, 1996.

Hall, Kira, and Mary Bucholtz. *Gender Articulated: Language and the Socially Constructed Self*. New York and London: Routledge, 1995.

Horn, Stacy. *Cyberville*. New York: Warner Books, 1998.

Hudson, David. *ReWired*. Indianapolis: Macmillan Technical Publishing, 1997.

Huitema, Christian. *IPv6: The New Internet Protocol*. Upper Saddle River, NJ: Prentice Hall PTR, 1996.

Jones, Steven G. *Cybersociety 2.0*. Thousand Oaks, CA: Sage Publications, 1998.

Kelly, Kevin. *New Rules for the New Economy*. London: Fourth Estate, 1998.

Kiesler, Sara. *Culture of the Internet*. Mahwah, NJ: Lawrence Erlbaum Associates, 1997.

Kurtz, Howard. *Media Circus*. New York: Times Books, 1993–1994.

Leonard, Andrew. *'Bots: the Origin of a New Species*. San Francisco: Wired Books, 1997.

Levinson, Paul. *Digital McLuhan*. London: Routledge, 1999.

Ludlow, Peter. *High Noon on the Electronic Frontier: Conceptual Issues in Cyberspace*. Cambridge, MA: MIT Press, 1996.

McGrath, Melanie. *Hard, Soft, and Wet*. London: HarperCollins, 1997.

Naughton, John. *A Brief History of the Future: The Origins of the Internet*. London: Weidenfeld and Nicolson, 1999.

Noble, David F. *The Religion of Technology*. London: Penguin Books, 1999.

Norman, Donald A. *The Invisible Computer: Why Good Products Can Fail, the Personal Computer Is So Complex, and Information Appliances Are the Solution*. Cambridge, MA: MIT Press, 1998.

Peterson, Ivars. *Fatal Defect*. New York: Vintage, 1996.

Pool, Robert. *Beyond Engineering*. Oxford: Oxford University Press, 1997.

Pratkanis, Anthony, and Elliot Aronson. *The Age of Propaganda*. New York: W. H. Freeman, 1992.

Reid, Robert H. *Architects of the Web*. New York: John Wiley and Sons, 1997.

Rifkin, Jeremy. *The End of Work*. New York: Tarcher Putnam, 1995.

Schneier, Bruce, and David Banisar. *The Electronic Privacy Papers*. New York: Wiley Computer Publishing, 1997.

Shapiro, Carol, and Hal R. Varian. *Information Rules: A Strategic Guide to the Network Economy*. Cambridge, MA: Harvard Business School Press, 1999.

Sinclair, Carla. *Signal to Noise*. San Francisco: HarperEdge, 1997.

Sinha, Indra. *The Cybergypsies: A Frank Account of Love, Life, and Travels on the Electronic Frontier*. London: Scribner, 1999.

Stefik, Mark. *Internet Dreams*. Cambridge, MA: MIT Press, 1996.

———. *The Internet Edge*. Cambridge, MA: MIT Press, 1999.

Stross, Randall E. *The Microsoft Way: The Real Story of How Bill Gates Outsmarts the Competition*. London: Warner Books, 1998.

Swisher, Kara. *aol.com*. New York: Times Business Books, 1998.

Tapscott, Don. *Growing Up Digital*. New York: McGraw-Hill, 1998.

———. *The Digital Economy*. New York: McGraw-Hill, 1996.

Tenner, Edward. *Why Things Bite Back*. New York: Vintage, 1997.

Turkle, Sherry. *Life on the Screen: Identity in the Age of the Internet*. New York: Simon and Schuster, 1995.

Ullman, Ellen. *Close to the Machine*. San Francisco: City Lights Books, 1997.

Wallace, Jonathan, and Mark Mangan. *Sex, Laws, and Cyberspace*. New York: Henry Holt, 1996.

Wriston, Walter B. *The Twilight of Sovereignty*. New York: Charles Scribner's Sons, 1992.

Index

Addiction (Internet), 4, 9
Alcoholics Anonymous, 176
alt.folklore.urban, 106
alt.showbiz.gossip, 9–12
alt.usenet.cabal, 56
AlterNIC, 46, 57, 60
Amazon.com, *xii*, 15, 71, 114, 140–141,
    142, 143, 144–145, 151, 166
America Online (AOL), 1, 18, 24, 26, 27,
    38, 68–71, 136, 141, 143, 167, 177,
    178
Anderson, Ross, 123, 173–174
Anonymity, 157
ARPAnet, 35–36
ASCII, 20, 26, 30, 90
Association for Computing Machinery
    (ACM), 41, 102, 103–104, 131, 133
Astrology, 144
AT&T, 67, 84–85, 101, 153, 155, 177

Baker, Nicholson, 119
Banner ads, 144, 164
Baran, Paul, 36
Barlow, John Perry, 105
Bellovin, Steve, 59–64
Berners-Lee, Tim, 55, 92–93, 137
Bezos, Jeff, 140
Biometrics, 153, 169–172
Blaze, Matt, 59–64, 155
Bolt, Beranek, and Newman (BBN), 35
Borg, Anitam, 134
Borsook, Paulina, 40, 54, 185
Bowden, Caspar, 173
Brand, Russell, 176
Breeder reactor, 6
Broadband, 38, 63, 65, 148, 167, 178,
    183–184
Brown, Andrew, 15, 54

Browser wars, 68–71, 72, 74–75
Bruckman, Amy, 22, 25
Bumgardner, Jim, 20, 21

Cagri, Mahir, 148
Cavoukian, Ann, 171
CDNow, 142
Censorship, 154
Center for Democracy and Technology
    (CDT), 124
Cerf, Vinton, 35, 56, 37, 128
Child Online Protection Act (COPA), 161,
    177
Cisler, Steve, 29
CIX (Compulink Information eXchange),
    183
Cohen, Julie E., 122
Communications Decency Act , 177
Community, online, 14–31, 141, 143,
    157–158, 178
Compulink Information eXchange. *See*
    CIX
CompuServe, 24, 26, 28, 38, 68, 98, 107,
    141, 177
Computers, Freedom, and Privacy (CFP)
    1995, 175, 176
    1998, 2, 59–64, 171
    1999, 39–40, 122, 124, 154, 164, 172,
    173
Consumer Project on Technology, 72–73,
    77, 115
Cook, Gordon (*Cook Report on Internet*),
    54, 56
Copy protection, 104, 109–110
Copyright, 80–81, 95–116, 122
Council of Registrars (CORE), 48
Cryptography, *xii*, 80, 102–103, 109, 122,
    155, 158, 168, 171–173

Curtis, Pavel, 24, 28, 29
Cybersquatting, 50, 52, 100, 114, 115
Cyclades network, 36–37

Data protection laws, 165–166, 170, 172, 174, 175
Databases
  copyright in, 100–101, 108, 115
  privacy and, 164–166, 172–174
Davies, Donald, 36, 38
Davies, Simon, 156, 161–162, 173
Daytraders, 3–4
Defense Advanced Projects Research Agency (DARPA), 35
Denninger, Karl, 46
Department of Commerce (DoC), 54, 81
  digital divide studies, 129–130
Department of Justice, 67–79, 90, 102
Department of Trade and Industry (DTI, UK), 156
Depression, 4–5
Dibbell, Julian, 29
Digital divide, 128–139, 182
  Department of Commerce studies, 129–130
Digital Millennium Copyright Act, 100, 102, 103, 158
Digital signatures, 168
Divx, 111, 149
Dog, on the Internet everyone knows you're a, 18, 135
Domain name system (DNS), 12, 28, 42–58, 60, 115
Drudge, Matt, 5, 9–12
DSM-IV, 7
DVD (and copyright), 99, 110, 158
Dyson, Esther, 105, 135, 145

"Easter Eggs," 86–87
eBay, 15, 120, 141
Ebert, Roger, 110
Echelon (global surveillance program), 174
Ecommerce, 140–153
eDNS, 46, 57
Enfopol, 173
Environmental Protection Agency (EPA), 123–125
European Union, 77, 100, 137, 145, 180
  privacy directive of, 159–160

Farber, David, 50, 101–102
Farmer, Randy, 24
Federal Trade Commission, 160
Feinstein, Senator Dianne (D-California), 6
First Amendment, 106, 162
Foundation for Information Policy Research (FIPR), 123, 156, 173
France, Elizabeth (UK data protection registrar), 165, 173
Free software, 70, 77, 80–94
  defined, 81–82
FreeBSD, 85
Froomkin, A. Michael, 53, 115
Furby, 80, 108

Garrin, Paul, 47
Gates, Bill, 13, 14, 67, 68, 75, 82–83
  Personal Wealth Clock, 73
Gilmore, John, 57, 91
Global User ID (GUID), 159, 168
GNU, 89, 92
Godwin, Mike, 14, 15
Goldberg, Ivan K., 6–7
Graham, Benjamin, 153
Griffiths, Mark, 7–8

Habitat, 21
Hacking, 6, 82, 65, 149
  defined, 81
Heath, Don, 50
Heaven's Gate, 1
Henshall, John, x
Hitchhiker's Guide to the Galaxy, 76, 115, 174
Hoffman, Donna, 50–51, 52, 58, 129–131
Holub, David, 26
Hooked, 26–27, 30
Hudson, David, 185
Human Genome Project, 95

IBM, 40, 67, 73, 77–78, 86, 98, 135, 142, 152, 160
ICANNWatch, 53, 102
ICQ, 183
Identity theft, 168
Intellectual property rights, 95–116
International Standards Organization (ISO), 44

International Telecommunications Union (ITU), 43, 49, 50
International Traffic in Arms Regulations (ITAR), 81, 155, 177
Internet Ad-Hoc Committee (IAHC), 48, 49, 53, 57, 59
Internet Architecture Board (IAB), 59
Internet Assigned Numbers Authority (IANA), 48
Internet Corporation for Assigned Names and Numbers (ICANN), 41, 43, 47, 52–58, 62, 115, 135
Internet Engineering Task Force (IETF), 48, 59
Internet Relay Chat (IRC), 18, 27
Internet Society (ISOC), 48, 50
InterNIC, 47, 53, 54
Ivins, Molly, 139

Jackson, Judge Thomas Penfield, 67, 68, 72, 73, 75, 78, 79
Jacobson, Bob, 22
Java, 40, 61, 65, 73–76, 143, 163

Kahn, Mimi, 26
Kahn, Robert E., 35
Kashpureff, Eugene, 12, 47, 61
Katz, Bruce, 18, 25, 26
Kiesler, Sara, 4
Kim, Amy Jo, 15–16
Kollock, Peter, 27, 29
Kraut, Robert, 4

LambdaMOO, 25, 28–29
Language, 138
LaRouche, Lyndon, 3
Lehrer, Tom, 1
Leonard, Andrew, 79
Lessig, Lawrence, 27, 151
Linux, 65, 79, 80, 90, 91
    why it should be called GNU-Linux, 85–86
Love, James, 72–73, 77, 115
Lucasfilms, 21

Mackenzie, Alex, 35–37
Magaziner, Ira, 32
Marx Brothers, 66, 74
Metcalfe, Bob, 60

Micropayments, 167
Microsoft, 15, 23, 40, 51, 65, 67–79, 82, 86, 90, 102, 134, 135, 167, 178
MI6, *xii*, 2
Mockapetris, Paul, 42
Morningstar, Chip, 24
Morton, David, 63, 65
Motion Picture Association of American (MPAA), 116
MP3, 99, 105. 107, 115, 116, 148, 152

Napster, 148, 149, 152
National Basketball Association, 100
National Physical Laboratory (NPL), 36
National Science Foundation (NSF), 47
Need to Know (Now) (NTK), 5
Netscape, 26, 68 –70, 73, 74, 91, 120
Network Associates, 47
Network Solutions (NSI), 44–46, 49, 51, 60, 61
No Electronic Theft (NET) Act, 100, 101
Noble, David F., 126–127
Norman, Donald, 93, 139, 178
Nostradamus, 2
Novak, Tom, 129–131

Online trading, 3–4, 146–147
Open source software, 70, 77, 79, 80–94
    defined, 82
Open Systems Interconnection (OSI), 34–35
Orwell, George, *xi*, 66, 165, 172, 174

Packet-switching, 36
Palace, The, 20–22
Patents, 95–116, 151
PGP, 81, 155
Pickering, Congressman Chip (R-MS), 35
Policy '98 conference, 41, 131, 132
Post, David, 35
Postel, Jon, 32–35, 42–43, 48, 53, 55, 57, 58, 62
Pouzin, Louis, 37
Privacy, *xii*, 65, 96, 137, 154–176
Privacy International, 156, 161
Proven, Liam, 84

Raymond, Eric S., 77, 81, 86–87, 89, 92, 93

Real Names, 114
rec.sport.tennis, 135
Recording Industry Association of
   America, 116
Red Hat, 78, 91, 94, 147
Request for Comments (RFC), 33–35,
   55, 84
Rheingold, Howard, 17, 29
Rossetto, Louis, 185
Rutt, Jim, 53–54
Ryman, Geoff, 136, 152

Salon.com, 11, 87, 106, 111, 148
Samuelson, Pamela 96, 99, 109, 112
Scantlebury, Roger, 36
Schifreen, Robert, 6
Secure Digital Music Initiative (SDMI),
   105, 149
Securities and Exchange Commission
   (SEC), 91, 123
Slashdot (/.), 15, 67, 91, 152
Software licenses, 112–113
Spainhower, Rebecca, 29
Spoofing, 47
Stallman, Richard, 83–84, 87–88, 91,
   94, 97
Stefik, Marc, 104, 109
Stock market bubble, 153
Sturgeon's Law, 186
Sweeney, Latanya, 158, 164

Tasini v. New York Times, 108
Taxes, 145, 160
Torvalds, Linus, 89
TRUSTe, 161
Trusted systems, 104
Tupperware, 30
Turkle, Sherry, 6, 129

Uniform Commercial Code, 112–113
UNIX, 15, 40, 65, 79, 85, 92
Usenet, 2, 13, 17, 24, 38, 59, 113, 135,
   138, 152, 158

Van der Leun, Gerard, 19, 24, 28
Varian, Hal, 58
Virtual Diplomacy, 179, 186

Wassenaar Arrangement, 157
Weblogs, 15
WELL (Whole Earth 'Lectronic Link),
   The, 14–15, 17, 18, 20, 22–23, 26,
   28, 30, 54
Williams, Gail, 15, 20
Wired, 47, 113, 180, 185
Wired News, 24, 50, 96, 106, 117, 134,
   149
Wireless, 166
Wireless Application Protocol (WAP),
   166, 183
Women in technology, 133–135
World Health Organization (WHO), 43, 48
World Intellectual Property Organization
   (WIPO), 48, 55, 100, 102, 114–115
World Wide Web Consortium (W3C), 55,
   57, 135
Worlds Away (now Avaterra), 21, 25, 27,
   28, 30

XML, 137

Yahoo!, 70, 101, 112, 122, 141, 143, 183
Yes, Minister, 172
Young, Kimberly S., 4, 7

Zero Knowledge, 157
Zimmermann, Phil, 155

About the Author

Wendy M. Grossman is an American freelance writer based in London, where she writes for the *Daily Telegraph* and *Scientific American*, among many other publications. Her books include *net.wars* (1997), which looks at the development of the Net as a commercial medium from 1993 to 1996—what you might call the border wars between cyberspace and real life. The full text of *net.wars* is available online at http://www.nyupress.nyu.edu/netwars.html).

She is also founder of the British magazine *The Skeptic* (http://www.skeptic.org.uk), one of the moderators of the Fleet Street online forum for U.K. media (http://www.fleetstreet.org.uk), and a former full-time folksinger. The MP3s of her 1980 album *Roseville Fair* are on her Web site (http://www.pelicancrossing.net).

She is a graduate of Cornell University, where she was primarily known for running the folk club, performing in Cornell Savoyards and Sage Chapel choir, and wandering around the campus playing a pennywhistle. She recommends checking the mood button on her Web site before sending email—and ensuring that HTML is turned off and there are no attached files.